Public Policy Implementation

PUBLIC POLICY STUDIES: A MULTI-VOLUME TREATISE, VOLUME 3

Editor: Stuart Nagel, *Department of Political Science, University of Illinois*

PUBLIC POLICY STUDIES
A Multi-Volume Treatise

General Editor: Stuart Nagel, Department of Political Science, University of Illinois

To Jeff
a constant source of joy

Public Policy Implementation

Edited by GEORGE C. EDWARDS, III

Department of Political Science
Texas A & M University

 JAI PRESS INC.

Greenwich, Connecticut   *London, England*

Library of Congress Cataloging in Publication Data
Main entry under title:

Public policy implementation.

  (Public policy studies ; v. 3)
  Includes bibliographies and index.
  1. Policy sciences—Addresses, essays, lectures.
2. Administrative agencies—United States—Planning—
Addresses, essays, lectures.   I. Edwards, George C.
II. Series: Public policy studies (Greenwich, Conn.) ;
v. 3.
H97.P795   1984   361.6   84-25056
ISBN 0-89232-453-8

CONTENTS

INTRODUCTION

Public policies are rarely self-executing. The Supreme Court may hand down a decision to desegregate schools, Congress may pass legislation to restrict immigration, or the president may order troops to rescue U.S. hostages in Tehran—yet little progress toward accomplishing these goals may occur. Without effective implementation policymakers' decisions will not be carried out successfully.

The study of policy implementation is crucial for the study of public administration and public policy. Policy implementation is the stage of policymaking between the establishment of a policy, such as the passage of a legislative act, the issuing of an executive order, the handing down of a judicial decision, or the promulgation of a regulatory rule, and the consequences of the policy for the people whom it affects. If a policy is inappropriate, if it cannot alleviate the problem for which it was designed, it will probably be a failure no matter how well implemented. But even a brilliant policy poorly implemented may fail to achieve the goals of its designers.

There is no lack of implementation problems, even in the provision of the most routine services. For example, a recent study by the General Accounting Office found that compliance with drinking water standards by tne nation's 215,000 drinking water systems "in literally thousands of cases appears to be the exception rather than the rule" (*Congressional Quarterly*, 1982:976).

At times implementation failures can be spectacular, as in the case of the Three Mile Island nuclear plant. It is equally important to note that both the President's Commission on the Accident at Three Mile Island and the Nuclear Regulatory Commission's own study concluded that the principal problem in the near-disaster was not one of engineering or hardware. Rather, it was a failure of organization and management (Sills, 1981; see also *Newsweek*, 1983:13).

The consumers of public policy are not alone in being concerned about implementation. The frustration leaders, too, face in dealing with implementation is eloquently represented in the plaintive response of one of our century's most notable autocrats, Chairman Mao Tse-tung, to compliments from President Nixon:

> Nixon: The Chairman's writings moved a nation and have changed the world.
> Mao: I have not been able to change it. I have only been able to change a few
>   places in the vicinity of Peking (quoted in Kissinger, 1979:1063).

OVERVIEW

Each essay in this book focuses on a crucial issue in the study of public policy implementation. Authors were selected for the special expertise and insights they bring to their topics, and their contributions are designed to have theoretical and analytical rather than descriptive focuses. Thus, these essays are relevant to many substantive policy areas.

Many of the authors also address prescriptive as well as analytical questions—in other words, they go beyond explaining the causes of implementation problems to examine or develop possible solutions. Such work is essential if we are to substantially improve the provision of public services without wasting scarce resources on seemingly plausible but actually unsatisfactory solutions.

In the remainder of this introduction, I will briefly outline each chapter that follows, freely admitting that these few paragraphs cannot do justice to the complexity and richness of the arguments that await the reader.

In our first essay Frank Thompson points out that overhead control is an important model for effective policy implementation. Among other things, this model is based on the notion that elected executives, legislators, and judges should exercise substantial control over bureaucratic actions through precise policy mandates and vigilant oversight.

Yet the contribution of the overhead control model to effective policy implementation is unclear. On the one hand, if implementation directives are not specific, implementors may be confused about what they should do, and they will have discretion to impose their own views on the implementation of policies, views that may be different from those of their superiors. Conversely, very specific implementation communications may overwhelm implementors with detail, leading to goal displacement, rigidity, or circumvention of regulations. It may also make it more difficult for officials in the field to adapt programs to meet the needs of particular circumstances. In addition, we cannot assume that the overhead model is always feasible.

So when is the overhead model likely to be the most effective approach to implementation? In investigating this question, Professor Thompson develops a four-celled typology of implementation based on the overhead control model's dimensions of statutory precision and oversight. Then he posits five conditions that influence the utility of each type of implementation. These conditions include the degree to which there is (1) a well-understood technology that is not bottom heavy, (2) environmental stability, (3) a tempered commitment to the policy within the implementing agency, (4) a debilitating sociopolitical milieu, and (5) efficacious overhead institutions.

From a cost–benefit perspective, the model of tight overhead control is attractive in only a limited number of cases. Similarly, a model that is based on precise statutes and limited oversight is rarely appropriate. Thus, most policies are implemented under conditions in which looser control is likely to produce the most effective implementation.

If implementors are well disposed toward a particular policy, they are more likely to carry it out as the original decision makers intended. But when implementors' attitudes or perspectives differ from the decision makers', the process of implementing a policy becomes infinitely more complicated. Those who implement policies are in many ways independent of their nominal superiors who directly participate in the original policy decisions. As a result of various grant and revenue sharing programs and the nature of our judicial system, many national and state policies are ultimately implemented by officials or judges of another jurisdiction. This magnifies the independence of implementors, and independence provides them with opportunities to use their discretion.

In Chapter 2 Lawrence Baum compares the effectiveness of appellate courts and legislatures in having their policies enacted as they desire. First, he examines the authority of the two institutions as a factor in affecting implementors' behavior. Although he finds that the authority of appellate courts is stronger and has greater effect than that of legislatures, the most significant point is that the authority of policy enactors is a relatively weak force in administrative policy implementation.

Professor Baum then turns his attention to the capacities of each institution to intervene in policy implementation, stressing both the availability and use of tools to influence implementors. He finds that legislatures have greater potential to influence the dispositions of implementors than do appellate courts. Nevertheless, legislatures do not often exploit this potential, undermining their ability to affect implementation. Obviously, the chances of influencing implementors' dispositions are greatest if courts and legislatures work together.

Barry Mitnick and Robert Backoff argue in Chapter 3 that policy implementation can be best understood as a system of implementation relations between policy enactors and implementing agents. They develop a typology of implementation relations and conclude that these are driven by incentive relations. Therefore they feel that problems in implementation can usefully be analyzed in terms of incentive failures.

Relying on an extensive review of the incentive-related literature, the authors determine the requisites for an adequate conceptualization of incentive relations and incentive systems. They then develop an incentive systems model, elaborate on its components and relationships, and show that incentive systems are key components of other models of implementation.

Finally, Professor Mitnick and Backoff provide a seven-stage model describing the process of analyzing incentive systems that may be applied to both theory-building and intervention and design in implementation. Thus, their incentive systems model sensitizes us to both the factors that drive behavior and the levels that can potentially be used to manipulate it.

Implementation is often intergovernmental activity, and the federal grant-in-aid is a primary mechanism for promoting policies, including fiscal support, fiscal stimulation and innovation, and the redress of inequalities. In Chapter 4 Robert Stein reviews the nature and types of federal grants and finds that they often do not work as intended. His task, then, is to increase our understanding of compliance with federal grants-in-aid requirements.

The author's review of the literature helps him to develop an evolutionary model of grant implementation. This model focuses on four aspects of the implementation of intergovernmental policy: utilization/participation, allocation of aid, donor–recipient negotiations, and feedback to the legislative process. Professor Stein emphasizes that programs not only grow fiscally, but they also change structurally to accommodate the preferences of recipients and the desire of the federal government to achieve greater compliance. Therefore, grant implementation is the product of a dynamic process in which each actor seeks to achieve different goals through the common mechanism of the federal grant.

Chapter 5 also sheds lights on the issues of the monitoring and control of the activities of local government units that administer federal programs. Frederick Lazin and Samuel Aroni provide a case study of the U.S. Department of Housing and Urban Development's (HUD) implementation of the Housing Assistance Plan (HAP) component of the Housing and Community Development Act of 1974 in Los Angeles. The HAP is supposed to coordinate housing policy with other aspects of urban policy.

The authors found that HUD regularly approved HAPs that it knew contained incorrect and unrealistic data about Los Angeles's housing conditions, needs, and goals. It adopted a service orientation and refused to hold up federal funds, regardless of the city's inflated goals and poor record in implementing its housing plan. The fact that HUD's own regulations were unclear and inconsistent and thus maximized the discretion officials had in evaluating HAPs, that HUD lacked the resources to produce an accurate picture of Los Angeles's housing conditions and needs, and that HUD's senior officials wanted to avoid a fight with local officials all contributed to this situation.

Urban public services are perhaps the most vital services that governments provide. Civilized society is difficult to imagine without police and fire protection, schools, parks, water, sewerage refuse collection, and so on. In Chapter 6 Ken Mladenka argues that the implementation of these routine public services occurs in an environment containing many complicating factors, including depending on state and federal resources, private sector influences, movement of citizens to the suburbs, citizen involvement in decision making, conflict over basic human values, conflicting needs and demands for service, the divisible nature of municipal services, insulation of the bureaucracy from political control, the tremendous discretion enjoyed by the street-level bureaucrat, and the multiple stages of the service delivery process.

Professor Mladenka then turns to a discussion of how competing conceptions of equity further hamper successful implementation. Equity involves justice and fairness, and what constitutes fairness is open to a variety of differing interpretations, a situation fraught with opportunities for political conflict. The author argues that the political risks inherent in conscious choices about equity standards intimidate public officials, so they abdicate responsibility for these major political decisions to the bureaucracy. Bureaucrats, in turn, solve the distributional puzzle by reducing it to a level that is susceptible to the application of technical-rational criteria. Administrators structure and routinize equity outcomes by concealing the distinctly political dimensions of their choices in decision rules based on professional norms.

The 1980s have seen a substantial increase in interest in fundamental changes in the way we implement policy. One technique that falls in this category is market reform. Market reform advocates believe that the political system is in many cases the wrong locus for allocating resources or resolving problems. They see the political process as inefficient and ineffective and recommend employing economic incentives and private markets to replace or complement government programs. Such an approach, they argue, would permit the use of more appropriate incentives, require less information, reduce political disputes, lessen the use of coercion, and enhance free choice.

In Chapter 7 Mark Rushefsky examines these arguments. He finds that an underlying assumption of the market reform advocates is that the incentives built into the system will automatically influence various parties to move in desired directions (e.g., select cost-efficient plans, reduce pollution to optimal levels). But because of this "automatic" assumption—the "invisible hand" of Adam Smith—market reformers have not seriously considered implementation problems. Similarly, the implementation literature has had little to say about market reform, primarily because of its focus on government programs.

Professor Rushefsky argues that market reform is faced with four sets of implementation problems. First, it is based on an extremely complex program theory. Second, the complexity of the program requires that numerous actors behave appropriately, which may not happen. Third, opposition to market reform exists because many actors are adversely affected by it, and they will seek to limit the impacts during implementation, much as occurs with other government programs. Finally, the politics that market reformers decry remains because affected actors, especially those whose interests are most directly affected, will seek to fix the rules within which competition occurs. Thus, the role of government persists, even though it has a different focus than in the implementation of standard programs.

A second prominent proposal for the improvement of policy implementation is "contracting out," which refers to the practice of having public services supplied either by other governmental jurisdictions or by private (profit or nonprofit) organizations instead of delivering the service through a government unit's own personnel. In Chapter 8 Ruth Hoogland DeHoog investigates the utility of contracting out as a solution to implementation problems. Employing the theoretical perspectives of the economics of market imperfection, the politics of cooptation, and the process of organizational decision making, she suggests that the various conditions assumed by contracting adherents are unlikely to occur in the real world. Consequently, many of the positive expectations of contracting are unlikely to materialize either. Indeed, contracting could even exacerbate the already serious problems of government.

The major difficulty with the contracting prescriptions, she argues, is that too often proponents offer them as panaceas for the current ills of government with little explicit recognition of the requisite conditions and realities of implementation. At least four general deficiencies are evident in the contracting prescriptions: (1) they overlook the motivational and organizational contexts of the contracting participants; (2) they fail to recognize the critical role that the service environment can play in contracting, both in terms of the pool of potential providers and the inputs and feedback of service consumers; (3) they often assume that quasi-market mechanisms will operate almost automatically, without exploring how and why contracting is actually utilized, what procedures are critical in producing the expected benefits, and under which conditions contracting works best; and (4) they typically have not fully considered the effect of wide-scale contracting on public policy implementation and the private agencies that provide public services.

The author concludes that many of the same problems that plague in-house supply of services will also characterize contractual arrangements for service provision. She then discusses the conditions under which contracting out is likely to be most successful.

Collectively the essays in this book provide a degree of optimism for those concerned with improving policy implementation, certainly one of the most intractable problems of government. They help us both to better understand the process of implementation itself and to evaluate proposed solutions. Equally important, the authors demonstrate how high quality scholarship based on solid social science foundations can contribute much to governing. It is to these contributions that we now turn.

George C. Edwards III

REFERENCES

Congressional Quarterly (1982) "Congress facing pressures to loosen, tighten federal safe drinking water statute." (May 1).

Kissinger, H. (1979) White House Years. Boston: Little, Brown.

Newsweek (1983) "The lessons learned at Three Mile Island." (June 27).

Sills, D. L. (1981) "Comment." American Political Science Review 75(March):143–45.

PART I

COMMUNICATION AND CONTROL

POLICY IMPLEMENTATION AND OVERHEAD CONTROL

Frank J. Thompson

INTRODUCTION

Overhead control continues to captivate many analysts concerned with the effective implementation of public policy. This model possesses a clear normative thrust. It holds that the traditional institutions of oversight, elected executives, legislators, and the judiciary, ought to exert substantial control over the implementation process.[1]

Precise policy mandates presumably comprise one appropriate path to control. A number of analysts have extolled such statutes as a potent catalyst for effective implementation. In this regard, Sabatier and Mazmanian (1979:487) argue that, given a sound underlying theory, a program's prospects improve when "policy objectives are precise and clearly ranked both internally (within the specific statute) and in the overall program of the implementing agencies." Another study asserts "that the surest way to avoid intraorganizational implementation problems is to establish a specific mandate and provide sufficient resources . . ." (Montjoy and O'Toole, 1979:473). Yet another analysis suggests that being specific about what is to be achieved and how constitutes "a necessary first step toward effective implementation" (Nakamura and Smallwood, 1980:33). Observers credit precise mandates with giving an agency a major weapon to turn against those who oppose its mission. Specific statutes also win praise for reducing the prospects that an agency's officials will dissipate energy in skirmishes over the interpretation of the law. Then, too, such mandates are thought to expedite evaluation and, thereby, the detection and correction of errors.

The contribution to effective implementation of the oversight that follows a law's approval has garnered less explicit consideration. Several observers have, however, come close to endorsing such oversight as a requisite of successful implementation. Sabatier and Mazmanian (1979:493) posit, for instance, that "implementing officials cannot necessarily be trusted to act in a manner consistent with statutory objectives. What is also required is constant oversight and intervention from supportive constituency groups and legislative (and executive) sovereigns." In this regard, they favor granting groups ample opportunity to appeal agency decisions to the courts as well as other devices designed to increase oversight.

Interest in finding a fixer has also directed attention toward the role of overhead actors in implementation. A fixer is some official or group that monitors a program carefully and intervenes to repair it when malfunctions occur. Following Bardach's (1977) insightful study of a California assemblyman's role in helping a mental health program through troubled waters, students of implementation have often looked to the legislative branch for fixers. Top political executives have, however, also been nominated for this ameliorative role (e.g., Sabatier and Mazmanian, 1979:497; Williams, 1980:108).

The allure of the overhead model of effective implementation receives a further boost from its compatibility with traditional theories of democracy. It seems consistent with ideals about the rule of law and the thwarting of unaccountable bureaucratic power (Finer, 1965; Lowi, 1969; Bensel, 1980). In essence, the overhead model eradicates the classic tension between efficiency and accountability. The citizenry can have its cake and eat it too.

In sketching the overhead model of effective implementation, it is important to avoid caricature. No single author has etched an elaborate theory of effective implementation via overhead control, and virtually all analysts acknowledge the importance of other variables in explaining implementation success. Moreover, some students of implementation are openly skeptical of the presumed correlation between overhead control and cost-effective implementation. Edwards (1980:26) observes, for instance, that "implementators need flexibility and can be hampered by overly specific instructions." Majone and Wildavsky (1979:189) go even further when they assert that "We require the impossible when we expect our bureaucrats to be at the same time literal executors and successful implementers of policy mandates." These and other analysts remain sensitive to how precise laws and concerted oversight can spawn premature programming, the proliferation of red tape, and rigidity (e.g., Berman, 1978; Menzel, 1981; Stout, 1980). While the overhead control model can hardly claim uniform endorsement among students of implementation, it nevertheless continues to serve as the fulcrum for much discussion. Moreover, it exerts a powerful prescriptive pull among the citizenry and elected officials. Popular political rhetoric tends to exalt the virtues of this model.

The debate over the potential and limitations of the overhead model in policy implementation deserves continued scrutiny. This essay strives to cast light on the subject by developing a typology of implementation based on the model's two major dimensions and by exploring the conditions under which each of the types becomes more attractive as a vehicle for cost-effective implementation. As Figure 1 indicates, statutory precision comprises one critical dimension of the matrix. Such precision is a function of the degree to which legislation defines objectives, quantifies them, specifies timetables for obtaining them, indicates priorities where multiple objectives exist, and spells out the administrative structure to be used in implementing the program.[2] Oversight comprises the second dimension. It increases to the degree that elected officials, their appointed staffs, and the courts spend more time reviewing the activities of implementing agencies.[3] The dimensions of precision and oversight are both continua. Ideally, researchers could pinpoint the exact location of a program along each continuum. Given current measurement problems and the need to get beyond the trees to see the forest, however, this analysis dichotomizes the two dimensions. As the diagram indicates, four

| | | *Statutory Precision* | |
		Limited	*Great*
Oversight	*Great*	Up-for-grabs implementation	Controlled implementation
	Limited	Buffered implementation	Prophylactic implementation

Figure 1. Types of Implementation Based on the Overhead Model

types of implementation emerge—controlled, prophylactic, up-for-grabs, and buffered implementation.

The next four sections of this essay consider in turn each of these types of implementation, focusing in particular on the conditions that heighten their appeal. As will become apparent, the controlled model of implementation seems likely to have prescriptive appeal in only a limited number of cases from the perspective of cost-effectiveness. A final section considers the implications of this conclusion for those concerned about both achieving more benefits per dollar spent and democratic accountability.

CONTROLLED IMPLEMENTATION

Controlled implementation features precise statutory mandates and much oversight activity. It embodies Finer's dictum that the course of action of public servants ought to be determined "to the most minute degree that is technically feasible" (1965:77). What factors heighten the allure of this model? Abjuring any claim to comprehensiveness, the following conditions play that role: (1) a well-understood technology that is not bottom heavy; (2) moderate environmental stability; (3) the absence of tempered commitment to the policy within the implementing agency; (4) a debilitating sociopolitical milieu; and (5) efficacious overhead institutions.[4]

Certain Technology

A well-understood technology that is not bottom heavy enhances the applicability of controlled implementation (Berman, 1978). Policy objectives vary considerably in terms of uncertainty over how to accomplish them. Certain aspects of assembling weapons for defense or of guaranteeing income under Social Security pose few technological mysteries. At least in the abstract, there seems to be little reason why Congress could not draft detailed legislation spelling out how to procure certain conventional weapons and to achieve income maintenance goals. In other spheres, however, the appropriate technology remains shrouded in fog. How can one set up a device to determine whether physicians paid by Medicare or Medicaid provide too much or too little service? Given fundamental ambiguities about what constitutes quality medical care, the precise specification of a system to achieve this end continues to divide and bemuse experts in the area. When a problem demands a bottom heavy technology, controlled implementation also becomes less feasible. Such a technology features heavy dependence on discretionary decisions at the street level (Elmore, 1980; Lipsky, 1980). Mental health, medical, or educational programs, for instance, often require that lower-level "professionals" make judgments about the particular needs of a client. Efforts to program the decisions of these street-level employees may well create dysfunctional rigidities.

Paradoxically, the more certain and less bottom heavy the technology, the more satisfactorily can the control model be applied but the less need exists for it in many cases. Where a technology is widely understood, clarification of goals may well be all that is required. A statute could be less precise about means because of the pervasive understanding about how to accomplish the task.

Moderate Environmental Stability

At least moderate environmental stability also enhances the appeal of the control model (Berman, 1978; Sabatier and Mazmanian, 1979). Rapid change in social, political, or economic conditions can quickly convert a sound policy hypothesis embedded in a precise statute into an invalid one. Consider, for instance, the Medicaid program which seeks to provide health care to those on welfare and to other indigent groups. The federal subsidy needed to entice effective state participation in this program could change markedly as economic conditions shift and as tax revolts or other political phenomena surface. To be sure, the oversight endemic to controlled implementation may help policymakers cope with some of these changes. Through constant monitoring, they may modify precise statutes in response to new conditions. But in the face of very rapid change, it seems unlikely that lawmakers, given their crowded agendas, will be able to adjust rapidly enough.

Absence of Tempered Commitment

A dearth of tempered commitment within the implementing agency also boosts the appeal of controlled implementation. Tempered commitment exists within an implementing agency when its key personnel strike a reasonable balance between dogma (or zealotry) and skepticism (or hostility). Where such commitment exists, officials stand ready to do their utmost to implement the law while simultaneously striving to make the program workable. In doing so, policy gets treated as hypothesis.

Commitment does not get translated into blind advocacy of obsolete techniques. In the spirit of science, officials remain open to information that certain initiatives do not work and of the potential need to formulate alternative policy hypotheses.

Other things being equal, the absence of tempered commitment necessitates more control by oversight actors if prospects for cost-effective implementation are to improve. In this regard, precise statutes and vigorous oversight may prove salutary in a number of respects. Where substantial opposition to a program exists within the implementing agency, these factors may convince managers that they need to comply despite their reservations about the program. In the face of dissension within an agency over the desirability of the policy, precise statutes and vigorous oversight may help the supportive coalition within the agency gain the upper hand. Controlled implementation may also inhibit dysfunctional performance by program zealots. This zealousness need not take the form of "overfeasance," i.e., going beyond the law in support of the program (Finer, 1965:180). It may simply mean staunch adherence to techniques that no longer function very effectively. Many officials in the Veterans Administration medical system, for instance, have remained firmly committed to the delivery of hospital-based acute care that employs the most sophisticated medical hardware. In fact, however, much evidence suggests that their aging clientele suffers from chronic and other diseases that are not particularly receptive to this form of treatment (Thompson and Campbell, 1981).

While controlled implementation probably makes more sense where tempered commitment does not exist, it essentially makes the best of a bad situation. The more rule bound and compliance oriented the implementation process becomes, the less likely are administrators to use their own initiative and abilities (Elmore, 1980:17). The risk runs high that administrators will play it by the book. Unless the statute and oversight are unusually sensible, this propensity may well breed rigidity. Administrators may apply rules even when they understand that these rules will undermine program effectiveness.

In considering the implications of commitment for the applicability of controlled implementation, we should emphasize that one must go beyond the federal bureaucracy in analyzing agency cultures. State and local governments often win critical roles in the implementation drama. Moreover, "indirect" or "third-party government" has often assumed center stage as private contractors on the "margins of the state" play pivotal roles (Salamon, 1981; Sharkansky, 1979). For instance, two major domestic programs in the United States, Medicaid and Medicare, rely heavily on private insurance companies for implementation.

Debilitating Sociopolitical Milieu

A debilitating sociopolitical milieu also heightens the appeal of controlled implementation. A debilitating milieu can spring from strong opposition to the goals of the program by the group targeted for attention (a common feature of many regulatory programs). Sabatier and Mazmanian (1979:485) have argued in this regard that the more opposed the target group is, the more critical it becomes to structure the statute precisely. It needs to be stressed, however, that a program's allies can also weaken it. The Medicare program, for instance, hardly endures serious opposition. Physicians and hospitals quickly came to see it as a major source of income. Rather than opposing the program, however, they have undermined its cost-effectiveness by practices that inflate the costs of the medical care they provide. Hence, the concept of a debilitating milieu needs to be extended beyond opposition of the target group. Whenever the preponderance of forces in a task environment places pressure on the agency to behave in ways that fail to foster cost-effectiveness, such a milieu exists.

Not all analysts would agree that a debilitating sociopolitical milieu increases the allure of controlled implementation. Berman (1978), for instance, argues that a "programmed approach" to administration becomes more suitable where there is little resistance to policy goals. He sees considerable advantage in administrators negotiating a compromise with opponents rather than seeking in more hierarchical fashion to prevail. But if one assumes a plausible policy hypothesis, the notion of negotiating differences during the implementation process becomes much less appealing. In most cases, sound policy (e.g., enforcing civil rights) may require a strong element of coercion by those with legitimate claims to authority (Bullock, 1980; Sabatier, 1975). One must recognize that the cost-effectiveness of a program can be negotiated away for the sake of environmental tranquillity.

One reason why controlled implementation looms as more important in a debilitating milieu is the low status of public bureaucracies in the United States. One observer has gone so far as to suggest that "the ineffectiveness and inefficiency" of the public sector is a belief "so widely and firmly held that one . . . can regard it as a unifying theme of our national creed: something that might be inserted after we hold these truths to be self-evident" (Waldo, 1980:17). While some view the low status of the federal bureaucracy as a means for curtailing bureaucratic arrogance, in fact the limited status of public agencies tends to heighten their need for succor from groups in their task environment. With limited prestige, officials in implementing agencies must often turn to statutory provisions or find allies among overhead actors if they are to resist group pressures inimical to cost-effectiveness.

Efficacious Overhead Actors

Controlled implementation becomes more enticing when overhead actors are efficacious. Their efficacy increases to the degree that they possess the capacity and incentive to formulate theoretically sound and coherent policies as well as to engage in error correction. Efficacious overhead institutions make the most of the knowledge base available in society to guide public policy development.

Any attempt to calibrate the efficacy of various overhead institutions confronts thorny empirical and normative questions. While answers to these questions must await further research and analysis, it seems pertinent to address some of the issues raised by the concept of efficacy through an examination of Congress. Among federal overhead institutions, Congress had probably fallen under the sharpest criticism by the end of the 1970s.

The need to forge coalitions has long provided some incentive for legislators to leave goals and means ambiguous. During the 1970s, however, the growth in congressional staffs precipitated greater attention to the details of legislation. But paying so much attention to trees can blind solons to the forest. The resulting legislation has in the view of one observer "been complicated, often contradictory, and more than occasionally filled with gaps" (Ornstein, 1981:381). Several factors account for this development. Ornstein (1981:369) notes, for example, that as many in Congress came to view the office as a steppingstone rather than a capstone to their careers, "the incentive for quick recognition has broadened" and "the formerly widespread pride in legislative craftsmanship has steadily declined."

More fundamentally, the fragmentation of power within Congress has probably undercut congressional efficacy in drafting laws. This fragmentation springs from a quest by members of Congress for personal clout that in turn tends to scatter power to subcommittees. While government by subcommittee enhances a legislator's own prospects for occupying a position with considerable leverage, it tends to weaken Congress as a formulator of precise statutes. Fragmentation has resulted in a situation in which many subcommittees can claim jurisdiction over a single bill. This has spawned a "bewildering array of access points" that groups can exploit to make sure that their concerns get taken into account (Davidson, 1981:121–123). The coalition formation process becomes less predictable and legislation increasingly seeks to satisfy a multitude of particular interests. The statutory sum of all the particular interests often fails to equal a coherent whole (see Sinclair, 1981:220).

Dysfunctional dynamics may become particularly evident in programs that explicitly allocate resources on a geographic basis. Here, the scattering of power makes it more difficult to forge multiple- as opposed to single-program logrolls (Arnold, 1979:210–11; 1981). Multiple-program coalitions derive from a willingness by members of Congress to support one another's most preferred program. Within each program, however, resources might still be allotted to areas of greatest need. Single-program coalitions, by contrast, depend on satisfying supporters within that program alone. Pressures to spread benefits broadly mount as less needy areas absorb disproportionate amounts of program resources. In sum, single-program logrolls heighten the risk that pork barrel dynamics will become more acute. Even when members of Congress firmly grasp the nature of a problem and the technology needed to ameliorate it, the marriage of policy precision and plausibility is often difficult to arrange.

Serious doubts also exist about the efficacy of Congress as a fixer of programs. To be sure, Congress has devoted more attention to oversight (Aberbach, 1979). Hearings have increased, the congressional staff has grown, the Congressional Budget Office has emerged, and the domain of the General Accounting Office has expanded. Moreover, Congress has moved steadily toward drafting statutes that require the bureaucracy to furnish information and obtain approval for certain administrative actions. During the decade of the 1970s, Congress adopted over 550 provisions in well over 300 federal statutes requiring congressional review of agency plans, projects, and rules (Gilmour, 1982:13). As a result of these developments, it may well be that the ability of Congress to detect errors of implementation has never been greater.

One cannot, however, necessarily equate increased congressional oversight with an enhanced tendency to repair programs. Lawmakers and their staffs may put their information to little use, a common phenomenon in organizations (Feldman and March, 1981:174). Then, too, knowledge of malfunctions need not produce insights as to how to remedy them. Learning can be difficult even among actors committed to correcting mistakes. More fundamentally, lawmakers may lack incentive to seek and use information most pertinent to fixing programs.

The fragmentation of power within Congress and the access it gives to interest groups can weaken legislative efficacy in this regard. Congressional intervention in administrative issues often has less to do with assuring that the bureaucracy follows the letter of the law or achieves cost-effectiveness than it does with advancing the cause of a particular interest group. Use of the legislative veto, for instance, has often featured this pattern (Gilmour, 1982).

The media also provide members of Congress with little incentive to get involved in fixing. As a rule, implementation problems do not make for interesting news stories. When the media do cover implementation, they tend to examine it in moralistic terms isolating cases of egregious abuse rather than more important, systemic issues. In the case of Medicare, for instance, the media devote far more attention to sporadic scandals than the seemingly dry but much more important technical issues concerning payment formulas and the inefficiencies they foster. A member of Congress who plunges into the significant details of implementation tends to win scant praise. Another who superficially grandstands over issues of bureaucratic performance often wins far more favorable publicity. The low status of public agencies further tempts members of Congress to raise their political capital by blaming or ridiculing the bureaucracy rather than by helping it diagnose and correct errors.

The popularity of casework may also divert Congress from more fundamental efforts at fixing. Members of the legislative branch have grown increasingly interested in cultivating voters by offering a potpourri of constituent services. They frequently intercede on behalf of citizens who must deal with bureaucracy. Casework yields much political profit for legislators. It creates far fewer enemies than taking stands on issues that affect programs as a whole. It often does little, however, to strengthen their performance as program fixers (Fiorina, 1977). The emphasis on casework can lead to the triumph of Gresham's Law of Oversight where bad time drives out good.

Thus, increased oversight by Congress may do little to foster error correction. It may even open the door to error creation as certain factions in Congress side with groups bent on making a program less cost-effective. Or it may inhibit efforts by administrators or other overhead institutions to repair programs. On balance, the available evidence about the efficacy of Congress tends to weaken the case for controlled implementation as a springboard for cost-effectiveness.

The efficacy of other overhead actors no doubt varies from program to program and over time. Overall, however, the institutions of the presidency and the judiciary have tended to receive less consistently pessimistic assessments. To be sure, one can raise some efficacy issues. Consider, for instance, the institutions of the presidency. Aside from circumstances where ideological convictions may incite a president to sabotage a program that he dislikes, other factors may undermine efficacy. The office of the presidency has become so large and complex that it presents the chief executive with major problems of internal management (Heclo, 1981:162). Moreover, the networks for recruiting top political executives suffer from deficiencies. Fragmentary national party organizations have perennially been an uncertain source of political manpower for managing the bureaucracy. In recent years the demand for better qualified political executives has increased while the capacity of these networks to provide them has probably declined further (Heclo, 1977:94). While these factors may impair the fixing capacity of the presidency, however, the overall efficacy of this institution seems greater than that of Congress.

The courts, which have become increasingly involved in implementation, have also drawn criticism. Some assert that as generalists rather than policy experts, judges lack the capacity to interpret statutes in ways that will foster cost-effective implementation. They also note that the cases brought to court may shed light on only a tiny aspect of a program's operations. The judges may not be able to put the case and program in broader perspective. Then, too, when courts err, they must usually wait for other cases to be brought to correct the mistake.

The efficacy of the courts may well be much greater than these arguments allow, however, The trial records, legal briefs, and oral arguments upon which judges depend are often quite extensive. Thus, judges can often make an informed decision that takes into account the broader functioning of the program. In this regard, their generalist vision may help them avoid the pathologies of tunnel vision that often afflict policy experts. Judges are also buffered from immediate interest group pressures that would weaken cost-effectiveness. Furthermore, in as litigious a nation as the United States, the courts are likely to have plenty of opportunities to correct their errors (Baum, 1980). Hence, the balance sheet with respect to the efficacy of the courts in implementation remains mixed.

Whatever the level of efficacy among overhead institutions, it does comprise a critical intervening variable in determining the desirability of controlled implementation. It must be emphasized that not only the efficacy of *each* overhead institution, but also their *collective* efficacy is critical. The collective element brings to the fore the following potential problem: as more overhead institutions become involved, overall efficacy may well decline. Lawmaking and fixing may come to require an extraordinarily high degree of coordination. In essence, greater involvement by all overhead institutions could further fragment political authority and thereby heighten the potential for veto group pluralism, political stalemate, and ineffective implementation.

The appeal of controlled implementation varies, then, not only with certainty about technology, the level of environmental stability, the nature of commitment in the implementing agencies, and qualities of the sociopolitical milieu; it also hinges upon the efficacy of overhead actors. At times enough salutary conditions may be present to make a normative case for controlled implementation on grounds of cost-effectiveness. In many other circumstances, however, the case will be very weak.

PROPHYLACTIC IMPLEMENTATION

Prophylactic implementation features precise statutes and limited oversight. It requires great skill at anticipating and planning, at laying out a coherent, detailed statute. It stresses error prevention and deemphasizes error correction in that oversight actors do not monitor the program very much. Moreover, the precise law tends to tie the hands of administrators so that they cannot readily play the role of fixer.

Under what circumstances would this model be more attractive? To an even greater degree than in controlled implementation, a well-understood technology that did not depend on substantial discretion by street-level employees would be essential. Environmental stability would also be all the more critical. With capacity to correct errors so limited, officials would need to plan and hope that no change would arise to invalidate the program's underlying hypothesis.

Then, too, prophylactic implementation becomes more appealing when at least a moderate level of commitment exists within the implementing agencies. A strong sense of legal obligation may be the most pertinent component of this commitment since the model emphasizes compliance more than creativity and initiative on the part of administrators. The outright absence of commitment poses more of a threat for this model than for controlled implementation. With overhead actors quiescent, unsympathetic administrators would more readily come to believe that they could get away with sluggish implementation or sabotage. For similar reasons, prophylactic implementation also becomes more appealing where a sociopolitical milieu is not strongly debilitating. Precise statutory provisions can help implementing agencies resist some group pressures that would divert a program from cost-effectiveness. But without allies among overhead actors, the bureaucracy's ability to resist is likely to be quite limited. The low status of public agencies exacerbates this problem.

Finally, the allure of this form of implementation increases if the efficacy of overhead actors in drafting coherent, plausible statutes is quite high. Policymakers must possess an extraordinary capacity to process information and plan. Efficacy at error correction would be less necessary under this model.

Given prevailing conditions in American society, the prospects that the prophylactic model will hold widespread appeal as the handmaiden of effective policy seem slim. Whatever its limitations, controlled implementation provides more opportunity for overhead actors to correct mistakes than this model does.

UP-FOR-GRABS IMPLEMENTATION

Up-for-grabs implementation features imprecise statutes and considerable oversight. Those who view adaptation, evolution, and learning as central to implementation might well see considerable virtue in this model. To some degree, this perspective draws sustenance from choice theorists who have begun to distance themselves from the rational model of decision making. The rational model generally assumes that good decisions require clear goals. March (1978:595, 603), however, argues that when decision makers have confused and contradictory preferences, "precision misrepresents them." In this view, decision making involves guesses not only about the future consequences of various alternatives but also about preferences for these consequences. At times people learn what they want by doing it. Recognition of this phenomenon has driven students of choice to the conclusion that vague tastes or goals may at times be intelligent rather than stupid. Or, as one analyst has observed, "Implementation is no longer solely about getting what you once wanted but what you have since learned to prefer . . ." (Wildavsky, 1979:176). Under this model, then, fidelity to an original plan becomes less of a concern. Bargaining emerges as a possible route to a kind of "disorderly learning process" (Berman, 1978:9).

On the surface, then, up-for-grabs implementation may seem the perfect midwife for flexibility and learning. But as with other forms of implementation, pathologies can afflict it. Carried to an extreme, the model elevates drift to the level of principle (Elmore, 1978:226). Actors involved in this implementation game may spend enormous energy bargaining and jockeying for position with almost nothing to show for it in terms of providing services or goods to clients. As with the other models, one needs to probe the circumstances under which up-for-grabs implementation holds out greater promise.

Not surprisingly, uncertainty about appropriate technologies adds to the allure of this model. At times, lawmakers have little recourse other than to throw money at a problem in hopes of discovering an effective way of accomplishing some task. In the absence of clearly understood technologies, the desirability of filling statutes with highly precise statements of goals and means becomes questionable. Few decision makers can confidently articulate precise objectives without understanding what must be done to accomplish them. Hence, goal articulation can be premature even when a substantial consensus seems to exist among policymakers concerning desirable ends. Stout (1980:107–108), for instance, argues that "when causal knowledge is lacking, complete goal specification can inhibit the exploitation of unexpected opportunities" and thwart "trial-and-error strategies . . . to take advantage of discovered opportunities."

Fluid environmental conditions also add to the luster of up-for-grabs implementation. If pertinent social, economic, and political conditions are highly ephemeral, up-for-grabs implementation can allow for relatively rapid adjustments. It can fuel adoption of new techniques and expedite a renegotiation of the value assumptions that undergird the program. This renegotiation looms as important because altered conditions may spawn new preferences among policymakers.

Up-for-grabs implementation also becomes more enticing if at least a moderate level of tempered commitment to the program exists within the implementing agency. In the absence of such commitment, overhead actors may still be able to steer administrators in desirable directions. But the energy consumed in doing so will be greater. The burdens of program guidance and error correction will more squarely rest on the shoulders of overhead actors. A moderate level of tempered commitment assures that administrators will more readily treat policy as hypothesis; it thereby boosts prospects for creative adaptation.

The need for a measure of tempered commitment represents a marked change from the vision ensconced in either the controlled or prophylactic models. These approaches expect administrators to comply, to play it by the book. Up-for-grabs implementation places a higher value on administrators having initiative and intelligence. These administrators need to be sufficiently skilled at advocacy to get their concerns taken into account in the bargaining that usually accompanies such implementation.

Up-for-grabs implementation also deserves more consideration where the sociopolitical milieu is no more than moderately debilitating. Strong pressures against cost-effective implementation probably signal an inadequate basis on which to bargain creatively. Without a sense of shared interests, bargaining with these outside groups will probably not produce very sanguine results in terms of cost-effectiveness. If confronted with the need to resist intense debilitating pressures, administrators will not be able to defend themselves with precise statutory provisions. Instead, they will need to obtain vigorous support from overhead actors. Support of this intensity will probably be difficult to obtain.

A situation where overhead actors possess considerable capacity and incentive to engage in error correction also magnifies the appeal of up-for-grabs implementation. Efficacy in drafting precise statutes takes a back seat to fixing. It deserves note in this regard, however, that the model demands less of overhead actors as fixers than controlled implementation. Error correction under controlled implementation tends to require adjustments in statutory authority. These revisions require intervention by overhead actors and can be cumbersome to arrange. Under up-for-grabs implementation, in contrast, legislators can use more informal means to repair programs. Moreover, the vague statutes give managers within the implementing agencies a chance to play a more pivotal role in error correction. These officials may function quite effectively in this regard (Thompson, 1982).

Relative to controlled or prophylactic implementation, the conditions bolstering the allure of up-for-grabs implementation seem more likely to be present. The most persistent barriers to its applicability probably arise from the limited efficacy of overhead actors as fixers.

Some, of course, may question how any discussion of the cost-effectiveness of up-for-grabs implementation can be meaningful.[5] If statutes do not clearly enunciate goals, how can any judgment of cost-effectiveness be made? In fact, however, vague goals need not rule out such judgments. To be sure, the absence of clear statutory standards may impede summary proclamations that a program succeeded or failed. But such statements generally contribute more to caricature than understanding anyway. In the absence of precise statutory criteria an analyst need not totally depend on "muddling through" tests of performance where a policy is deemed "good" if key actors perceive this to be the case (Lindblom, 1959). Other modes of evaluation based on more systematic research can also take root. This evaluative research can be guided by the substantial consensus that usually exists at a given point concerning the *range of values* that deserve consideration in assessing a program.

Consider, for instance, the Emergency Health Personnel Act of 1970 (Redman, 1973; Thompson, 1982). This legislation ultimately led to the establishment of the National Health Service Corps, a group of physicians in the Public Health Service who were to work in critical shortage areas. The law was very vague about goals and means. Yet, although those monitoring the program often differed about the particular path it should follow, their discussions and debates revealed considerable consensus about a range of values that ought to be on the scorecard. Did the course taken by the National Health Service Corps allow it to target its resources on those who ordinarily faced the greatest barriers to obtaining medical care? Did it heighten the productivity of physicians involved in the program? Did it swell access to health care in rural areas? Did it bolster the access of the poor in the cities? Using analysis to answer any one of those questions would not permit definitive judgment as to whether the program succeeded or failed. But answering several of them sheds light on what the program did and did not do effectively. If one adopts the phrase, "Given value X, then the program accomplished Y at cost Z," evaluative judgment of cost-effectiveness based on systematic analysis can still be rendered.

BUFFERED IMPLEMENTATION

Imprecise statutes and limited oversight characterize buffered implementation. In some respects, the conditions contributing to the palatability of the up-for-grabs model also apply here. Uncertainty about appropriate technologies as well as environmental fluidity, for instance, enhance the appeal of this model as well as the up-for-grabs approach. But differences between the models also exist.

Buffered implementation places more of a premium on tempered commitment within the implementing agency. Since overhead actors refrain from much involvement in this implementation game, the initiative and creativity of officials in the implementing agencies become particularly momentous. The willingness to treat policy as hypothesis becomes all the more important. Administrators must be adroit at diagnosing the program's problems and pursuing error correction. Even if tempered commitment runs high within the implementing agencies, however, problems could still surface in the absence of a substantial consensus over which aspects of the program ought to have priority. In the presence of a vague statute, different goals and means might attract the allegiance of different quarters of the bureaucracy. Various bands of committed administrators might expend considerable energy fighting with one another over the definition of program goals and means. Thus, in addition to tempered commitment, buffered implementation probably requires homogeneous outlooks among officials within the implementing agencies or a means of rapidly resolving disagreements about proper statutory interpretations.

Is there reason to believe that administrators have the capacity and incentive to play the creative role required by buffered implementation? Not inevitably. Yet, various analyses hold out some hope in this regard.

Rein and Rabinovitz (1978:311–13) note, for instance, that the "rational-bureaucratic imperative" often becomes a major driving force in implementation. While a concern with "institutional maintenance, protection and growth" lies at the heart of this imperative, it also reflects a concern born of considerable experience and expertise as to what is reasonable, workable, and just. Then, too, while troubled by issues of accountability when administrators take the lead in formulating policy goals and means, Nakamura and Smallwood (1980:115, 141) conclude that "in terms of producing results and getting things done," this approach "is one of the most efficient of all the implementation scenarios." More specifically some analyses suggest that implementing agencies serve as a useful check on the propensity of Congress to capitulate to pork barrel politics. This brand of politics diverts money from needy locales in order to distribute benefits broadly to many congressional districts. One of the leading students of the pork barrel notes that bureaucrats are much less susceptible to such politics and, given adequate discretion, "are much more likely than congressman to target funds according to need" (Arnold, 1981:185). An analysis of the National Health Service Corps supports this view. In this case, program administrators deflected congressional pressures to spread resources broadly and managed to assign medical personnel in ways that enhanced prospects that those in greatest need would obtain care (Thompson, 1982).

In shaping policy one cannot assume that managers will ignore the preferences of overhead actors. In the United States an imperative to stay within the general parameters of the law seems strong (Rein and Rabinovitz, 1978). Various analyses also suggest that the presidency exerts a powerful pull in shaping the behavior of those in implementing agencies (e.g., Rourke, 1981:137; Cole and Caputo, 1979). One must guard, then, against letting popular stereotypes about the incapacities or obstinacy of implementing agencies obscure the potential for creative management that often exists within these organizations.

The sociopolitical milieu of the implementing agencies also bears on the appeal of the buffered approach. In general the allure of the model tends to grow if these agencies confront a task environment relatively free of group pressures inimical to cost-effective implementation. As Yates (1982:128) has observed, "The absence of intense constituency pressure may well make it easier to organize and manage the work of an agency and pursue the norms of the efficiency model." Where debilitating pressures buffet administration, the low prestige of public agencies means that they will often succumb. The absence of precise statutory authority and of helpful overhead actors can leave administrators naked in their efforts to defend their program.

Finally, the appeal of buffered implementation swells when overhead actors can claim only limited efficacy as formulators of policy mandates or as the handmaidens of error correction. The approach expects little of elected officials and the judiciary.

Under some conditions, then, buffered implementation yields cost-effective implementation. Despite its virtues in certain contexts, however, buffered implementation has tended to receive less attention than the other models as a desirable approach to implementation.

COST-EFFECTIVE IMPLEMENTATION AND DEMOCRACY

This essay has used the variables of statutory precision and oversight to demarcate four approaches to implementation: controlled, prophylactic, up-for-grabs, and buffered. Table 1 provides an overview of those conditions that enhance the piquancy of each form. These conditions incorporate concerns with technology, environmental stability, tempered commitment, the presence or absence of a debilitating sociopolitical milieu, and the efficacy of overhead actors. Minimal prospects exist that all five of these factors will uniformly point toward the suitability of one type of implementation. But consideration of the various conditions can at least alert us to potential trade-offs in the use of one or the other of these models.

While acknowledging that all four types of implementation deserve continued consideration, subsequent analyses might usefully focus more attention on models other than controlled implementation. Both from the perspective of traditional democratic norms and theories of rational decision making, controlled implementation has dominated prescriptive thinking. It would probably be better to recognize that "Public organizations are particularly susceptible to generalizing control to inappropriate realms partly because of demands for bureaucrats to be 'in control' of their organizations and accountable to a superior authority" (Stout, 1980:13). Useful as it is under some circumstances, the emphasis on compliance endemic to the controlled model will often fail to yield greater cost-effectiveness. The potential virtues of other models deserve more study.

For some, of course, any claims on behalf of up-for-grabs or, especially, buffered implementation may seem to represent a kind of political apostasy. What about democratic theory? Even if circumstances point to the cost-effectiveness of buffered implementation, should we prefer the controlled model on grounds of accountability? In some

Table 1. Types of Implementation and Some Conditions Regarding Them

Type	Technology	Environmental Stability	Implementing Agency	Sociopolitical Milieu	Overhead Actors
Controlled	Certain; not bottom heavy	Moderately high	Absence of tempered commitment either in the form of hostility or zealotry	Substantial opposition to cost-effective implementation from groups in the task environment; in sum, a debilitating sociopolitical milieu	The capacity and incentive to formulate coherent policy is moderately high; efficacy in terms of error correction is very high
Prophylactic	Very certain; not bottom heavy	Very high	A moderate level of commitment; strong sense of obligation to obey the law	A milieu that is not strongly debilitating	The capacity and incentive to formulate coherent policy is extremely high; efficacy with respect to error correction is low
Up-for-grabs	Uncertain; often bottom heavy	Low	A moderately high level of tempered commitment	No more than moderate opposition to cost-effective implementation from groups in the task environment	The capacity and incentive to formulate coherent policy is low, but the propensity to engage in error correction is moderately high
Buffered	Uncertain; often bottom heavy	Low	Widespread consensus within the implementing agency; very high level of tempered commitment	Limited, if any, opposition to cost-effective implemention from groups in the task environment	The capacity and incentive to formulate coherent policy and engage in error correction are low

cases, probably so. Beyond some threshold, implementing agencies can
become too autonomous and immune to overhead control. It deserves
emphasis, however, that many of the programs that feature buffered
implementation are probably subject to "big loose control." Even those
who express concern about the extension of bureaucratic policymaking
acknowledge that sufficient mechanisms often exist to inhibit "bull in a
china shop behavior" by agencies. The problem is not usually one of
"unchecked rampaging bureaucracy" (Yates, 1982:152, 167). Or, as
Kaufman (1981:2) observes, "violations of idealized hierarchical norms
do not necessarily free bureaucrats from restraints or place them in a
dominant position. . . ."

In gauging whether big loose control applies to a given case of buffered implementation, the degree to which decision making in that arena
features "silent politics" becomes central (Yates, 1982).[6] The problem of
silent politics becomes acute in the absence of vigorous oversight if little
prospect exists that overhead actors will acquire information about a
program. Often, however, dynamics exist that provide elected officials
with this information even when they spend little time at oversight.
Certain procedures endemic to the operation of government, such as the
budgetary process, usually guarantee the routine transmission of some
information. Beyond this, however, interest groups, the specialized media, and conflict among agencies often generate useful evidence.

Compared to other Western democracies, citizens and interest groups
in the United States have considerable formal access to information
about the decisions of public agencies. Various procedural requirements
reinforce the strong cultural bias in this direction. The Freedom of
Information Act and the Administrative Procedures Act, for instance,
give outside groups access to much information. In the case of regulatory agencies, the emphasis on judicialized procedures, putting disputes
on the record, represents a marked contrast to the more informal and
closed bargaining style that often accompanies regulatory decision making in European democracies (e.g., Kelman, 1981). In view of these
procedural requirements and cultural norms, it is little wonder that
public sector management has been likened to operating in a goldfish
bowl. Interest groups and citizens can, therefore, often obtain evidence
about agency behavior and supply it to the courts or elected officials.

Prospects that interest groups will funnel information in this way increase when implementing agencies have diverse constituencies. In this
regard, a trend toward heterogeneity may well exist. The 1960s and
1970s spawned a proliferation of interest groups, many of which sought
to represent previously submerged interests such as environmental preservation (Rourke, 1981). These groups monitor the bureaucracy and

have encouraged the development of a highly specialized press that reports agency developments to a specialized set of readers. The *Occupational Safety and Health Reporter*, for instance, appears weekly and follows government developments in the policy sphere suggested by its title. Hence, constituency groups become more informed. More fundamentally, the heterogeneity of agency constituencies means that when administrators make a decision that pleases one group, they will often draw biting criticism from another. Such conflict usually unleashes a flow of information to overhead actors.

Overlap and competition among implementing agencies also yields information. Where agency officials do not exclusively control the operation of some program, other agencies may fight with them over issues of program management. To be sure, bureaucrats face strong incentives to stabilize their environments by forging consensus on a given domain among interested agencies. Yates (1982) has in this regard noted a strong bias toward "segmented pluralism" whereby bureaucrats strive to carve out and control a particular policy segment. But if administrators prefer this conflict-dampening arrangement, other forces may well thwart their ability to accomplish it. As governmental programs have multiplied, the tendency for agency jurisdictions to overlap and generate conflict may well have risen (Rourke, 1981:139).

Information-generating dynamics will not, of course, characterize all implementing agencies. For some programs, such as defense, foreign intelligence, and law enforcement, secrecy remains a vital component of an effective technology. Vigorous oversight thereby becomes pivotal if overhead actors are to obtain information. Buffered implementation in these instances is more likely to cross the line from big, loose control to lack of accountability. For many other social and regulatory policies, however, buffered implementation may not precipitate this transgression.

Clearly, concerns with democratic accountability cannot be dismissed in considering the potential cost-effectiveness of the four types of implementation discussed here. At a time when the view runs rampant that government cannot make things work, however, it may well be that greater success in fostering cost-effective implementation would do at least as much to buttress the credibility and legitimacy of government as efforts to increase accountability. Any quest for accountability needs to be carefully focused on policy spheres where big, loose control seems most threatened in the absence of vigorous oversight.

Aside from reconciling cost-effectiveness with democratic norms, an important research agenda remains. The propositions embedded in this essay cry out for empirical examination. Dealing with implementation and its relationship to policy outcomes poses enormously complex methodological problems. But through the use of a range of research techniques, from econometric methods to intensive case analyses, theory development can occur (Williams, 1982). While this research will probably not give birth to *the* laws of implementation, it should allow us to upgrade the content of the ongoing debate over the uses and misuses of controlled implementation.

ACKNOWLEDGMENTS

My thanks to Richard W. Campbell and George Edwards for helpful comments on an earlier draft.

NOTES

1. I have also referred to this as the hierarchy assumption (Thompson, 1982).

2. For an effort to define statutory specificity in quantitative terms, see Rosenbaum (1980).

3. This definition derives from that of Aberbach (1979).

4. In addition to these factors, some analysts have considered the degree of change sought by a statute to be a critical contingency. Berman (1978:17) argues that "all other things being equal, policy involving minor change can be more effectively or more efficiently implemented using a programmed approach." This approach entails giving more detailed instructions to administrators. Berman suggests that minor changes tend to be ignored unless specifically required. Major changes, by contrast, involve efforts to "ameliorate resistance to change by inviting extensive participation in the decision process." Sabatier and Mazmanian (1979:485) reach a different conclusion, however. They suggest that the greater the mandated change, the greater must usually be the statutory structuring of the implementation process. This essay takes the view that both sides to this debate may be correct in certain circumstances. These circumstances can largely be defined by the five factors analyzed here (e.g., tempered commitment within the implementing agency). Relative to these five variables, the degree of change sought does not appear to be as important an explanatory factor.

5. The same question could, of course, be raised with respect to buffered implementation.

6. Of course, critical problems could also arise if administrators explicitly refused to obey clear instructions from overhead actors that have a firm foundation in law.

REFERENCES

Aberbach, J. D. (1979) "Changes in congressional oversight." American Behavioral Scientist 22:493–515.

Arnold, R. D. (1979) Congress and the Bureaucracy. New Haven, Conn.: Yale University Press.

Arnold, R. D. (1981) "The local roots of domestic policy." In T. E. Mann and N. J. Ornstein (eds.), The New Congress. Washington, D. C.: American Enterprise Institute.

Bardach, E. (1977) The Implementation Game. Cambridge, Mass.: MIT Press.

Baum, L. (1980) "The influence of legislatures and appellate courts over the policy implementation process." Policy Studies Journal 8:560–74.

Bensel, R. F. (1980) "Creating the statutory state: the implications of a rule of law standard in American politics." American Political Science Reivew 74:735–44.

Berman, P. (1978) "Designing implementation to match policy situation: a contingency analysis of programmed and adaptive implementation." New York: Paper delivered at the American Political Science Association Convention.

Bullock, III, C. S. (1980) "The office for civil rights and implementation of desegregation programs in the public schools." Policy Studies Journal 8:597–616.

Cole, R. L. and Caputo D. A. (1979) "Presidential control of the senior Civil Service: assessing the strategies of the Nixon years." American Political Science Review 73:399–413.

Davidson, R. H. (1981) "Subcommitte government: new channels for policy making." In T. E. Mann and N. J. Ornstein (eds.), The New Congress. Washington, D.C.: American Enterprise Institute.

Edwards, III, G. C. (1980) Implementing Public Policy. Washington, D.C.: Congressional Quarterly, Inc.

Elmore, R. F. (1978) "Organizational models of social program implementation." Public Policy 26:185–228.

Elmore, R. F. (1980) Complexity and Control: What Legislators and Administrators Can Do About Implementing Public Policy. Washington, D.C.: National Institute of Education.

Feldman, M. S. and J. G. March (1981) "Information in organizations as signal and symbol." Administrative Science Quarterly 26:171–86.

Finer, H. (1965) "Administrative responsibility in democratic government." In F. E. Rourke (ed.), Bureaucratic Power in National Politics. Boston: Little, Brown.

Fiorina, M. P. (1977) Congress: Keystone of the Washington Establishment. New Haven, Conn.: Yale University Press.

Gilmour, R. S. (1982) "The congressional veto: shifting the balance of administrative control." Journal of Policy Analysis and Management 2:13–25.

Heclo, H. (1977) A Government of Strangers. Washington: Brookings Institution.

Heclo, H. (1981) "The changing Presidential Office." In A. J. Meltsner (ed.), Politics and the Oval Office. San Francisco: Institute for Contemporary Studies.

Kaufman, H. (1981) "Fear of bureaucracy: a raging pandemic." Public Administration Review 41:1–9.

Kelman, S. (1981) Regulating America, Regulating Sweden. Cambridge, Mass.: MIT Press.

Lindblom, C. E. (1959) "The science of muddling through." *Public Administration Review.* 19:79–88.

Lipsky, M. (1980) Street-Level Bureaucracy. New York: Russell Sage Foundation.

Lowi, T. (1969) The End of Liberalism. New York: Norton.

Majone, C. and A. Wildavsky (1979) "Implementation as evolution." In J. L. Pressman and A. Wildavsky (eds.), Implementation, 2nd ed. Berkeley: University of California Press.

March, J. G. (1978) "Bounded rationality, ambiguity, and the engineering of choice." The Bell Journal of Economics 9:587–608.

Menzel, D. C. (1981) "Implementation of the federal surface mining control and reclamation act of 1977." Public Administration Review 41:212–218.

Montjoy, R. S. and L. J. O'Toole, Jr. (1979) "Toward a theory of policy implementation: an organizational perspective." Public Administration Review 39:465–76.

Nakamura, R. T. and F. Smallwood (1980) The Politics of Policy Implementation. New York: St. Martin's Press.

Ornstein, N. J. (1981) "The House and the Senate in a new Congress." In T. E. Mann and N. J. Ornstein (eds.), The New Congress. Washington, D.C.: American Enterprise Institute.

Redman, E. (1973) The Dance of Legislation. New York: Simon & Schuster.

Rein, M., and F. F. Rabinovitz, (1978) "Implementation: a theoretical perspective." In W. D. Burnham and M. W. Weinberg (eds.), American Politics and Public Policy. Cambridge, Mass.: MIT Press.

Rosenbaum, N. (1980) "Statutory structure and policy implementation: The case of wetlands regulation." Policy Studies Journal 8:575–96.

Rourke, F. E. (1981) "Grappling with the bureaucracy." In A. J. Meltsner (ed.), Politics and the Oval Office. San Francisco: Institute for Contemporary Studies.

Sabatier, P. (1975) "Social movements and regulatory agencies: toward a more adequate—and less pessimistic—theory of 'Clientele Capture.'" Policy Sciences 6:301–42.

Sabatier, P. and D. Mazmanian (1979) "The conditions of effective implementation: a guide to accomplishing policy objectives." Policy Analysis 5:481–504.

Salamon, L. M. (1981) "Rethinking public management: third-party government and the changing forms of government action." Washington, D.C.: Urban Institute Working Paper.

Sharkansky, I. (1979) Wither the State? Chatham, N.J.: Chatham House.

Sinclair, B. (1981) "Coping with uncertainty: building coalitions in the house and the senate." In T. E. Mann and N. J. Ornstein (eds.), The New Congress. Washington, D.C.: American Enterprise Institute.

Stout, Jr., R. (1980) Management or Control? Bloomington: Indiana University Press.

Thompson, F. J. and R. W. Campbell (1981) "Implementation and service error: veterans administration health care and the commercial market option." Journal of Health Politics, Policy and Law 6:419–43.

Thompson, F. J. (1982) "Bureaucratic discretion and the National Health Service Corps." Political Science Quarterly 97:427–45.

Waldo, D. (1980) The Enterprise of Public Administration. Novato, Cal.: Chandler & Sharp.

Wildavsky, A. (1979) "Implementation in context." In J. L. Pressman and A. Wildavsky (eds.), Implementation, 2nd ed. Berkeley: University of California Press.

Williams, W. (1980) The Implementation Perspective. Berkeley: University of California Press.

Williams, W. et al. (1982) Studying Implementation. Chatham, N.J.: Chatham House.

Yates, D. (1982) Bureaucratic Democracy. Cambridge, Mass.: Harvard University Press.

PART II

DISPOSITIONS AND INCENTIVES

LEGISLATURES, COURTS, AND THE DISPOSITIONS OF POLICY IMPLEMENTORS

Lawrence Baum

INTRODUCTION

Legislatures and appellate courts both enact policies that must be implemented elsewhere in government. In both instances the implementation process is inherently problematic. Indeed, one major enterprise of social scientists in recent years has been documentation of failures in the implementation of legislative and judicial policies.

Comparison of these two implementation processes is difficult, in part because they tend to differ in some important respects. Statutes are carried out primarily by administrators, while judges often have primary responsibility for implementing the decisions of higher courts. The scope of court decisions and thus of what they require from implementors usually is narrower than the scope of legislation. These differences help to explain the limited integration that exists between the scholarly work on the implementation of statutes and the work on implementation of judicial decisions.[1]

When scholars do make comparisons, they frequently depict the implementation of judicial policies as uniquely problematic. One student of policy implementation concluded that "Judicial decisions seem particularly prone to slippage in implementation" (Edwards, 1980:153). A recent critic of judicial activism bases much of his criticism on courts' failures to achieve effective implementation of their policies. These failures, in turn, provide one basis for his conclusion that courts should play a more limited role in making social policy (Horowitz, 1977).

Quite appropriately, these judgments have been made tentatively; we know too little about the two implementation processes to reach firm conclusions. One virtue of the efforts at comparison that have been made so far is their reminder of the need for further comparative analyses of implementation processes. Such analyses would have obvious scholarly value, both for the understanding of policy implementation and for the understanding of courts and legislatures as political institutions. They also would have practical value for their implications about the appropriate spheres of judicial and legislative policy activity.

More specifically, a better determination of the relative success of courts and legislatures in obtaining effective implementation of their policies would help in judging whether the current wave of judicial activism represents an overreaching from which courts should retreat. For instance, if courts prove to be relatively ineffective in implementing policies that mandate racial equality, they might limit their activity in that field so that efforts to secure equality can focus on legislative action. Similarly, the Supreme Court might accept the argument that legislative remedies for police misconduct will be more effective than those that courts have established.[2] On the other hand, if courts fare well in comparison with legislatures, that finding might reinforce judges' confidence in activist policymaking.

This essay constitutes one effort to compare the implementation of policies enacted by appellate courts and by legislatures.[3] Its scope as a comparison is limited. First, the essay is concerned only with what may be considered the first stage of the implementation process, in which public officials responsible for implementation take action. I will not consider later stages involving nongovernmental responses to policies and the ultimate impact of those policies.[4]

Second, I take what might be called a *compliance perspective* on the behavior of implementors. My interest is in the behavior of policy implementors in relation to the policies established in appellate court decisions or statutes, and the ultimate "dependent variable" is the extent to which policy implementors follow the dictates of enacted policies. This perspective is a narrow one, and it provides only a partial view of the implementation process (see Ripley and Franklin, 1982:10), but it addresses an issue central to policy implementation.

Finally, the essay focuses on what some students of implementation have called the dispositions of implementors (Edwards, 1980:ch. 4; Van Meter and Van Horn, 1975:472–74). By dispositions I mean the inclinations of officials responsible for implementation toward the policy choices that they face. Put most simply, to what extent will implementors want to do what a policy enactor has asked of them? Officials' dispositions, of course, are not the only factor that determines their behavior. Even where those responsible for implementation are positively disposed toward their mandate, problems of capability or of communication may result in implementation behavior that runs counter to the intentions of the policy enactor (Kaufman, 1973:2; Van Meter and Van Horn, 1975:478–83). But the dispositions of implementors undoubtedly are a central factor, ordinarily *the* central factor, in determining their behavior.[5]

The issue with which I am concerned, of course, is the comparative one: how does the identity of the policy enactor as a court or a legislature affect the dispositions of implementors toward their choices? Presumably, an implementor's disposition will be based primarily on attitudes toward the enacted policy itself. These attitudes may be based both on whether the policy accords with the implementor's conception of good policy (which I will refer to as policy preferences) and on its relationship with the self-interests of individual officials and their institutions (which I will refer to as interests). But the identity of the policy enactor can affect the implementor's calculations in at least two ways. First, the enactor may take actions that alter the preferences or interests of those responsible for implementation. Second, implementors' attitudes toward the enacting institution may help to shape their dispositions toward their policy choices.

These two considerations provide the basis for the two major inquiries of this essay, presented in the two sections that follow. First, I will consider the authority of legislatures and appellate courts as a factor that may influence the behavior of policy implementors. At first glance, courts might seem to have an advantage in this respect. Then, I will consider the capacities of legislatures and appellate courts to intervene in the implementation process so as to shape the dispositions of implementors. Here, legislatures would seem to be at a considerable advantage. A concluding section will discuss the significance of the findings on these two issues for the roles of courts and legislatures in the policy process.

AUTHORITY IN THE IMPLEMENTATION PROCESS

The concept of authority has been used in several ways in the study of social and political institutions (Simon, 1947; Peabody, 1964; Dornbusch and Scott, 1975).[6] For purposes of this essay authority may be defined as the perceived right of a policy enactor to have its policies carried out; the greater the authority that an implementor ascribes to an enactor, the greater the obligation that that person will feel to follow the enacted policy.[7] In an organizational setting authority usually derives from the subordination of one person to another, but authority can exist without subordination. Supreme Court justices may accept congressional authority to adopt statutes that are binding on the judiciary, while members of Congress accept the Court's authority to establish binding interpretations of the Constitution, even though neither group acknowledges the general superiority of the other.

For a considerable time much of the writing on American government assumed the overwhelming force of authority on judges and bureaucrats as policy implementors. This theme was connected with a formalistic conception of governmental behavior. Because administrators and judges had a legal duty to carry out relevant statutes and higher court decisions, it was widely assumed that these officials fully accepted this duty. As a result, the dispositions of implementors toward policies were thought to be of little importance, because they were largely negated by acceptance of legislative and judicial authority (see Nakamura and Smallwood, 1980:7–10).

This theme faded as scholars developed a more realistic understanding of bureaucratic and judicial behavior. In the process there has been some tendency to discard authority altogether as a troublesome and perhaps irrelevant concept. Even if more attention had been given to authority, however, our understanding of its impact in the policy implementation process might be limited; the degree to which officials accept other institutions' authority is not easy to determine, and the impact of authority on actual behavior is even less susceptible to measurement. Certainly any examination of legislative and judicial authority at this time must be largely speculative.

For comparative purposes it will be useful to examine judicial and bureaucratic implementors separately. For each group we can attempt to assess the authority of legislatures and appellate courts generally and comparatively. Because we know a little more about authority as a force on judges, it will be appropriate to begin with them.

Judges

Among students of judicial behavior the authority of legislatures and higher courts has been debated a good deal, though in terms of a larger debate about judges' adherence to "law." The "legal realists" of the 1920s and 1930s challenged the traditional assumption that judges gave complete fealty to law. Since that time many scholars have argued that judges tend to follow the policies that accord with their preferences, giving little regard to the body of law that supposedly is binding if the applicable law is inconsistent with their preferences (Frank, 1930; Spaeth, 1979). This view in turn has been challenged by scholars who argue that the law constitutes an important constraining or structuring influence on judges' policy choices (Brigham, 1978; O'Neill, 1981).[8]

I side cautiously with the latter group, because it seems to me that judges' training and career experiences and the context in which they decide cases attach real authority to the legislation and court decisions that they are asked to implement. As law students future judges are imbued with the principle of adherence to statutes and to the rulings of higher courts (Becker, 1964:ch. 5). This principle is presented as one that has practical as well as symbolic value; adherence to the intentions of policy enactors makes the law more uniform and more susceptible to prediction.[9] In their research and argumentation on cases lawyers operate on the assumption that judges will follow the policies that legislatures and higher courts enact as law. By the time an attorney becomes a judge, the habit of thinking in terms of hierarchical authority within the judicial system and in terms of statutory authority for courts is likely to be firmly established.

This habit then will be reinforced by the inputs that a judge receives and by the judge's own mode of speaking and writing. Attorneys' oral arguments and written briefs are based on a principle of legislative and higher court authority. The same generally is true of intracourt discussions on appellate courts. The judge's own decisions and opinions necessarily express adherence to that principle, and they are judged by the legal community largely in terms of that principle.[10]

The strength of this mode of thinking as a constraint should not be exaggerated. Judges hardly become automatons who follow ruling law blindly without taking other considerations into account. Indeed, the evidence that their own preferences have a fundamental impact on their decisions is overwhelming (Goldman and Jahnige, 1976:159–74).[11] The ambiguity of the situation is suggested by the occasional statements of judges that they have followed the dictates of statutes or higher court decisions despite their own contrary preferences. Most such statements deserve to be taken at face value, as indications that adherence to authority plays a significant part in at least some judges' decisional processes. But they also indicate that judges are not imprisoned by the legal framework in which they analyze policy choices; they can and do weigh legal authority against their own dispositions.

The basic strengths of legislative and judicial authority for judges are difficult to compare. In one sense statutes carry a more fundamental authority. Most rulings of higher courts constitute interpretations of something else, a constitution or a statute. Lower court judges can make their own analyses of constitutional or statutory provisions, and they may conclude that a higher court's interpretation of a provision is faulty. At the extreme, they may reject altogether a superior court's interpretative approach. One state supreme court justice said of the Supreme Court and the Constitution, "They're destroying it, and we're upholding it" (Lichtenstein, 1975).

In contrast, statutes themselves constitute the law that courts are called upon to interpret. Under some circumstances judges reject statutes as constitutionally invalid, but far more often statutes are accepted as legitimate and used by judges as the frameworks for decision. For this reason a judge might give more weight to a statutory command than to the command of a higher court, though the difference may not be great.

Judges' acceptance of the authority of legislatures and higher courts probably is strengthened by their own need for authority. For a judge to deny the principle of obedience to formally binding law is to undercut the judge's own basis for expecting obedience from legally subordinate officials and from litigants. This motivation should be particularly helpful to higher courts, because judges may perceive the principle of hierarchical authority within the judiciary as a unitary principle that cannot admit exceptions.[12] Whether judges think explicitly in these terms very often is uncertain, but implicit recognition of judges' shared dependence on the authority attached to their decisions may help to explain the infrequency of direct challenges by judges to the legal authority of appellate decisions and statutes.

The impact of authority on judges' behavior is reduced a good deal by the substantial discretion that higher court decisions and statutes frequently provide. Discretion may be provided either deliberately or inadvertently. In either case it can give judges so inclined the capacity to subvert the spirit of the law that they apply while expressing obedience to its letter. Perhaps the classic example of this phenomenon was the use of the "all deliberate speed" formula by Southern federal judges to help prevent the desegregation of public schools (Peltason, 1971). But other court decisions and statutes have suffered from similar problems in a less dramatic way.

This use of discretion may have a latent function as well, that of helping judges to preserve a feeling of autonomy and to maximize their own power by increasing their control over uncertainty (see Crozier, 1964:ch. 6). This function may be particularly important in relations between higher and lower courts, because lower court judges tend to resent the control exerted over them by judges on superior courts (Carp and Wheeler, 1972:377–78).[13]

It is uncertain whether legislative or judicial policies tend to provide more discretion to judges, in part because they provide discretion in somewhat different ways. Legislation increasingly is written in broad and somewhat vague terms, so that its specification falls to judges as well as administrators (Lowi, 1979). Judicial decisions also may suffer from overgenerality. But the greater problem is that judicial policies are established in the context of specific cases, and an opinion may not be clear about the general principles to be drawn from the specific decision. However one might compare the level of discretion typically provided by the two kinds of policies, the frequent existence of substantial discretion seems to weaken authority substantially as a force for faithful implementation of both judicial and legislative policies.

In general, the similarities between the authority of legislatures and that of higher courts for judges appear to outweigh the differences. Both statutes and higher court decisions can be expected to receive more favorable responses than judges' policy preferences and interests alone would dictate. One likely impact is to reduce the frequency of openly negative responses to enacted policies; another is to secure compliance with the spirit of a policy that falls within a judge's "zone of indifference" (see Simon, 1947:133–34). These and other effects are limited, however, by the discretion that legislatures and higher courts usually pass on to judges as policy implementors. The differences that have been noted between the authority of the two sets of policy enactors may work to the net advantage of one, but that advantage seems likely to be relatively small at most.

Administrators

There is little explicit concern with legislative or judicial authority in recent scholarship on policy implementation by administrators. This lack of concern reflects a growing awareness of the gap between enactments and implementation behavior. That awareness has led students of implementation to discard concepts that imply a centripetal force between enactor and implementor (Lipsky, 1978). Perhaps few scholars would argue that authority plays no role in administrative implementation, but most are silent as to what role it does play. As a result, it is necessary to proceed with even greater caution as we turn to authority in the administrative sector.

The basis for enactors' authority is weaker in the bureaucracy than in the judiciary in at least one important respect. Most administrators are not lawyers performing judicial functions. As a result, the socialization, decisional style, and environment that support legal authority in the courts are absent in most sectors of the bureaucracy. The numbers of lawyers and quasi-judicial activities in the bureaucracy are sufficient to constitute an important exception to this rule, but they are an exception nonetheless.

The backgrounds and roles of administrators seem likely to weaken their acceptance of legislative and judicial authority in a second way. Almost by definition, most administrators are specialists who develop experience and expertise in the particular areas of policy with which they deal. A good many middle-level and upper-level bureaucrats are specialists by profession—medical doctors, engineers, economists, and the like. Specialists, especially those whose expertise is associated with a profession, tend to accord the greatest authority to people who share their expertise. The authority of legal superiors who lack this expertise is reduced accordingly (Gouldner, 1959:413–16; Hall, 1972:222–24; Kaufman, 1981:117–18). It follows that the authority of legislatures will suffer from this division of loyalties. Judicial authority probably will suffer even more, because most judges are the quintessential generalists with relatively little access to specialized expertise as a basis for their decisions.

What basis remains for legislative or judicial authority? The legislature retains the advantage that the formal role of the bureaucracy is primarily one of implementing statutes. We would expect most administrators to accept with little question the proposition that they are responsible for statutory implementation.

This advantage is limited when the legislature and bureaucracy are at different levels of government. The authority of Congress for a state administrator must be shared with that of the state legislature and even of the parallel federal administrative agency, and it is doubtful that most state administrators see their primary task as that of following federal statutes. This is a significant problem for Congress because a high proportion of federal programs involve state and local implementation (though perhaps not as high as a reading of policy implementation studies might suggest).

Judicial authority for most administrators would seem to be rather limited, for two reasons. First, the legal obligation of administrators to follow a court-established doctrine that has not been applied directly to them is uncertain. If a state supreme court holds that one state agency must abandon a particular procedure, another agency with exactly the same procedure may not be acting "illegally" in a strict sense if it adheres to the status quo.

Second, courts are quite peripheral to most administrators. A classroom teacher who is not trained as an attorney, whose thinking is not legally oriented, and whose primary sources of direction are administrative and legislative is unlikely to accord much authority to courts on a professional basis. To some extent we can expect administrators to share attitudes of the general public toward the courts and the duty to obey court decisions. Evidence on these attitudes from survey research is ambiguous and somewhat indirect (see Sarat, 1977). One negative sign for the courts is the finding in some studies that the people who are most knowledgeable about courts also are the least supportive of them (Dolbeare, 1967; but see Murphy et al., 1973).

Despite these weaknesses, courts clearly do carry some authority for administrators. After the Supreme Court's decisions in the early 1960s prohibiting certain school religious practices, for instance, some school officials felt an obligation to eliminate those practices even prior to the threat of a direct court order (R. Johnson, 1967; Muir, 1967). Apparently courts, at least the Supreme Court, have enough general legitimacy so that authority attaches to their rulings even for some nonlawyer administrators.

The discretion that court decisions and statutes provide is likely to be a major source of authority slippage in the administrative sector as it is in the courts. Effective discretion is likely to be even greater in the bureaucracy, because long chains of communication and officials' lack of expertise facilitate selective misunderstanding of what legal provisions mandate. Police officers, for instance, often gain only a vague sense of appellate court requirements for searches and questioning of suspects (Wasby, 1976), so that the discretion that they perceive is substantially greater than what the court decisions provide.

Another kind of discretion expands administrators' freedom even more. Courts may have a good deal of leeway in interpreting legal mandates, but specific judges must respond to those mandates formally in specific cases. Frequently this is not the case in the bureaucracy, where the identity of those responsible for action, the time for their response, and the manner in which it is to be made may be quite unclear. As a result, officials may be able to avoid facing a conflict between their own preferences or interests and the authority that they attach to legislative and judicial mandates. If a school system's religious observances are challenged implicitly by a U.S. Supreme Court decision, responsive action can be delayed and the buck passed so that no explicit decision on continuation or termination of the observances is ever made (see Birkby, 1966).

In one sense this kind of discretion will tend to be even greater for statutes than it is for court decisions. Judicial rulings usually are relatively narrow in what they require of administrators: a particular action must be taken or, more often, a particular practice must be eliminated. Statutes tend to assign broader responsibilities, such as the administration of a general program. The broader the responsibilities, the easier it is to avoid confronting specific legal requirements encased within those responsibilities. Within a law as broad as the Elementary and Secondary Education Act a particular requirement that administrators would prefer to avoid facing may be easy to avoid. This difference between statutes and judicial decisions is a tendency rather than something approaching an absolute rule, but it is a strong enough tendency to reduce the impact of legislative authority significantly.

Conclusions

In several respects, then, authority seems to be a relatively weak force in administrative policy implementation. In that sense the lack of attention that students of this process give to authority may be justified. Yet we know too little to make firm judgments. In particular, it is uncertain how much the formal roles of administrators as executors of legislation affect their behavior. These roles undoubtedly bias bureaucrats in favor of carrying out legislative mandates, but the extent of the bias, the strength of legislative authority, is unclear. Primarily because of this factor, legislatures seem to have an advantage over courts in this respect, but the degree of advantage cannot be specified.

It does seem to be clear that the authority of policy enactors is stronger and has a greater effect in the judiciary than it does in the bureaucracy. This difference gives an advantage to courts as policy enactors, since they rely more on lower courts for implementation and less on administrative agencies than do legislatures. When courts and legislatures try to do the same things through the same branches, of course, this advantage disappears. Perhaps the most important implication of this analysis, then, is that we have no strong evidence that authority is a stronger force for faithful implementation when policies are enacted by courts rather than by legislatures.

INTERVENING IN THE IMPLEMENTATION PROCESS

The authority attached to statutes or to judicial decisions provides policy enactors with a passive kind of influence over the process of policy implementation. In this section I will consider a more active form of influence, one that stems from enactors' direct intervention in the implementation process. My concern is the capacity of a legislature or appellate court to influence the dispositions of policy implementors. Influence over dispositions is not the only way in which an enactor can intervene in the implementation process.[14] But it is of particular significance, in part because it relates to a crucial issue: if the officials responsible for implementing a policy are inclined against carrying it out faithfully, is the situation hopeless? The scholarly literature on policy implementation documents the frequency with which implementors do not want to do what is asked of them; what, if anything, can enactors do about this problem?[15]

Efforts by policy enactors to deal with this problem can come at two different stages. A legislature or court can attempt to dispose implementors more positively toward a policy after difficulties in implementation have begun to arise. Alternatively, the original policy may be framed in such a way as to increase the chances that implementors will be positively disposed toward it. In assessing the capacities of legislatures and appellate courts for influence, we need to consider possible action at both stages of the policy process.

In this context the term "capacity" is susceptible to two somewhat different meanings. On the one hand, it can refer to an institution's potential capability for influencing the implementation process. Alternatively, it can refer to the actual use of that capability in practice. It will be useful to analyze legislative and judicial capacities in both respects. First, I will survey the tools that are available to each institution; then, I will consider the extent to which those tools actually are used. Only by considering capacities in both respects can we obtain a full sense of the relative strength of courts and legislatures in policy implementation.

The influence that policy enactors may exert over the dispositions of implementors, of course, can take a variety of forms. I will focus on three forms that seem especially important. The first is influence over the policy preferences or interests of a set of policy implementors. The second is the strengthening of authority as an influence over implementors' behavior. The third is causing a policy to be implemented by officials who are more favorably disposed toward the policy than are some alternative officials. Each of these will be examined in turn in terms of the potential capabilities of legislatures and courts to utilize them. I then will discuss their use in practice.

Preferences and Interests

The ability to influence the policy preferences or interests of those assigned to implement a policy is a valuable tool, but such influence is not easily obtained. Preferences about policy are likely to be particularly intractable (see Tullock, 1965:120–21). Judges and administrators develop strong views about the policy questions with which they deal, and it will not be easy for another policymaker to alter those views.

This difficulty becomes clear when we consider efforts at persuasion by courts. Some scholars have argued that where the Supreme Court is more persuasive, in terms of the reasoning in its opinion, its policies will receive a more positive response (see Wasby, 1970:246–51). But such influence seems plausible only for an official whose views on a policy issue are weak. On issues that engage strong feelings, it is doubtful that the Court could change the minds of judges or administrators with well-written opinions. One popular sport among legal commentators has been criticism of the Court's opinion in *Roe* v. *Wade*[16] for its weak logic, accompanied by suggestions for an alternative rationale for the decision (Perry, 1976; Regan, 1979). But it is doubtful that a better argued opinion would have produced support for the Court's policy from people who were morally opposed to abortion. The same could be said of *Brown* v. *Board of Education.*[17] If Chief Justice Warren had omitted the references to sociological evidence that disturbed some commentators, would Alabama have desegregated its schools? Even where an official's views on an issue are weakly held, a court will not necessarily be successful in changing those views. Administrators especially may fail to be swayed by a seemingly persuasive opinion because they never see the opinion itself.

Influence over officials' interests seems more promising, because a court or legislature may be able to add additional elements to an implementor's preexisting calculus. Legislatures do possess a significant stock of mechanisms with which to influence the interests of policy implementors. These mechanisms are most applicable to courts and administrative agencies at the same level of government as a legislature, but they also have some relevance to administrators at a lower level.

Perhaps the most fundamental legislative power is budgetary. Through the capacity to appropriate money, legislatures can make the implementation of their policies more attractive. For instance, an administrative agency can be given funds for additional personnel to encourage a commitment to agency resources to a new program. Legislatures also can use their power to withhold funds as a means to secure the desired behavior from implementors. In a particularly clear example, as a member of the House Robert Dole once proposed that an increase in Supreme Court salaries be made contingent on the Court's rescinding a major reapportionment decision (Schmidhauser and Berg, 1972:10). The drastic character of this sanction limits its practicality (Edwards, 1980:67–70), but it does add to the legislature's power over implementing agencies.

The significance of the budgetary power can be illustrated in the intergovernmental context, specifically in categorical grant programs. By providing federal aid money conditionally, Congress has had some success in securing acceptance of federal policies from state and local governments (see Derthick, 1970). Perhaps the most noteworthy of its successes was the use of federal education grants as leverage with which to secure the beginnings of meaningful school desegregation in the Deep South (see Rodgers and Bullock, 1972:Ch. 4).

The budget power can be used in more diverse ways within a single level of government. Most generally, the centrality of funding for government agencies requires them to concern themselves with the legislature and with legislators' evaluations of their policy behavior (Wildavsky, 1979). This is true of courts as well as administrative agencies, because courts too are dependent upon legislative appropriations (see Yarwood and Canon, 1980).

The budget is only the most important case of legislation that affects a policy implementor. Some goals of every administrative agency and court could be advanced or retarded by legislative action. The Supreme Court, for instance, has sought a reduction of its mandatory jurisdiction so that it can cope with its caseload more effectively. The legislature's capacity to respond to these concerns positively or negatively provides an additional broad type of leverage, to the extent that legislators choose to use it.

Legislative powers to investigate and publicize the work of courts and administrative agencies also are significant. These powers allow legislators to embarrass an agency and its officials, and, in some instances—the congressional confrontation with the Environmental Protection Agency in 1983, for example—the resulting embarrassment may have massive effects on the agency. The investigative power also underlines the substantive powers that legislatures hold and provides opportunities for their use.

These legislative tools add up to a good deal of capability to influence the interests of officials. Because these tools exist, legislatures and legislators command the attention of the other branches. Not surprisingly, administrative officials devote much of their effort and concern to the legislature (Wright, 1967; Kaufman, 1981:47–57, 164–67). While the strength of some of these tools is attenuated when a legislature must cross jurisdictional lines, Congress has real power even in dealing with state and local bureaucracies.

In contrast, appellate courts' mechanisms to influence the interests of lower court judges and administrators are quite limited. The legislative powers discussed have at most weak equivalents in the judiciary. Even a supreme court holds little or no budgetary power over lower courts, and its rule-making power for the judiciary is narrower than the legislature's power to adopt statutes. A supreme court lacks even these limited powers over courts in another jurisdiction and over administrative agencies.

In its relations with lower courts, the primary sanction available to an appellate court is the power to reverse errant decisions. This sanction may be strengthened with criticism of the court that departed from applicable appellate policy. Reversal is a significant sanction because judges and others tend to treat reversal rates as indicators of judicial competence (Schick, 1970:141–53; Grossman and Wasby, 1972:571). But it also is relatively mild; even a judge who is very concerned with reversal rates could afford one or two reversals as the price for adherence to a favored policy. Because the primary impact of reversal is symbolic rather than concrete, it carries less sting for a judge who questions the authority of a superior court. In that sense it is least helpful when it is most needed.

For administrative agencies a court's primary source of leverage is the possibility that failure to implement a policy faithfully will lead to a legal challenge and an adverse judicial ruling. There are elements of both strength and weakness in this possibility. The strength lies primarily in the costs of a lawsuit and of a legal defeat for an agency and its jurisdiction under some circumstances. The monetary costs of a desegregation suit for a losing school district, for instance, can be enormous. In addition, defeats in "institutional reform" cases involving schools or prisons can lead to a loss of autonomy for the administrators of an institution (see Alabama Law Review, 1981).

The weakness lies primarily in the ability of administrators to minimize the likelihood that they will pay monetary costs or lose autonomy if they initially refuse to follow a judicial policy. If a school board has continued the use of proscribed religious practices in hopes that no challenge will be made, it can react to such a challenge by agreeing to change its practices; in this instance its recalcitrance will have won time and lost little. Under some circumstances even a legal defeat will cost little. As many observers have noted, police officers may not be greatly disturbed if cases are thrown out of court due to their failure to follow evidentiary rules, because that action has no direct effect on them (Skolnick, 1966:Ch. 10; Oaks, 1970).[18]

The capacity of courts to alter the self-interest of implementing officials and their institutions, then, seems rather limited in both an absolute and a relative sense. Legislatures are in a far better position, it would appear, to influence implementors in this way. The actual use of these legislative and judicial powers remains to be examined.

Strengthening Authority

In the last section I suggested that both courts and legislatures benefit from the authority attached to their policies. Particularly for judges as implementors, the perception that enacted policies ought to be followed appears to increase the faithfulness of policy implementation. It follows that anything that a policy enactor could do to strengthen its authority or the impact of that authority should be beneficial.

The prospects for strengthening perceptions of authority in themselves, like the prospects for changing implementors' policy preferences, seem rather limited. Students of the judicial process have pointed to actions that an appellate court can take to enhance its authority, actions that range from increasing the esteem of subordinate judges for a court or its members (Murphy, 1964:98–104) to avoiding intramural dissensus. But there is no evidence that such tactics have a substantial effect.[19] Perhaps the one action most likely to preserve and enhance judicial authority is to avoid unpopular policies. The Warren Court's liberal decisions on civil liberties issues may well have weakened its authority for some conservative-minded officials. But to avoid unpopular policies in order to maintain authority is to give up a great deal, so that this is not a very practical strategy.[20] Although not much seems to be written about the possibility of a parallel strategy for legislatures, enhancement of authority seems equally unpromising for them.

A more promising route is to increase the impact of institutional authority by reducing the discretion that policies provide. I argued in the preceding section that discretion allows policy implementors to reconcile their acceptance of an enactor's authority with evasion of the spirit of its policies. If this is correct, reduction of discretion probably is important as a means to convert authority into faithful implementation. This is the argument of one commentator about school desegregation, where the "all deliberate speed" formula maximized discretion and thereby promoted evasion (Peltason, 1971:244–47).[21]

The relative narrowness of the typical policy enacted by appellate courts may give them an advantage over legislatures in this respect. The broad sweep of many legislative policies makes detailed specification of policy implementation very difficult (Shapiro, 1968:3–5). If our concern is with legislatures and appellate courts as alternative enactors of the same policy, of course, this difference is irrelevant. More important is the question as to how fully the two types of institutions use opportunities to reduce implementors' discretion by specifying and clarifying policies.

Selecting Favorable Implementors

Perhaps the primary limitation of the strategies discussed so far is that the dispositions of a particular implementor tend to resist change. For this reason it seems more effective to avoid or eliminate the problem of negatively disposed officials by choosing implementors whose inclinations are more positive.

Legislatures have some capacity to use this strategy. For a policy to be implemented at the same level of government, a legislature can specify that it be implemented by one agency rather than another. On issues of unusual importance the legislature can go one step further and create a new agency to carry out a particular program, as Congress did in setting up such agencies as the Equal Employment Opportunity Commission and the Office of Economic Opportunity, although to create agencies very frequently is impractical. Another option is to reallocate responsibilities from public agencies to the private sector: one recent example occurred in the area of job training, in which the Job Partnership Act of 1982 "privatized" programs that had existed under the Comprehensive Employment and Training Act (Corrigan, 1983). A legislature can even design a new type of agency for a new program, as Congress did when it created the independent regulatory commission.

Legislatures also have some control over personnel. They can establish criteria for the selection of administrators and judges, as in the common state requirement that occupational regulatory boards be staffed by members of the occupations in question. At a more specific level, the requirement that most high officials obtain confirmation from the legislature provides legislators with the opportunity to reject nominees who displease them. Through the use of senatorial courtesy and its state-level equivalents, this negative power has been converted into a positive power to help choose nominees originally (see Harris, 1953).

The powers of courts in this area are so limited as to be almost meaningless. Under special circumstances an appellate court can help to determine which courts or individual judges are responsible for implementing a policy. For instance, in an extreme case an appellate remand of a case could direct the case to a new judge rather than one who had displayed recalcitrance toward the appellate court's policy. Informally, an occasional judge who is well connected politically may be able to influence appointments to lower courts (see Murphy, 1964:113–20). In relation to administrators, courts' powers are even weaker. Here, too, the legislature is at a great advantage.

Using Mechanisms for Influence

The central remaining question is how much these tools for influence over the implementation process actually are used. Most important, to what extent does the legislative advantage in potential capability for influence translate into an actual advantage in practice? Because this question focuses on the legislature, I will turn first to that branch.

Assessment of legislatures' use of influence mechanisms is difficult, because the reality is ambiguous. But it is possible to make a meaningful assessment by looking at what is required to make effective use of these mechanisms. Three kinds of requirements seem most important: (1) identification of problems and solutions in the implementation process; (2) the ability to act in response to actual or potential problems; and (3) most fundamentally, interest on the part of legislators in acting to improve implementation.

Identification of problems and solutions in implementation can involve two different kinds of tasks. One is surveillance of the implementation process to locate weaknesses that result from negatively disposed officials (or any other unfavorable factor). The inherent difficulty that a legislature faces in this surveillance process is well understood: it is an enormous task to keep tabs on the vast array of administrative and judicial activities. In recent years Congress has improved its means to accomplish this task, with a growth in committee staff and in the activity of the General Accounting Office and other staff agencies (Kaufman, 1981:54–57). To a lesser extent the same developments also have occurred in state legislatures, though the pace of change has varied a good deal among the states. Still, surveillance necessarily is quite imperfect.

The other task is the design of legislative action to correct or prevent implementation problems. The difficulty here lies in the existing state of knowledge about program design to achieve desired implementation behavior. Academic students of policy implementation have only a limited sense of causes and effects in implementation, so it would be unreasonable to expect even the best informed legislator to be certain about how to address problems. For instance, in 1983, some critics of the Environmental Protection Agency's policies argued that the EPA would follow congressional intent more faithfully if it were made an independent agency, shielded from presidential influence. Political scientists would have reason to urge caution in considering such a change, but they are not in a position to offer definitive judgments about its impact. In this and other situations, legislators must do a certain amount of stumbling in the dark.

The ability to act in the interest of effective implementation suffers from the effects of legislative inertia. The heart of the problem is the sheer difficulty of passing legislation.[22] In the initial adoption of a program, supportive legislators need to concentrate on building coalitions under what often are unfavorable circumstances. In that situation, attention to details that will improve a policy's implementation may be limited. Further, provisions that would enhance the likelihood of faithful implementation sometimes are sacrificed in order to secure passage. An administrative agency may be given broad responsibilities to handle with limited resources, so that its officials have little incentive to take those responsibilities seriously. Legislative language may be made deliberately vague in order to avoid hard choices that might alienate potential supporters.

Once a program has been established and a problem identified, the difficulty may lie in getting the problem on the legislative agenda. When significant legislation on an issue is adopted, legislators and other interested parties may perceive that the issue has been resolved, and other issues may take its place on the institutional agenda. Only certain kinds of dramatic problems, which are not necessarily the most important, are likely to make their way easily onto the agenda.

Even if this barrier is overcome, inertia and outright opposition may prevent the adoption of corrective legislation. This outcome is especially likely if the political coalition that was responsible for the original legislation has dissipated. It is easy to say that legislative ambiguities should be clarified or that administrative responsibilities should be taken from resistant agencies, but it may prove impossible to obtain the needed support for such action.

The task of getting implementation issues on the agenda has been reduced somewhat by the development of devices that help to force these issues onto the agenda. One example is the review of some adminstrative agencies under "sunset" legislation that has been adopted in about two-thirds of the states, although the existence of review provisions does not guarantee that the legislature actually will undertake review of the implementation behavior of agencies. Some forms of the legislative veto have a similar effect by requiring legislative action to make administrative regulations effective or creating a short period for Congress to consider regulations before they become effective (see Ripley and Franklin, 1980:74–75). But the Supreme Court has indicated that at least a large portion of the legislative veto provisions at the federal level are unconstitutional.

Of course, it is not necessary to get implementation issues on the full legislative agenda to secure changes in implementation behavior. A great deal of adjustment in administrative policies occurs through informal interaction between administrators and legislative committees. This role of committees has been formalized in the procedures that now exist in most states under which administrative agency rules must be reviewed by committees. In some states, the review committee can even suspend or veto rules (Ethridge, 1981:3). The existence of such procedures greatly increases the legislature's ability to act to change policy implementation.

The interest of legislators in improving implementation is the most fundamental factor because it underlies everything else. If legislators are highly interested in obtaining administrative and judicial compliance with legislative mandates, their powers are sufficient to allow them considerable impact. If legislators give low priority to implementation, then they are likely to make little difference no matter what means of influence are available to them.

In general, legislators seem to give a low priority to effective implementation. This low priority frequently is noted by students of legislative oversight over the executive branch (Scher, 1963; Ogul, 1976). The general absence of a strong interest in improving implementation is not accidental; rather, it follows from the limited utility of this task in helping legislators to achieve their primary goals (see Mayhew, 1974; Fenno, 1973).

Legislators' lack of interest in implementation should not be exaggerated. Clearly, nearly all legislators are concerned with the implementation process to some degree. Moreover, even if only a relative few are motivated to focus on implementation, their efforts may be sufficient to create a meaningful institutional commitment (Rosenthal, 1981). Still, the fact that legislators focus their attention elsewhere reduces their collective capability to make good on their potential role (see Ripley and Franklin, 1980:222–29).

Further, much of the attention that legislators pay to the implementation process is narrow and particularized. The effort that legislators and their staffs put into constituency service involving the bureaucracy typifies this pattern; such service has payoffs that broader concerns about the effectiveness of policy implementation do not. Similarly, scrutiny of agency budget requests provides an opportunity to seek changes in administrative policy, but the changes that are sought generally seem to be narrow and often constituency-oriented (Wildavsky, 1979). Thus, there is a kind of paradox: legislators intervene continually in the bureaucracy and impose their presence on administrators in an overwhelming way, but the form that much of their intervention takes ensures that it has only a peripheral impact on the effectiveness with which legislation is carried out.[23]

The impact of all these factors is not so great as to render the legislature's powers meaningless.[24] Legislatures do act to achieve faithful implementation of their policies,[25] and the frequency of such action probably has increased along with the general institutional strength of Congress and state legislatures. But a yawning gap remains between legislative powers of intervention in the implementation process and the use that those powers actually receive.

The gap between available powers and their actual use necessarily is more limited in the judiciary, simply because the powers themselves are far more limited. Still, the gap can be compared in "proportionate" terms. In establishing a policy initially, courts suffer from limitations similar to those of legislatures. Reduction of implementors' discretion is a good example. Factors such as the desire to reach a consensual decision may lead to lack of clarity in a court's opinion. Occasionally, of course, a court cannot mass majority support behind a particular opinion, and the resulting ambiguity widens the discretion of lower courts and administrators tremendously.[26] This problem has no direct parallel for statutes, except to the extent that the legislative history is ambiguous because legislators disagree on the intent behind a provision.[27]

To the extent that courts can remedy problems after a policy is established, they may be in a better position than legislatures to make use of their remedial powers. This is because the litigation process provides a regularized mechanism to bring implementation problems to a court's attention and to allow the court to respond. In this sense at least, the imprisonment of courts within the adjudicative process constitutes a partial advantage.

This advantage seems most useful for clarification of a court's intentions in enacting a policy. When an appellate policy is ambiguous, so long as the policy is the subject of future litigation the court is likely to be confronted with demands to resolve the ambiguity. If the court is so inclined, it can do so by accepting a new case and rendering a clarifying decision. This is a fairly routine process in the judiciary. When the U.S. Supreme Court made unclear its policy on the closing of criminal trials to the press, within a year it was given and took the opportunity to eliminate confusion.[28] Appellate courts do not always act so quickly— the Supreme Court maintained its ambiguous position on the timing of school desegregation for more than a decade—but their record probably is better than that of legislatures.

Because courts are weaker in mechanisms to affect dispositions in other ways, this apparent advantage means less in those other areas. Even there, however, courts may benefit from the effectiveness of feedback mechanisms. For instance, victims of lower-court recalcitrance have an incentive and a channel to inform higher courts of that problem, so that reversal of the offending court probably is more likely than corrective legislative action in an analogous situation.

Conclusions

Certain conclusions follow fairly clearly from the discussion in this section. In the abstract, legislatures have a much greater capacity to influence the dispositions of judges and administrators than do appellate courts. Even the legislative capacity is somewhat limited, because so much of what goes into the dispositions of implementors is beyond the control of any policy enactor. But such potent mechanisms as the budgetary power do provide very meaningful leverage for legislatures.

This means that where a legislature as an institution is committed to a goal, it can achieve results in the implementation process that would be impossible for an appellate court. The issue of voting rights for black citizens provides a good example. A series of U.S. Supreme Court decisions reinforcing the Fifteenth Amendment proved insufficient to give most blacks in the Deep South the ability to register to vote. The first congressional efforts, beginning with the Civil Rights Act of 1957, also were unsuccessful. Ultimately, with the Voting Rights Act of 1965, Congress was successful. To achieve this success, it had to adopt some extreme measures, the most important of which was the authorization of federal voting registrars to replace resistant local registrars. It would have been very difficult and perhaps impossible for the Supreme Court to have done the same.

The second conclusion is that that kind of legislative behavior is the exception rather than the rule. Congress and state legislatures seldom feel a strong commitment to the success of a particular policy, so that they fail to make use of their powers over the implementation process.

As a result, in practice the advantage of legislatures over courts is substantially more limited than it would appear to be in the abstract.

It may be tempting to minimize the importance of this factor, because the legislative weaknesses that I have discussed are potentially remediable. Indeed, to some extent they actually have been remedied, most importantly in the improvement of legislative oversight over the implementation process. In that sense the legislature's problems seem less fundamental than those of the judiciary. But some of the sources of these problems, such as legislators' lack of incentives to engage in effective oversight, are deeply rooted and not easily eliminated. For this reason it is not clear that legislatures actually are in a much better position to influence the implementation process than are appellate courts.

DISCUSSION

This essay has focused on a comparison between legislatures and appellate courts as policy enactors in terms of their impact on the dispositions of implementors toward their policies. Differences between the two types of enactors in this respect might appear in the context of their authority or their capability to intervene in the implementation process, so both of these areas were canvassed.

The discussion of authority as a force for faithful implementation of policies was quite tentative, because of our limited understanding of its operation. It appears, however, that appellate courts lack a significant advantage over legislatures in their authority for judges and administrators. Indeed, differences in authority acceptance seem to lie primarily in the identities of implementors rather than in the identities of enactors; by their training and experience judges are more inclined to accept the authority of legally superior institutions than are administrators. Even where the abstract acceptance of authority is high, its impact in practice may be reduced by the use of discretion to evade the spirit of enacted policies. For this reason authority seems to have only a moderate effect on implementation behavior in any arena.

The capacity of courts to intervene in the implementation process is a limited one both in the abstract and in practice, because courts lack a stock of powerful mechanisms with which to shape the dispositions of policy implementors. In the abstract legislatures are enormously stronger, because they possess tools as potent as the budget power. But legislatures regularly fail to make use of these tools because of a lack of commitment to improvement of policy implementation as well as other weaknesses that arise in practice. In situations in which legislators are strongly committed to the success of a policy, their capacity to affect the choices made by policy implementors is quite substantial; where that commitment is lacking, the actual differences between legislatures and courts in this respect may be rather minimal.

Taken together, the discussions of authority and of intervention in the implementation process underline the shared weaknesses of legislative and judicial policy enactors. If the officials who are responsible for carrying out a policy are negatively inclined on the basis of their preferences or interests, their implementation of that policy is likely to remain a good deal less than perfect. The sad stories related by the scholarly literature on policy implementation serve as testimony on these shared weaknesses.

What implications does this exploration of the implementation process have for the allocation of responsibilities between appellate courts and legislatures? If the issue is the relative capacities of courts and legislatures to make effective policy, the concerns of this essay represent only one small part of that issue, and other aspects of it are equally important (see Horowitz, 1977). On the basis of the concerns of this essay alone, however, at least two tentative conclusions are possible.

First, a fully committed legislature seems more likely than even an equally committed court to obtain faithful implementation of its policies where the initial circumstances are basically unfavorable. If neither an appellate court nor a legislature can be confident of rescuing a bad situation, specifically, where those officials responsible for implementing a policy have strong reasons to subvert that policy, the chances of a successful rescue are greater for a legislature that is willing to use its powers fully than they are for a similarly determined court.

Second, it follows that the chances of success are even greater when the two branches work together to achieve a mutually desired result. The history of federal policy on voting rights for black citizens and on school desegregation often is interpreted as evidence of congressional strength relative to that of the U.S. Supreme Court, and this interpretation seems quite appropriate in light of the contribution of Congress to the achievement of civil rights goals. But this history also underlines the value of collaboration, because the relatively weak Supreme Court (and Fifth Circuit Court of Appeals) did make important contributions to the successful outcome through such means as reducing the legal discretion available to Southern officials.[29] While these two policies are anything but typical, they illustrate the impact that legislatures and appellate courts can have when they pool their strengths. In that sense an emphasis on differences between legislatures and appellate courts in their positions as policy enactors is inappropriate; if both are weak, then this shared weakness makes collaboration between them important. For that reason one important line of inquiry may be the conditions under which courts and legislatures—for instance, the Supreme Court and Congress—work together to achieve mutually agreeable results in the implementation process.

One continuing theme of this essay has been our lack of knowledge about the comparative positions of appellate courts and legislatures as enactors of public policy. What we think we know about this issue is based primarily upon speculation and comparison of two separate bodies of research. While no research strategy will produce definitive answers quickly, the most productive strategy is one that compares legislatures and courts directly and empirically. There has not been much research of that type (but see Giles, 1975; Reedy, 1982). Only when such research becomes common will we be able to move beyond our rather unsatisfactory current knowledge of legislatures and courts in the policy implementation process.

NOTES

1. This limited integration also derives from the general separation between the study of courts and the study of other political institutions (see Baum, 1983). The integration between the two literatures on implementation does seem to be increasing, at least to the extent that students of implementation from a public policy perspective, who are responsible for most of the literature on the implementation of statutes, increasingly are taking judicial policies into account in general analyses of the implementation process. See Edwards (1980), Nakamura and Smallwood (1980), and Mazmanian and Sabatier (1983).

2. In this regard, see Chief Justice Burger's argument in his dissent in *Bivens* v. *Six Unknown Federal Narcotics Agents*, 403 U.S. 388, 411–427 (1971).

3. As such, it constitutes a continuation of the inquiry reflected in Baum (1981).

4. The distinction between public and private sectors has become more confused with the increasing participation of private individuals and institutions in the implementation of public policies. The most important form of such participation is the "contracting out" of government programs to private organizations, a practice that is quite common. In fiscal 1982, the federal government spent an estimated $147 billion on contracts (Keep, 1983:888), and local governments use private organizations to provide a wide array of services (Fisk et al., 1978). To make the analysis more manageable, I will concern myself only with government institutions as implementors, though this limitation leaves out an important part of the implementation process that is relevant to the concerns of this essay.

5. Both conceptually and empirically, implementors' dispositions are intertwined with their capabilities and with the process of communicating policies to them. Only in extreme cases, when policy is not communicated at all or when it is literally impossible to do what an enactor asks, are dispositions entirely separate from these other factors. As a result, any discussions of officials' dispositions as an element in the implementation process, including the discussion in this essay, will deal with these other elements as well.

6. In this section the analysis of authority as it affects the implementation process owes much to ideas Richard Pacelle developed. See Pacelle and Baum (1982).

7. Because of this connection, at some points I will refer to the authority that is attached to enacted policies.

8. A more specific version of this debate has occurred in the study of the implementation of U.S. Supreme Court decisions by lower courts and administrative agencies. Some scholars have emphasized the strength of the Court's authority (Petrick, 1968), while others have argued that this authority has limited impact (Levine and Becker, 1970).

9. This point merits emphasis, because it makes the principle much less vulnerable than it would be if it simply had symbolic value. Lack of uniformity in the law disturbs people in the legal community in part because it looks untidy, but in part also because it seems to violate the right to equal treatment under the law and the right to be able to predict the legal consequences of one's behavior. In this light phenomena such as the current concern about the existence of unresolved conflicts among federal courts of appeals are understandable.

10. This was true even of Jerome Frank, a leading legal realist, whose appointment to a federal judgeship on the Second Circuit Court of Appeals in New York City was likened "to the choice of a heretic to be a bishop of the Church of Rome" (Seagle, 1943:664). While Frank was not an entirely conventional judge, his opinions did not look fundamentally different from those of other judges. If this reflected only a reluctant adherence to expected form, it is nonetheless significant. If it reflected an acceptance of the value of adherence to law as at least one operating principle for judicial decisions, it is even more significant as an indication of the strength of legal authority as a structuring principle for judicial action. On Frank's work as a judge, see Schick (1970).

11. However, the scholarly work on judicial decision making probably underestimates the importance of ruling law in decisions because of its focus on U.S. Supreme Court decisions and on sentencing decisions by trial judges. For quite different reasons, both types of decisions involve an unusually high level of discretion and thus room for judges to bring their preferences into play.

12. Some judges may perceive authority as separable in one respect. Because of the separation between federal and state court systems, the U.S. Supreme Court's power to dictate rules to state courts sometimes has been viewed as uncertain (Miller and Scheflin, 1967:290). Some evidence suggests that state judges are inclined less favorably toward the Supreme Court than are federal judges (Caldeira, 1977:218–19), and this difference may result from the gap between court systems.

13. Judges may use discretion to serve this function or its more direct function without their being fully conscious of what they are doing: judges need not be cynical or openly rebellious to take advantage of discretion for "subversive" purposes.

14. For a broader inventory of forms of intervention, see Sabatier and Mazmanian (1981).

15. In some respects my concern is similar to that of Walter Murphy (1964) in his pioneering examination of the ways in which policy-oriented U.S. Supreme Court justices can advance their goals.

16. 410 U.S. 113 (1973).

17. 347 U.S. 483 (1954), 349 U.S. 294 (1955).

18. The contempt power may come to mind as another, very potent, judicial tool. Aside from judges' reluctance to cite officials for contempt, this tool is weakened by its limited applicability; a contempt citation can be issued only after a direct court order. Disobedience of a general judicial policy could not be punished through the contempt power. On this and related powers, see Murphy (1964:108–10).

19. Even if there is an effect, of course, it might well be sufficiently subtle to frustrate efforts at measurement. On the matter of consensus and dissensus, there is a little evidence

that the degree of unanimity in U.S. Supreme Court decisions has no significant effect on responses to those decisions by lower courts (C. Johnson, 1979).

20.   A limited version of this strategy, in which the U.S. Supreme Court avoids certain controversial decisions in order to preserve its authority for what the justices deem more important matters, seems to be adopted occasionally. One example is the Court's avoidance of the interracial marriage issue in the mid-1950s (see Provine, 1980:59–61). The Court's celebrated "retreat" on economic regulation issues in the late 1930s and its less celebrated retreat on civil liberties issues in the late 1950s might be considered more substantial versions of this strategy, but they reflect primarily a concern with congressional power over the Court rather than the Court's authority over legal subordinates (see Murphy, 1962).

21.   Peltason also points out that the Court's issuance of an unambiguous mandate would have allowed Southern judges to claim that they had no choice but to enforce desegregation, thereby reducing local cricitism of the judges (and of school boards that complied). This would seem to be an important factor whenever there is a conflict between an enactor's authority and external pressures on implementors.

22.   Senator Russell Long perhaps has said it best: "It is absolutely beyond the power of any human mind to assess the various ways that something which appears destined to become law can fail to become law, but it happens all the time" (Masley, 1977).

23.   Indeed, a constituency orientation may cause members of Congress to work against faithful implementation of legislation. Efforts by federal administrative agencies to impose sanctions on state and local agencies that misuse federal grants are likely to be short-circuited by members who seek to protect the errant officials and the beneficiaries of the funds. Similarly, a study of regulatory review in Michigan found that it was used most frequently to reduce the aggressiveness of regulation. "The legislators involved were primarily concerned with preventing displeasure on the part of any important constituents" (Ethridge, 1981:19).

24.   Certainly the possibility of intervention in itself can extend the impact of legislative powers by giving implementors an incentive to follow legislative intent generally (see Johannes, 1979). To the extent that administrators expect the legislature to use its powers primarily on peripheral matters, however, they will focus their efforts on those matters, e.g., policies that provoke constituency complaints.

25.   Speaking of congressional instruments to reward or punish agencies, Herbert Kaufman concludes, "Congress can write a specific mandate or prohibition or authorization into a law, or reduce the funds available for a particular program or part of a program, or inquire into an individual action. Such things happen all the time . . ." (1981:164).

26.   An example is the U.S. Supreme Court's decision in *Regents* v. *Bakke*, 438 U.S. 265 (1978), the case dealing with affirmative action in medical school admissions, in which the five-member majority could not agree on an opinion. Such instances have grown more common in the Supreme Court in recent years.

27.   For a recent example of that problem, see Gailey and Weaver (1983).

28.   *Richmond Newspapers* v. *Virginia*, 488 U.S. 555 (1980).

29.   The U.S. Supreme Court also played a crucial role in getting civil rights issues on the congressional agenda, and that role also is relevant to an examination of the contributions of the two institutions.

REFERENCES

Alabama Law Review (1981) "Judicially managed institutional reform." Alabama Law Review 32:267–464.

Baum, L. (1981) "Comparing the implementation of legislative and judicial policies." Pp.

39–62 in D. A. Mazmanian and P. A. Sabatier (eds.), Effective Policy Implementation. Lexington, Mass.: Lexington Books.

——— (1983) "Judicial politics: still a distinctive field." Pp. 189–215 in A. W. Finifter (ed.), Political Science: The State of the Discipline. Washington, D.C.: American Political Science Association.

Becker, T. L. (1964) Political Behavioralism and Modern Jurisprudence. Chicago: Rand McNally.

Birkby, R. (1966) "The Supreme Court and the Bible Belt: Tennessee reaction to the 'Schempp' decision." Midwest Journal of Political Science 10:304–319.

Brigham, J. (1978) Constitutional Language: An Interpretation of Judicial Decision. Westport, Conn.: Greenwood Press.

Caldeira, G. A. (1977) "Judges judge the Supreme Court." Judicature 61:208–19.

Carp, R. and R. Wheeler (1972) "Sink or swim: the socialization of a federal district judge." Journal of Public Law 21:359–93.

Corrigan, R. (1983) "Private sector on the spot as it prepares to take over job training." National Journal 15:894–97.

Crozier, M. (1964) The Bureaucratic Phenomenon. Chicago: University of Chicago Press.

Derthick, M. (1970) The Influence of Federal Grants: Public Assistance in Massachusetts. Cambridge, Mass.: Harvard University Press.

Dolbeare, K. (1967) "The public views the Supreme Court." Pp. 194–212 in H. Jacob (ed.), Law, Politics, and the Federal Courts. Boston: Little, Brown.

Dornbusch, S. M. and W. R. Scott (1975) Evaluation and the Exercise of Authority. San Francisco: Jossey-Bass.

Edwards, III, G. C. (1980) Implementing Public Policy. Washington, D.C.: Congressional Quarterly Press.

Ethridge, M. (1981) "Legislative participation in policy implementation: an analysis of the Michigan experience." Presented at the Annual Meeting of the Midwest Political Science Association, Cincinnati, April.

Fenno, R. F. (1973) Congressmen in Committees. Boston: Little, Brown.

Fisk, D., H. Kiesling, and T. Muller (1978) Private Provision of Public Services: An Overview. Washington, D.C.: The Urban Institute.

Frank, J. (1930) Law and the Modern Mind. New York: Brentano's.

Gailey, P. and W. Weaver (1983) "A question of intent." The New York Times (April 14):12.

Giles, M. W. (1975) "H.E.W. versus the federal courts: a comparison of school desegregation enforcement." American Political Quarterly 3:81–90.

Goldman, S. and T. P. Jahnige (1976) The Federal Courts as a Political System, 2nd ed. New York: Harper & Row.

Gouldner, A. W. (1959) "Organizational analysis." Pp. 400–28 in R. K. Merton, L. Broom, and L. W. Cottrell (eds.), Sociology Today: Problems and Prospects. New York: Basic Books.

Grossman, J. B. and S. Wasby (1972) "The Senate and Supreme Court nominations: some reflections." Duke Law Journal 1972:557–91.

Hall, R. H. (1972) Organizations: Structure and Process. Englewood Cliffs, N.J.: Prentice-Hall.

Harris, J. (1953) The Advice and Consent of the Senate. Berkeley: University of California Press.

Horowitz, D. L. (1977) The Courts and Social Policy. Washington, D.C.: Brookings Institution.

Johannes, J. R. (1979) "Casework as a technique of U.S. congressional oversight of the executive." Legislative Studies Quarterly 4:321–51.

Johnson, C. A. (1979) "Lower court reactions to Supreme Court decisions: a quantitative examination." American Journal of Political Science 23:792–804.

Johnson, R. M. (1967) The Dynamics of Compliance. Evanston, Ill.: Northwestern University Press.

Kaufman, H. (1973) Administrative Feedback: Monitoring Subordinates' Behavior. Washington, D.C.: Brookings Institution.

_____ (1981) The Administrative Behavior of Federal Bureau Chiefs. Washington, D.C.: Brookings Institution.

Keep, P. M. (1983) "Business and federal employee unions battling over when to contract out." National Journal 15:888–91.

Levine, J. P. and T. L. Becker (1970) "Toward and beyond a theory of Supreme Court impact." American Behavioral Scientist 13:561–73.

Lichtenstein, G. (1975) "Utah's conservative court center of dispute over rulings." The New York Times (November 30):63.

Lipsky, M. (1978) "Standing the study of public policy implementation on its head." Pp. 391–402 in W. D. Burnham and M. W. Weinberg (eds.), American Politics and Public Policy. Cambridge, Mass.: MIT Press.

Lowi, T. J. (1979) The End of Liberalism, 2d ed. New York: Norton.

Masley, P. (1977) "The Capitol." Washington Post (April 23):A3.

Mayhew, D. R. (1974) Congress: The Electoral Connection. New Haven, Conn.: Yale University Press.

Mazmanian, D. A. and P. A. Sabatier (1983) Implementation and Public Policy. Glenview, Ill.: Scott, Foresman.

Miller, A. S. and A. W. Scheflin (1967) "The power of the Supreme Court in the age of the positive state: a preliminary excursus." Duke Law Journal 1967:273–320, 522–51.

Muir, W. K. (1967) Prayer in the Public Schools: Law and Attitude Change. Chicago: University of Chicago Press.

Murphy, W. (1959) "Lower court checks on Supreme Court power." American Political Science Review 53:1017–31.

_____ (1962) Congress and the Court. Chicago: University of Chicago Press.

_____ (1964) Elements of Judicial Strategy. Chicago: University of Chicago Press.

Murphy, W., J. Tanenhaus, and D. Kastner (1973) Public Evaluations of Constitutional Courts. Beverly Hills, Cal.: Sage Publications.

Nakamura, R. T. and F. Smallwood (1980) The Politics of Policy Implementation. New York: St. Martin's Press.

Oaks, D. H. (1970) "Studying the exclusionary rule in search and seizure." University of Chicago Law Review 37:665–757.

Ogul, M. S. (1976) Congress Oversees the Bureaucracy: Studies in Legislative Supervision. Pittsburgh: University of Pittsburgh Press.

O'Neill, T. J. (1981) "The language of equality in a constitutional order." American Political Science Review 75:626–35.

Pacelle, R. and L. Baum (1982) "Supreme Court authority and the judicial hierarchy: a study of remands." Presented at the Annual Meeting of the Midwest Political Science Association, Milwaukee, April/May.

Peabody, R. (1964) Organizational Authority. Chicago: Aldine-Atherton.

Peltason, J. W. (1971) Fifty-Eight Lonely Men: Southern Federal Judges and School Desegregation. Urbana: University of Illinois Press.

Perry, M. (1976) "Substantive due process revisited: reflections on (and beyond) recent cases." Northwestern University Law Review 71:417–69.

Petrick, M. J. (1968) "The Supreme Court and authority acceptance." Western Political Quarterly 21:5–19.

Provine, D. J. (1980) Case Selection in the United States Supreme Court. Chicago: University of Chicago Press.

Reedy, C. D. (1982) "The Supreme Court and Congress on abortion: an analysis of comparative institutional capacity." Presented at the Annual Meeting of the American Political Science Association, Denver, September.

Regan, D. (1979) "Rewriting *Roe v. Wade*." Michigan Law Review 77:1569–1646.

Ripley, R. B. and G. A. Franklin (1980) Congress, the Bureaucracy, and Public Policy, rev. ed. Homewood, Ill.: Dorsey Press.

—— (1982) Bureaucracy and Policy Implementation. Homewood, Ill.: Dorsey Press.

Rodgers, H. R. and C. S. Bullock III (1972) Law and Social Change: Civil Rights Laws and Their Consequences. New York: McGraw-Hill.

Rosenthal, A. (1981) "Legislative behavior and legislative oversight." Legislative Studies Quarterly 6:115–31.

Sabatier, P. A. and D. A. Mazmanian (1981) "The implementation of public policy: a framework of analysis." Pp. 3–35 in D. A. Mazmanian and P. A. Sabatier (eds.), Effective Policy Implementation. Lexington, Mass.: Lexington Books.

Sarat, A. (1977) "Studying American legal culture: an assessment of survey evidence." Law & Society Review 11:427–88.

Scher, S. (1963) "Conditions for legislative control." Journal of Politics 25:526–51.

Schick, M. (1970) Learned Hand's Court. Baltimore: Johns Hopkins University Press.

Schmidhauser, J. R. and L. L. Berg (1972) The Supreme Court and Congress: Conflict and Cooperation, 1945–1968. New York: Free Press.

Seagle, W. (1943) "Book review: 'If All Men Were Angels'." Virginia Law Review 29:664–71.

Shapiro, M. (1968) The Supreme Court and Administrative Agencies. New York: Free Press.

Simon, H. A. (1947) Administrative Behavior. New York: Macmillan.

Skolnick, J. A. (1966) Justice Without Trial: Law Enforcement in Democratic Society. New York: Wiley.

Spaeth, H. J. (1979) Supreme Court Policy Making: Explanation and Prediction. San Francisco: Freeman.

Tullock, G. (1965) The Politics of Bureaucracy. Washington, D.C.: Public Affairs Press.

Van Meter, D. S. and C. E. Van Horn (1975) "The policy implementation process: a conceptual framework." Administration and Society 6:445–88.

Wasby, S. L. (1970) The Impact of the United States Supreme Court: Some Perspectives. Homewood, Ill.: Dorsey Press.

—— (1976) Small Town Police and the Supreme Court: Hearing the Word. Lexington, Mass.: Lexington Books.

Wildavsky, A. (1979) The Politics of the Budgetary Process, 3rd ed. Boston: Little, Brown.

Wright, D. S. (1967) "Executive leadership in state administration." Midwest Journal of Political Science 11:1–26.

Yarwood, D. L. and B. C. Canon (1980) "On the Supreme Court's annual trek to the Capitol." Judicature 63:322–27.

THE INCENTIVE RELATION
IN IMPLEMENTATION

Barry M. Mitnick and Robert W. Backoff

INTRODUCTION

From one perspective, implementation is a game of agents: a central authority seeks to create agents—or to create subagents to perform programs—to realize the program goals of the central authority. From another perspective, implementation is a game of principals: willful and autonomous actors adapt programs in ways congruent with their interests and operations. A third view sees those implementing actors again as agents, this time molding programs to satisfy their clients or their most insistent constituencies. As the literature makes clear, implementation can occur in a complex network or system in which the actions of even obedient agents can produce unforeseen and perhaps undesired outcomes.

Thus Congress creates administrative agencies that delegate across the intergovernmental system, supposedly in order to achieve legislative goals. Those agencies, or the state and local bodies that implement federal directives, may, however, adapt programs to fit their own procedures or parochial self-interests. Finally, implementers may instead mold programs to satisfy what their clientele prefers.

Of course, in their pure forms these frames can be seen as caricatures; the literature is rich with theory and description that posit or observe mixed or altered versions. That literature does not necessarily provide us, however, with building blocks to systematic theory in implementation. What these frames do suggest to us is the central role of *relations* in implementation in contrast to a focus on atomistic factors like resource scarcity, environmental complexity, or goal clarity. Further, the core feature of such implementation relations is the pattern of *incentive relations* that exists among the actors. We shall argue in this paper that implementation is fruitfully understood as a time-varying system of attempted or achieved incentive relations.

We shall begin by considering the concept of *implementation relations*, developing a typology of basic relations. Consideration of the means of control and interaction in such relations leads us to consider the importance of incentives and the nature of *incentive failures* in implementation. The literature on incentives is then scanned for material relevant to development of a general incentive systems approach; from this review, the requisites for such a model are identified. We then introduce the key concept of the *incentive relation* and use it to develop a general sorting/mapping model of incentive systems. This model is applied to several major models in the implementation literature, demonstrating their key incentive elements and relationships. Finally, we present a seven-stage model of incentive system analysis and show its relevance in implementation settings. The model discusses the process of sorting a set of perceived implementation phenomena into the incentive system framework and analyzing the resulting incentive system constructions.

IMPLEMENTATION RELATIONS

One of the outstanding features of the implementation literature, and the source of occasional complaints, is the presence of numerous inventories of factors affecting implementation. Some are part of theoretical constructions or discussions of various kinds; some have received empirical study. For example, Rein and Rabinovitz (1977) consider the saliency, clarity, and consistency of goals; the complexity in administration; and the kind, level, and timing of resource allocations. Van Meter and Van Horn (1975) relate standards/objectives and resources of the policy; interorganization communication and enforcement activities; characteristics of the implementing agencies; economic, social, and political conditions; and the disposition of the implementers to implementation performance. Mazmanian and Sabatier (1983) identify three classes of factors: tractability of the problem (e.g., technical difficulty, extent of behavioral change required), statutory variables (e.g., clear objectives, adequate causal theory), and nonstatutory variables (e.g., public support, commitment and leadership skill); and present a framework in which these factors interact and six general conditions of effective implementation. There are many other such analyses.

Although the literature contains a number of these inventories, some with conceptual frameworks that locate the factors identified and discuss their roles, few approaches provide the means to systematically identify and sort behaviors or relations in implementation and to provide a systematic understanding of the nature of (and the alternatives that exist within) implementation systems. Although analysis of "games" in implementation can be appealing and contribute to our understanding of behavior (e.g., Bardach, 1977), we should try to lay out the basic dimensions that limit the space of the phenomena, whether it be implementation behaviors (see Sorg, 1978, 1983) or structural possibilities in implementation relationships. Only in this way can we approach serious theory-building in the area.

Hence our concern over implementation relations. Rein and Rabinovitz (1977) identify three major patterns of such relations, which they term the legal, the rational-bureaucratic, and the consensual imperatives. Roughly speaking, the legal imperative describes relations in which implementation is to be responsive to the dictates of the legislative statute; the rational-bureaucratic imperative covers situations in which implementation is to be responsive to bureaucratic self-interest and process, including consistency, workability, and aspects of organization maintenance and professionalism; and the consensual imperative deals with relations in which implementation is to be sensitive to the wishes of the agency's clientele, i.e., those affected by the legislation. [On implementation relations, cf. Nakamura and Smallwood (1980) on "implementation linkages."]

As "imperatives," these three types can be thought of as alternative instructions for identifying referents for choice of behaviors by implementers. The imperatives imply the existence of *relations* between implementers and those who implicitly or explicitly direct the implementation. These "directors" of implementation are located in the law or legislature, the bureaucracy, or the clientele.

Given the apparent importance of these alternative implementation situations, should we not consider an analytical approach to implementation that is constructed explicitly in the context of *relations*? Indeed, the implementation variables discussed by Rein and Rabinovitz (1977) can be treated easily in an explicitly relational context: the sender of instructions sends them (or they are received) with a certain saliency, clarity, and consistency; the resources sent or possessed are of a certain kind, level, and timing; and the implementation situation is often characterized by a network of relations [on the concept of "implementation situation," see Sorg (1978); we largely follow his conceptualization]. That network is said to span various levels and display a number of participants in the relational positions of senders and receivers of implementation instructions.

Implementation Relations as Agent–Principal Relations

Indeed, the game metaphor is perhaps so attractive in implementation studies because implementation often features what can be thought of as games of control in a network of agents and principals. An *agent* is a party in the nominal position of acting to benefit some *principal*. Nominally, the legislature creates a bureaucratic agent (or agents) through delegation; this agent is to realize the legislature's wishes regarding a policy or program (legal imperative). This could require the adaptation of the implementing agent-bureau to the demands of the policy/program (and, by implication, adaptation as well by the policy/program's clientele). In practice, the bureaucratic agent often either adapts its legislative instructions to what is workable, consistent, and serves the interests of its members (rational-bureaucratic imperative) or adapts it to the friendly, if demanding, prescriptions of the alternative principals that it serves, i.e., its clientele (consensual imperative). Of course, these are pure types; mixed results characterized by mutual adaptation (Berman and McLaughlin, 1974) can occur. Given the types we have described, this can mean adaptation of both the policy/program and the bureau and/or clientele.

If the relations are of agents and principals, why not map these relations systematically through considering the logical possibilities of agency (i.e., agent–principal behavior) in implementation? In this way we can perhaps begin to meet the objection raised earlier, i.e., we can move in at least some respects from sometimes randomly constructed inventories to systematically generated relations in the space of implementation possibilities.

In looking at implementation relations as agent–principal relations, we are making use of a developing body of research on the *theory of agency* (e.g., Ross, 1973; Mitnick, 1973, 1974; Jensen and Meckling, 1976; Baiman, 1982). This work seeks to identify and model the generalizations that may govern the huge variety of agent–principal relationships in society (e.g., lawyer–client, doctor–patient, industry–regulator, legislator–constituency, and so on). Principals typically face problems in controlling agents who may not know the principal's preferences perfectly and may prefer behavior that is inconsistent with these preferences. The literature has, for example, explored a variety of reward strategies to control the agent and to elicit from the agent truthful reports about the state of the world and the agent's own behavior. The costs of policing agents to be perfectly faithful, however, may exceed the benefits to be gained therefrom.

In this context, the three referents for the implementer discussed above can be seen as potential principals. In the case where the implementing bureau acts for bureaucratic purposes (i.e., acts for itself in some respects), we do not necessarily see problems, however, in keeping the agent–principal distinction. A variety of individual self-interest and group goals or norms can serve as the preferences of the "principal." The bureau's goal structure need not be viewed as monolithic. Actors in or for the bureau may potentially refer, therefore, to any of a number of such goals that may be analytically "located" anywhere in the bureau system. In some cases, of course, it is possible that the analytical distinction of agent and principal has no reflection in a physical or a formal institutional difference.

Having identified the three relevant sets of principal preferences, we must still specify the agent dimensions.

Implementing-Agent Dimensions

As a game of control, implementation can frequently be treated as a study in compliance and adaptation. Halperin (1974:238; see also Kaufman, 1973; Van Meter and Van Horn, 1975) identifies three basic sources of noncompliance: (1) implementers may not know what it is that they are expected to do; (2) implementers may be unable to do what they think they are supposed to do; and (3) implementers may not want to do what they believe they have been told to do. Note that these sources of noncompliance deal only with the superior-to-subordinate (implementer) relationship; overall noncompliance can also result where implementation occurs in a system (e.g., an intergovernmental system) even if each constituent relation functions with internal compliance (on sources of noncompliance, see, e.g., Anderson, 1979; Coombs, 1980; Diver, 1980; McKean, 1980). In such cases, the initial "instructions" may not have taken emergent phenomena in the system into account. Emergent phenomena can, of course, characterize the system level without being "visible" in any system component; by their nature, such phenomena are attached to the system as a unit and not its parts. The qualities of implementation in an intergovernmental system, for example, may be different from those between any pair of governmental units or within any governmental unit.

Following Halperin in part, we can create a typology of implementation relations by "crossing" possible principals with certain dimensions of implementers. In the agent–principal context, we shall refer to implementers as "implementing agents." The principals thus include legislative or statutory, bureau (individual self-interest and group or bureau-level goals such as norms of administrative procedure and professionalism), and target group or clientele referents. The implementing-agent dimensions consist of agent knowledge sources, agent disposition, and agent capability (see Figure 1).

Agent Knowledge.   We have divided the implementer's knowledge of what is desired of him into *policy goals* and *policy design* (or *program*). "Policy" itself is used ambiguously in the literature to refer both to objectives and to courses of action; we merely make these two meanings explicit. Implementers may receive, have, or create for themselves knowledge of the goals of the public policy, i.e., the desired end-states, as well as knowledge of the activities or procedures or design, i.e., the means prescribed for achieving those ends. Policies can vary in the explicitness with which goals and designs are conveyed. Some policies contain little more than vague goals, permitting implementers great discretion; others prescribe in detail what the implementer is supposed to do. Note that discretion can exist with respect to *both* goals and designs. A policy may have specific goals and vague program specification; it may also have vague goals but specific program description. [On "policy," cf. Kerr, 1976.]

In regulation, for example, there is a recurring debate over the desirability of varying degrees of specificity in goals and in program design in the statute handed the regulatory body. This carries over to the regulations established under the statute (if permitted by the statute). So-called performance standards are specific on goals but vague on compliance requirements, supposedly allowing regulated parties to respond most efficiently and innovatively. Design standards, on the other hand, specify compliance behaviors fully, supposedly assuring that possibly recalcitrant and inexpert regulated parties will do what it takes to comply. In theory, ironically, explicit goals would not be necessary under comprehensive design standards since the regulated party need not know what the goals of his efforts are. If the statute as well as the regulations are strong on design and weak on goals, the regulatory body's efforts and those of the regulated entity can be displaced into program achieve-

Referent Principal Preference Set

for the Implementing Agent

Implementing Agent Knowledge, Disposition, and Capability			Statute/ Legislature	Implementing Bureau:		Clientele/ Target Group
				Individual Self-Interest	Group Goals/Norms	
Agent seeks or knows principal's preferences re policy goals and/or design	Agent* Agrees	Agent can do**	(Legal Imperative)			
		Agent can't do				
	Agent Disagrees	Agent can do				
		Agent can't do				
Agent decides principal's preferences re policy goals and/or design	Agent Agrees	Agent can do		(Rational-Bureaucratic Imperative)		(Consensual Imperative)
		Agent can't do				
	Agent Disagrees	Agent can do		Null		
		Agent can't do		Null		

Figure 1. Basic Implementation Relations.

65

ment without regard to goal definition or even use of goals in activity evaluation; the goals are superfluous. When technology and other environmental conditions change, when the regulated party is atypical in some respects, or when the policy design is inappropriate in general, problems can result. [On specificity of goals, see, e.g., Rosenbaum (1980); Thompson (1981).]

We shall presume that the implementing agent either (1) seeks or knows the principal's preferences regarding policy goals or policy design, or (2) creates, i.e., decides by himself what the principal's preferences are regarding policy goals or policy design. In the first case, definition of the principal's preferences is done by the principal; in the second case, it is done by the implementing agent. Since it makes a difference where policy goals, policy designs, or both, are determined, we shall retain the distinction through the typology.

Agent Disposition. Either the implementing agent agrees with the principal's preferences for policy goals or policy design, whoever defines them, or he does not. Now, of course, as with the other polar distinctions made for knowledge and for capability, degrees of each are certainly possible. The implementing agent may partly decide the principal's preferences, may be in moderate agreement with them, and be only fair in his capability in performing the indicated design activities. The typology seeks to bound the space of possibilities by identifying pure (and even extreme) types. Having done so, we can introduce the realistic complexity of variation.

Agent Capability. Either the implementing agent can perform the design activities specified in the principal's preferences, or he can not. Note that the implementing agent may be led to define or not to define the principal's preferences, to agree or disagree with them, and to be able to act for them or not because of factors outside the strict implementing agent-to-principal dyad. Other actors and network or systemic factors could play a role.

Many, but perhaps not all, of the implementation relations defined in the typology of Figure 1 are discussed in the literature. The realization of the "legal imperative" of Rein and Rabinovitz (1977) is a kind of nominal baseline: the agent seeks or knows the policy goals and design, agrees with them, and can perform the requisite design activities. Relations responding to the bureaucratic imperative typically feature bureau definition of the policy aspects with respect to bureau referents, agreement with these policy aspects, and capability to perform them as designed (after all) by the bureau. The categories in which the bureau decides with respect to its own referent yet disagrees with the preferences so derived seem logically null. Situations reflecting the consensual imperative would seem to require that the agent decide on the principal's policy preferences, that it agree with them (those of target or clientele groups), and that it can perform the design activities indicated by them (i.e., in Figure 1, "can do" them).

We have specified that each of the three basic imperatives falls in a "can do" category, because we can presume in the simplest case that agent and principal in deciding on policy, and agent in agreeing, are rational. Of course, in an imperfect world, it may happen that the bureau cannot perform the designed activities; these should not be null categories.

Any deviation from the legal imperative in policy goals and/or design implies the possibility of change in the policy, by definition. Because the typology is set up this way, it can be used to depict the "mutual adaptation" (Berman and McLaughlin, 1974) and "policy evolution" (Majone and Wildavsky, 1978) aspects that are said to characterize real-world implementation. Furthermore, the typology permits us to identify workable and unworkable relations marked by apparent policy conflicts. By distinguishing policy goals from policy design or program we can include, for example, relations in which the implementer may agree with the goals set by the statute (or by the clientele or the bureau itself) but use his discretion to create different, perhaps more efficient, more effective, more innovative, or more self-serving policy designs. If organizations can act a little like the "garbage can" of Cohen et al. (1972), they can conceivably behave with consistency to goals set by statute using their own preferred tool kit of program methods.

Johnson and O'Connor (1979) describe a public welfare bureaucracy in which workers may have poor knowledge and even dislike for the program designs set for them, yet act in (presumedly creative) ways responsive to the needs of their clientele. In this case, the analysts assume that the broad goals of the policy coincide with the interests of the clientele for whom it was established. Thus, the policy goals themselves are achieved in spite of likely noncompliance with the policy design.

To use the typology of Figure 1, we must therefore disaggregate policies, tracing both policy goals and policy design through the typology dimensions. For policy goals and design in Johnson and O'Connor's welfare bureaucracy, we have what appears to be a consensual imperative in that workers choose a client referent and devise ways to achieve it. But the goals component coincides with that intended by the statute; in that sense, we have a legal imperative. Indeed, we speculate that workers may have chosen their jobs because they presumed something (correctly) about the (at least nominal) goals of the organization. So we have a legal imperative on goals and a consensual imperative on goals and design, with the positions on goals coinciding.

"Mutual adaptation" specifies change in both the policy and the implementer. We can, as before, distinguish changes in goals or design in the policy. Changes in the implementer may occur where there is agreement to (at least part of) a policy design specified by a principal different from the implementer; we presume that implementing bureaucracies are less likely to impose change on themselves. Even where the policy design comes from outside, it is possible, of course, that it coincides with a policy design already used by the implementer, e.g., one already in the bureaucratic tool box. At any rate, deviations from the legal imperative imply adaptation on at least one side; it is apparent from the rationale for the typology that adaptation of some kind is likely to be the most frequent result.

Similarly, policy evolution or reformulation is clearly implied by the logic of Figure 1. Conditions promoting it include some or all of the following cases: when the agent decides, when the agent disagrees, when the agent cannot perform the design, and when the implementing agent chooses as referent a principal other than the legislature, i.e., the statute. Each case may provide the opportunity for policy reformulation. The direction of policy reformulation depends on which agent deviations from the pure legal imperative response occur.

Although the typology suggests how policy reformulation can occur, by itself it is a static representation. To take account of the fact that policies, and policy implementation, evolve over time, we need an additional theoretical premise. *Implementation can be viewed as a potentially changing series of implementation relations.* The typology can be used to supply a series of descriptive snapshots over time, tracing the implementation relations that exist at any moment. Policies that begin to be implemented as the legal imperative suggests may, for example, evolve so that clientele referents become predominant (and the policy design is adjusted accordingly). A version of this in the context of government regulation is termed "capture."

The typology is descriptive; it does not tell us *why* implementation relations change. To understand why certain relations and not others form, and why certain changes and not others occur, we must look further. Focusing on the *relation* as building block, we ask, what holds it together? If this is a game of control, why is control effective (or ineffective)? To address this question, we introduce the concept of *incentive failures* in implementation.

INCENTIVE FAILURES AND IMPLEMENTATION

The game of control in agent–principal relations is conducted through the incentive system, broadly construed. Because of information, reward, preference, and capability variations, agents may not perform as their principals desire. These and other factors must be included in the general concept of the incentive relationship that exists between agents and principals. While the nominal implementing agent–principal relation features the classic control problem, we need not restrict ourselves merely to hierarchical control aspects. As the literature notes, implementation often occurs in a system in which both original policy goals and contextual conditions for implementation are changing [cf., for example, Berman (1978) on micro and macro implementation; see also Berman (1980) on programmed vs. adaptive implementation]. Goal incompatibility between implementing agent and principal is meaningful as a source of implementation "failure," however, only if goals are stable. Indeed, we need not talk in this context of "implementation failure" at all. Such evaluative analysis is completely dependent on the referent goal set (e.g., statute, bureau norms, clientele goals, process criteria, original vs. evolved goals, and so on).

"Incentive failures" as a concept refers to failures in the analytically identified incentive relation or complex incentive system that exists in an implementation or other setting. Given whatever principals and principal goals are set, does the incentive system function to achieve them? If it does not, what are the source or sources of failure? It may be that failure to achieve the nominal principal's goals (i.e., the original statutory goals) may be held as desirable; there can exist alternative competing principals and principal goals in a complex network of incentive relations. Thus, an incentive failures approach does not necessarily bias the analysis toward static hierarchical situations in which we can only examine whether or why the statute's prescriptions are (or are not) being followed. It is our argument that *every adequate model of implementation must have incentive relationships as a key component, implicitly or explicitly.* Later in this paper we shall define "incentive relation" at length and present an incentive system framework and a model for incentive system analysis in implementation.

Incentive failures may be distinguished on the basis of whether their sources are inside or outside the implementing agent-to-nominal principal relation. *Intra-agency failures* can occur both in the core incentive relation between implementer and principal (e.g., in such aspects of the incentive relation as the clarity of the principal's goals and how they are

communicated to the agent, the poor design of rewards or their nonar-
rival, the inability of the implementer to respond as requested) and in
the context of the agent–principal relationship (e.g., aspects of the organizational setting and the wider environment that affect the relation's
core factors directly). *Extra-agency failures* can result from the existence
of competitive agency relationships as well as from noncompetitive systemic or emergent factors. In situations that economists term "moral
hazard," for example, alternative reward sources (i.e., competing relationships) reduce the degree of contingency existing between a reward
and the behavior required of the agent; the reward can be received
whether or not the agent performs as the principal desires. In moral
hazard, the agent's behavior is not observable by the principal. Examples
of moral hazard are well-described in the insurance and the health and
welfare support literatures. Extra-agency incentive failures can also be
produced as a result of such systemic or emergent factors as implementation network coordination or performance problems. In other words,
the system in which the particular implementer and principal are embedded (e.g., an intergovernmental system) fails to produce outcomes
on which ultimate success of the local implementation efforts is
dependent.

From the perspective of Figure 1's implementation relations, incentive
failures may conceivably be produced where the agent has a faulty
knowledge of the principal's preferences, where the agent disagrees with
the principal's preferences, and where the agent cannot perform as
indicated. Incentive failures may occur with respect to the statute as
principal if alternative principals are chosen. Note again, however, that
these conditions do *not* necessarily imply failures; they can also contribute to policy adaptations or evolution that may lead to implementation
consistent with policy goals (if not designs).

Incentive failure as a description and an explanation of implementation problems appears by implication throughout the implementation
literature. Later in this paper we shall show how several major implementation models can be decomposed (at least in part) and the elements
sorted into the categories of the incentive system framework we develop.
To illustrate the relevance of incentive failures to implementation, we
shall briefly consider a few of the existing discussions of problematic
behavior in implementation.

Edwards (1980:107–114), for example, discusses a number of incentive problems in implementation. In the public sector the reward mechanism is often constrained [an aspect of what we shall later call the sender
(principal)–receiver (agent) relation]; pay increases go mostly across the
board, promotions are based on seniority, rewards are tied to individual.

not program, performance, and all members in the group cannot be rewarded (e.g., promoted). Competing sources of reward(i.e., potential principals) exist, with important referents stemming from individual self-interested behavior in bureaucratic settings. This includes peer pressure to conform (social reward control), underperformance to demonstrate need for a larger budget (with its consequent rewards), and goal displacement. The latter can result where goals and policy designs are vague and perhaps diverse and the measures of performance are poor. Since it is hard to evaluate what has been achieved with respect to the policy goals, bureaucrats emphasize whatever it is that is measured. All of these aspects can be treated comfortably within an incentive failures approach and, indeed, within the incentive systems framework presented later in this paper.

Bardach (1977) argues in part that implementation behavior can be seen as consisting of games of control within implementation relations, with incentive failures as a key element. Such "implementation games" should then be interpretable using the incentive failures perspective. Bardach's games often feature self-interested bureaucrats manipulating the system to obtain available rewards. Since it is difficult for nominal principals to monitor bureaucratic agents, budgets are successfully inflated, sometimes with both bureau and clientele benefiting ("diversion of resources" games). In "deflection of goals" games, participants alter policy goals or designs to satisfy bureaucratic or clientele interests. In what we shall call "avoidance-of-control" games, behavior reflecting either tokenism or massive resistance seeks to subvert the program. Here the implementing agents clearly disagree with the policy goals or design; the strategies that Bardach discusses to overcome this disagreement include manipulation of incentives/sanctions. Bardach's "dissipation of energies" games deal with bargaining by the implementing agent to get preferred rewards in policy areas or jurisdictional control, avoiding situations that are not rewarding (or protecting escape routes from such situations), or achieving personal image enhancement. It should be apparent that incentive failure aspects pervade these "games."

Incentive failure aspects are also evidenced, to take a related example, in Sorg's (1983) typology of implementer behaviors. The typology is based on whether there is a behavioral intention to conform, whether (and what kind of) compliance occurs, the covertness or overtness of the behavior, and the target of the behavior, including as targets policy goals/designs or other actors (such as the implementer or the client). Unlike some writers, Sorg (1983) worries about the nature of the behavior, i.e., the kinds of compliant/noncompliant adaptations in policy goals or designs that occur (addition, subtraction, substitution). The approach seems somewhat complementary to the general incentive failure/implementation relations approach we have presented. Implementing agents that agree or disagree with the policy goals or designs adopt behaviors presumably consistent with their interests or those of their principals or target groups. Incentive failure notions seem naturally to fit into such a setting.

Thus, we propose that a perspective grounded in incentive systems in implementation relations should be fruitful as an approach to implementation. We need to know, however, how to define and structure incentive systems and how to analyze their behavior.

THE INCENTIVES LITERATURE RELEVANT TO IMPLEMENTATION

Although it is apparent that many problem areas in implementation are consistent with an incentive failures approach, as yet we have neither defined "incentive" nor suggested how the elements of incentive relationships are arrayed. To help us do this, we turn now to the enormous literature that bears on incentives. We cannot hope to do it justice in this short space, but we can highlight certain especially relevant models. These include models that treat organizations as systems of incentives, that include general approaches to individual behavior in organizations, that present partial approaches to such behavior, or that address interorganizational or systemic behavior.

Organizations as Systems of Incentives

Chester Barnard (1938), in an approach that has inspired others but has never been fully developed, was the first to suggest the usefulness of regarding each organization as an "economy of incentives." He saw the organization "executive" as faced with the task of carefully administering scarce incentives to individuals in order to induce the contributions from them that are required for the functioning of the organization. He provided an elaborate list of important incentives, but the individual incentives are often vaguely defined and overlapping and the list is not exhaustive. Barnard also stopped short of a systematic framework that relates the incentives to varieties of behavior. His notion of "contribution," which is seen as a response to incentives, is left quite vague; he defines it obliquely as "activities constituting organization" (Barnard, 1938:75), though he gives a number of examples.

Herbert Simon and others (Simon, 1945; Simon et al., 1950; March and Simon, 1958) revived the essentials of Barnard's approach in presenting an "inducements–contributions" model. Although somewhat more specific and systematic than Barnard's approach, this model did not substantially advance the "economy of incentives" perspective. March and Simon (1958) distinguished between productivity within an organization, on the one hand, and joining and staying with an organization, on the other, noting that the determinants of the two phenomena are different. They applied the inducements–contributions model primarily to the analysis of joining and staying, with the implication that it is less applicable to the tendency to perform or produce within the organization. There is consequently some concern about the approach's relevance for implementation. Furthermore, their model of the determinants of turnover, joining, and staying was not clearly a derivation from the inducements–contributions model. Although they offered no systematic suggestions concerning what the major inducements (incentives) might be, they gave suggestions as to the measurement of inducements and contributions. Thus, the inducements–contributions approach remains more of a broad, undeveloped perspective than a systematic model.

The original incentive systems approach has been more fully developed by James Q. Wilson (Clark and Wilson, 1961; Wilson, 1973), and his work has inspired a number of empirical studies in political science. As with the efforts of March and Simon, however, most of this development and testing has focused on determinants of joining and staying with an organization. While such an emphasis might be quite appropriate to certain important purposes, such as analysis of voluntary political organizations (where much of the empirical work was done), it is less appropriate to analysis of internal design and management problems in organizations, and especially in differentiating public and private organizations along these lines (Levine et al., 1975; Rainey et al., 1976). But Wilson's work and related research do represent the most promising effort to move an incentive systems approach in the direction of systematic theory, at least in the context of public sector or nonprofit organizations.

Clark and Wilson (1961) were among the very few authors in this stream of research to offer a reasonably clear typology of incentives (material, solidary, and purposive incentives), and to relate that typology to the behavior of individuals and organizations. They focus on the implications of the predominance of one of these types of incentive in an organization, including impacts on such matters as organizational change and interorganizational competition, which result from efforts by key organizational figures to provide a particular type of incentive.

Even though Wilson later elaborated this typology by differentiating solidary incentives into "specific solidary" incentives and "collective solidary" incentives, the categories remain far from inclusive. This typology excludes potentially important incentives such as power or intrinsic satisfactions (for instance, self-esteem, competence goals, and intellectual excitement).

Although this oversimplified typology, and the associated treatment of incentives, may have heuristic value for certain purposes, it omits important dimensions that would improve prediction and explanation of a broader set of phenomena. For example, more attention to the attributes or dispositions of the receivers of the incentives (or those to whom the incentive is offered) would be valuable; a person acting as agent for someone else, under a "fiduciary" norm, might respond to an incentive differently from a person acting purely on his or her own behalf (Mitnick, 1973, 1974, 1975a). This could be especially relevant in understanding control problems in implementation. The Clark and Wilson approaches also tend to omit consideration of the process by which an incentive transaction is converted into behavior or satisfaction on the part of the receiver. Still another oversimplification that arises in the application of this approach to incentive systems is the emphasis on the central role of key organizational figures—"the executive"—in providing and manipulating incentives; significant incentives transactions frequently bypass the executive (Georgiou, 1973; Mitnick, 1974, 1975a).

As noted, much of the development of the Clark and Wilson approach has moved in the direction of emphasis on joining and staying, although Wilson (1966) has offered some suggestions on the application of the model to innovation within organizations. Perhaps because the model is most appropriate for analysis of joining and staying, the more recent work by Wilson (1973), as well as the several empirical tests of the model, have focused on participation in voluntary political activities (see, e.g., Conway and Feigert, 1968; Hofstetter, 1971, 1973). Limitations of these empirical tests underscore the need for greater elaboration and specification of the incentive systems approach. As operationalizations of the incentive types, these empirical studies use questionnaire items calling for responses about the respondent's "reasons" or "motives" for political participation. One might question, however, whether a person's motives necessarily reflect on externally available incentives, whether the same categories apply to incentives and motives, and whether there might not be a complicated process of conversion between the two that makes it inappropriate to study incentives by reference to motives. The empirical studies have sometimes focused on purposive goals of various levels, leaving unclear the role of organizational goals, which were the main concern of Clark and Wilson. They have also given most of their empirical attention to voluntary political organizations, which raises questions concerning generalizability. [For a recent use of the Clark and Wilson model, cf. Moe (1980); see also Salisbury (1969).] The limitations of the empirical efforts reflect the limitations in the model and suggest the need for a more elaborate and carefully conceptualized incentive systems approach.

In addition to these general models of organizations as systems of incentives, there are a few approaches based in the organization development and design literatures. An incentive or reward system approach is adopted specifically because of its presumed utility in designing effective organizations or organizational interventions. Galbraith (1977), for example, attempts to build on the Barnard, March, and Simon tradition in his analysis of integrating individuals and organizations. He relates behaviors, including joining and remaining, dependable role behavior, effort above minimum, spontaneous behavior, and cooperative behavior, to reward system features, including rule compliance, system/group/ individual rewards, task involvement, and goal identification. An adequate incentive system theory will, of course, have to relate incentive system characteristics to performances. The behaviors that Galbraith addresses, while focusing on intraorganizational performances, are particularly meaningful in many implementation contexts, such as compliance.

Perhaps closest in spirit to the approach that we shall offer is Steven Kerr's work on organizational reward systems (1975, n.d.). Kerr (n.d.) has been developing an instrument to assess organizational reward systems. This has led him to focus on types of rewards (e.g., salary, promotion, private and prestigious office, and so on), types of reward sources or controllers (e.g., organization policy, top management, personnel division, automatically over time, and so on), and reward contingencies (e.g., individual performance, group performance, attendance, variable or fixed membership, and so on). His instrument permits him to map relationships among these three classes of factors for any particular organization setting and to thereby identify problematic patterns.

We feel that Kerr's analysis makes a good deal of intuitive sense and clearly possesses power in identifying problem areas and intervention needs. Kerr does not, however, present a systematic incentive system conceptualization. We shall try to take this next step. Kerr's three main categories—rewards, controllers, and contingencies—can be reconciled with our incentive relation framework, with each dimension sorted into a category in our model. Indeed, it would be essential to do exactly what

Kerr has done—lay out observed types in each category and develop an assessment instrument—in order to make an incentive systems approach operational. [For other incentives-related perspectives, cf. the "political economy" approach; Zald (1970); Wamsley and Zald (1973); also see the incentives approach of Knoke and Wright-Isak (1982).]

General Models of Individual Behavior in Organizations

Of particular interest are general models of individual behavior in organizations that have at least implicit relevance to incentives. Some of the more prominent of these are the following:

Rational Choice or "Positive Theory" Models.   Models of individual behavior employing the rational choice assumption, frequently with specification of goal or dispositional states, have received increasing attention in political science (e.g., Riker and Ordeshook, 1973) and sociology (e.g., Blau, 1964) and have been of continuing interest in economics, where the approach originated. Some of these models have concerned organizational behavior (e.g., Williamson, 1964; Niskanen, 1971; Migue and Belanger, 1974; Mitnick, 1974, 1975b, 1980a; Tullock, 1965; Downs, 1967). In these models, behavior is regarded as the result of individuals pursuing goals consistently (rationally) given certain distributions of goal satisfactions ("rewards" or "incentives") in their environments. Although sometimes criticized as unrealistic, simplistic, and lacking in predictive power (which is supposed to be a strength of the approach) (see, e.g., Hardin, 1976), these models are clearly relevant to incentives and implementation. Some provide major suggestions as to characteristic behaviors of individual personality types within bureaucracies (Downs, 1967) or concerning particularly important goals and incentives within bureaucracies (Niskanen, 1971).

Compliance Models.   Etzioni (1961) has offered a compliance-based model that bears great similarity to the approach of Clark and Wilson (1961; see also Wilson, 1973). Organizations are distinguished on the grounds of "compliance relationships" between an actor exercising power and one subject to it who responds with degrees of alienation or commitment. Power is distinguished according to the means of compliance, coercive (physical sanctions), remunerative (material rewards), and normative ["symbolic," including both prestige and ritual ("pure normative power") and social group pressures ("social power")]. This compares with Clark and Wilson's (1961) and Wilson's (1973) material, solidary, and purposive incentives. Compliance relations are determined by the kinds of power and of "involvement" (alienative, calculative, moral) that exist in the relations.

Etzioni's concept of compliance as a relationship is consistent with the general incentive relation conceptualization that we describe below; social systems are to be understood as systems of relations rather than as isolated elements transmitting or exchanging stimuli or valued objects. The focus on compliance makes it especially relevant to implementation; indeed, it is sometimes cited in the implementation literature.

Exchange Theory. It is a comment on the compartmentalization of the disciplines to observe the obvious familial relationship of exchange theory to such approaches as inducements–contributions models, rational choice models, compliance models, expectancy theories, and the transactions costs perspective. Although the work of a few researchers has spanned two or more of these areas, by and large each represents relatively distinct research traditions. Exchange theory has a venerable history in sociology (e.g., Thibaut and Kelley, 1959; Homans, 1961; Blau, 1964; Emerson, 1972; Marsden and Lin, 1982). Social exchange theory takes relations as units of analysis and considers such variables as rewards, costs, comparison levels (value standards), reinforcement patterns, exchange rules, norms, and so on (see, e.g., Emerson, 1976). Although it is perhaps best developed for the case of relations among individuals, exchange theory has also been applied extensively in group and interorganizational settings (see below).

The relevance of exchange theory to incentives and, consequently, to implementation is obvious; it could conceivably be viewed itself as a general incentive system approach to social behavior. The relational emphasis as well as the possibility of higher level applications make it especially consistent with our approach to implementation.

Transactions Costs Models. Oliver Williamson (1975, 1979, 1981) has developed an approach that employs arguments about the nature of transactions in institutional settings to explain the organization of those settings. "Critical dimensions" of transactions include uncertainty, frequency of transaction recurrence, and idiosyncratic aspects of investment by participants in the transaction (Williamson, 1979;239). The transactions occur under a variety of contractual arrangements and can be marked by strategic behavior provoked by opportunism, by problems resulting from small numbers of participants or potential participants, by bounded rationality, and by "impactedness of information," i.e., a condition in which "true underlying circumstances relevant to the transaction, or related set of transactions, are known to one or more parties

but cannot be costlessly discerned by or displayed for others" (Williamson, 1975:31).
The focus in the transactions cost approach is on the exchange, including whatever agreement (i.e., contract) governs it. We are less well-informed about particular characteristics or motivations of the actors (cf. Emerson's (1976) comments). The emphasis on a relation among parties in which performance is controlled at least partly by contract is consistent with our concerns about incentives and implementation. In general, agents and principals can operate under a variety of contractual arrangements; a variety of implicit or explicit contracts can govern implementer behavior for legislative, bureaucratic, or clientele principals [for another institutional approach, cf. Wolf (1979)].

Expectancy Theories.   The predominant models in the study of individual effort and motivation in work organizations are currently formulations of "expectancy theory." In its simplest form, as presented by Vroom (1964) in the earliest effort to apply the theory to work motivation, "motivation," and therefore effort, is a multiplicative function of (1) the individual's subjective probability estimates ("expectancies") concerning the attainment of "outcomes" (e.g., rewards or punishments) through his efforts; and (2) the "valences" of these outcomes for the individual, i.e., the extent to which he values them positively or negatively.

This simplified version has been subjected to various extensions and elaborations. For example, expectancies have been differentiated into expectancies that efforts will lead to performance and expectancies that performance will lead to outcomes (Campbell and Pritchard, 1976). Others have included additional variables, such as the individual's ability level (Lawler, 1971), and there have been numerous efforts to relax the specification that the model's components be multiplied together.

These efforts at modification have not resolved some problems with the theory, which have been pointed out in a number of critiques (see, for example, Behling et al., 1973; Campbell and Pritchard, 1976). Among many other complaints, critics have charged that expectancy theory is inadequate as a representation of human cognitive processes and that it has major conceptual shortcomings—for example, what are "outcomes" and how are they kept distinct from expectancies? These conceptual problems are related to measurement problems, and the theory has not fared well in empirical tests.

Like the incentive system approach, expectancy theory has a central assumption of rationality. Also like some versions of incentive theory, longer-term goals or objects of preference are not specified, so prediction of behavior in differing circumstances may not be possible. Some versions of expectancy theory come close to the simple statement that performance will occur when it is rational for the individual to perform, and some tests of the theory are virtually simple tests of rationality under highly limiting assumptions.

In spite of both discouragement due to these problems and a search for alternatives (Behling et al., 1973), the basic rationale of the theory is persuasive enough to command attention. Certainly, concepts similar to "expectancy" and "valence" must be considered for inclusion in any incentives model. The model is conducive to a focus on the *contingencies* of incentives (their relation to actions and behaviors), a consideration that is fundamental to the attractiveness or repulsiveness of incentives and to the design of incentive systems.

Attitude-Behavior Theory. Attitude-behavior models such as that of Fishbein and Ajzen (1975) are quite similar to expectancy theory. Their attitude-behavior model is structured like an expectancy formulation, but with different conceptualization of the component concepts, emphasizing primarily the prediction of behavioral intentions on the basis of attitudes. Although seldom applied in organizations (Mitchell and Nebeker, 1973), these alternative concepts may well prove more tractable and measurable than some of the vague concepts with which expectancy theory formulations are concerned, and thus the approach may supplant expectancy theory for certain purposes. Sorg (1978) has developed an application of this approach to implementation.

Operant Conditioning Models. A recent development, of increasing interest due to discouragement over expectancy theory, is the application of Skinnerian, operant, or behavior modification models to the analysis of behavior in work organizations (Behling et al., 1973). Although they take into account various of the phenomena related to incentives (i.e., the environment of the individual, his responses to it), such approaches are only roughly developed as yet. They might remain undeveloped, at least as formal models, since they tend to be based on explicit renunciation of many of the concepts frequently used in analysis of purposeful and rational behavior, such as motives or values. In a sense, they also renounce the possibility of their own development into a theory through their denial of any but the most general of constructs and of the possibility of specifying incentives or rewards ("reinforcements") except through actual tests in a highly specific context. Rather, such approaches tend to involve a set of statements about the effects on behavior of very general types of reinforcement and of certain schedules of reinforcement. Nevertheless, the arguments under these approaches raise important points concerning the development of certain responses over time, the effects of various patterns or schedules by which incentives are applied, and other variables with potential for inclusion in an incentive system approach.

Partial Models of Individual Behavior in Organizations

Other approaches concentrate on only one major factor among the many that are relevant to the impact of incentives in organizations. These include models that concentrate on independent variables, moderating variables, and dependent variables. We address them very briefly.

Needs Models.   Although the major models or theories of human needs (e.g., Maslow, 1954; Alderfer, 1969; McClelland, 1961) were not all devised for application to behavior in organizations, such applications frequently occur (see Lawler, 1973). Obviously, identification of fundamental human needs and their operation would be of great value to a theory of incentives. The immense variety of needs and means of their satisfaction, as well as measurement problems, create formidable theoretical difficulties, of course.

Goal-Setting Approaches.   The advancement of a theory by Locke (1968) and the emergence of techniques such as management by objectives (MbO) have created interest in the effects of goal-setting in organizations and the impacts on effort and performance of various goal attributes. Using a broad definition of "incentive" ("an external incentive is . . . an event or object external to the individual which can incite action"), Locke discusses task goals as mediators of the effects on performance, time limits, participation in decision making, competition, and praise or reproof. In addition, he hypothesizes that the level of difficulty and specificity of a goal are positively associated with level of performance, i.e., harder or more specific goals lead to better performance. Empirical research has provided only mixed support for Locke's theory, however.

Emphasis on incentives involves emphasis on external inducements and their contingencies on behaviors, and goal attributes certainly can influence the perceptions of such contingencies. These goal-setting and goal-attribute approaches are therefore relevant to an incentive system approach, particularly one intended for application to government or public organizations, which are often said to face particular difficulties due to vagueness and complexity of goals and performance measures (Rainey et al., 1976).

Equity Models. Much attention has been devoted to equity models (Adams, 1965; Walster et al., 1978), which posit a drive to reduce inequity in various types of exchanges. Inequity results from the perception of imbalance between individual contributions and receipts, especially as compared to the contributions and receipts of another. As applied to work behaviors and satisfactions, the models lead to such hypotheses as predictions of reduction in effort when an individual sees himself as underpaid in comparison to another and of increase in work effort when one sees himself overpaid as compared to another. Although such behavior has obvious relevance to implementation, there can be conceptual and measurement problems in the analysis of "equity" as a variable.

Self-concept (Self-esteem, Self-consistency) Approaches. Self-concept models (e.g., Korman, 1966; Lawler, 1973:92–93) posit that one's image of oneself strongly affects one's performance. Those who see themselves as poor performers will tend to perform poorly, which in turn will reinforce poor self-image. Lawler (1971) has tried to incorporate such factors into an expectancy model by noting that a given reward will be less motivating to an individual with low self-esteem, since he will have a lower expectation (expectancy) of achieving the reward. Thus, these approaches offer another important factor for consideration in constructing the component of an incentives model concerned with the attributes or dispositional state of an individual implementer.

Money as an Incentive. There is a voluminous literature on financial incentives, some reporting laboratory studies and some concerned with the practical problems of administering pay incentive plans in industry. Although the laboratory studies are limited in their generalizability and the practical discussions are often conceptually disorganized, there have been efforts at systematic conceptualization and analysis (e.g., Lawler, 1971). Frequent observations concerning the failure of pay incentive plans due to employee misunderstanding or opposition (and consequent problems in implementation) emphasize the importance to an incentives model of factors related to information about incentive contingencies. Since money is probably the most easily manipulable incentive, and the one that can most easily convert to other incentives (such as prestige, status), this literature will require attention in any incentives approach.

Studies of Effects of Properties of the Individual's Environment. As already noted, there have been attempts to include contextual or situational factors in models of behavior in organizations; these should help in understanding incentives and implementation. The properties that may prove useful include: group variables like norms; variables indicating aspects of task, group, or organizational leadership or its history that may affect individual behavior; aspects of job design, i.e., properties of the task, and aggregate organizational properties, such as climate, that may sometimes be used in modeling individual behavior.

Motivation–Hygiene (Two Factor) Theory.   Herzberg's motivation–hygiene theory (Herzberg et al., 1959) holds that job satisfaction is determined by intrinsic aspects of the job, such as achievement, recognition, advancement, and the work itself ("motivator"). Job *dis*satisfaction, on the other hand, is determined by extrinsic aspects of the job, such as salary, supervision, organizational policy, interpersonal relations, and job security ("hygiene" factors). Performance is said to depend on motivators and to be unrelated to hygiene factors, but there has been relatively little theoretical or empirical study of this linkage. The theory has remained one essentially concerned with determinants of job satisfaction. While this approach suggests some important incentives and incentive attributes, it has been subjected to severe criticism (Lawler, 1973:70–71) for oversimplification of the phenomena it purports to explain.

Satisfaction and Satisfaction–Performance Studies.   There have been innumerable studies of work satisfaction and its correlates, but there have also been continuing uncertainty and controversy over the relation of satisfaction to performance (see, e.g., Schwab and Cummings, 1970). Lawler (1973) suggests that the relationship is a matter of the contingency of rewards on performance; if rewards are tied to performance, then the satisfaction that results from receipt of rewards will vary with performance. If rewards are provided independently of performance, however, then one can be quite satisfied, regardless of one's performance. This suggests the importance of differentiating between satisfaction and performance in an incentive systems approach in implementation.

Models Relevant to Interorganizational or Systemic Behavior

The last 15 years have seen a veritable explosion of research on organization–environment and interorganizational relations [on organization–environment relations, see, e.g., Aldrich (1979)]. There are several bodies of work here that have relevance for incentives models; we can only sketch a few of the main areas. Researchers have begun to investigate the structure of interorganizational relations (e.g., Guetzkow, 1966; Litwak with Rothman, 1970; White, Boorman, and Breiger, 1976), identifying the "organization-set" with which a focal organization interacts (Evan, 1976). The nature of the interaction itself has attracted considerable attention with theorizing and empirical study of exchanges and consequent resource dependence (e.g., Levine and White, 1961; Pfeffer and Salancik, 1978; Van de Ven, 1976; Raelin, 1980). Exchange theoretical approaches developed for individual or abstract actors have been applied to networks of organizations (e.g., Cook, 1977; Laumann and Pappi, 1976; Marsden and Lin, 1982). The linkage roles between organizations and the external environment have received considerable attention (Adams, 1976; Leifer and Delbecq, 1978; Aldrich and Herker, 1977; Miles, 1980).

The personnel that inhabit these boundary-spanning roles can be viewed both as organizational agents who are subject to the organizational incentive system and as creators of agents in the environment (Mitnick, 1982a). As creators, boundary personnel can seek to manipulate the environmental incentive system so as to manufacture or maintain conditions favorable to the organization (e.g., keeping friends in Congress or developing a supply of regulators dependent on the organization's provision of information needed in regulation).

That material that deals, implicitly or explicitly, with the management of, or response to, exchanges with the environment, including other organizations, has obvious relevance to an incentive system approach. Exchanges can be modeled at both the individual and organizational levels, of course. What is less clear is how to treat emergent phenomena in a system of interaction. An incentive system approach should allow us to at least model the pattern of relations in the system; emergent phenomena should be a function of the particular pattern that occurs. As long as we are aware that system behavior cannot necessarily be extrapolated from behavior of a typical constituent relation, we can avoid the level-crossing fallacy. Indeed, we are better equipped to understand emergent phenomena if we understand the system of relations that produce them.

These approaches should be of particular benefit, of course, in understanding implementation in an intergovernmental system. They should help, for example, in identifying its elements (organization-sets of public and private sectors), characterizing exchanges (e.g., pattern of resource dependence among government bodies and target groups), and describing the structure and behavior of actors in linkage (i.e., boundary-spanning) roles, including key public and private facilitators.

Suggested List of Constituent Elements of an Incentives Approach

Our review has identified both strengths and weaknesses in the current writing related to incentives and behavior by individuals in organizations. The salient contributions that will be used to develop our incentive system approach are listed below. In parentheses we indicate a theoretical area or two (there may be additional ones) of research (or related scholar) that suggests (possibly by deficiency as noted above) inclusion as an element in our approach. For the convenience of the reader, we have ordered these elements according to whether they pertain to the sender of incentives, the sender–receiver relationship, the receiver of the incentives that may perform the desired behavior, or the setting in which the incentive relationship unfolds. These terms will take on additional meaning as they are discussed in the next section of the paper.

A. *Sender of Incentives*

1. A variety of entities can be considered providers of incentive stimuli and rewards; we do not want to limit our approach to incentives orginating from a single manipulating executive (e.g., Barnard, 1938). Individuals, groups, and organizations may provide incentives to the receiving system.

2. Senders may vary in the type of incentive stimuli or rewards they can or do provide; their control over the incentives may also vary.

B. *Nature of the Sender–Receiver Relation*

3. Attention must be placed on the nature of the historical (e.g., operant conditioning) as well as the current relationship between the sender and receiver of incentive messages and rewards.

4. Provision should be made for feedback from the receiver to the sender (e.g., operant conditioning models and performance leading to satisfaction models) and to the receiver itself on its own behavior.

5. A complete, exclusive classification of incentives that are potentially provided external to the receiver is useful [e.g., see Barnard (1938); Clark and Wilson (1961); Wilson (1973); Locke (1968)'s goal-setting theory; money as incentive theories).

6. The extent to which rewards are actually provided contingent on behavior (e.g., operant conditioning) and the extent to which the actual performances or outcomes are clearly specified should be recognized as significant factors in the approach.

C. *Receiver of Incentive Stimuli and Rewards (Punishments)*

7. The receivers may be a variety of entities, i.e., individuals, groups, or organizations. In our model we shall assume for purposes of illustra-

tion that the receiver system is an individual, but the approach should be more generalizable. Many of the points below apply to human receiver systems since the literature reviewed focused on individual behavior.

8. Receivers will vary in the extent of information they have on the incentive situation and the specific relation (e.g., expectancy and attitude-behavior theories).

9. Individuals have limits on their information processing abilities [e.g., Simon's (1945, 1947) "bounded rationality"; expectancy theory; attitude-behavior theory]. These limits should be specified.

10. Biological aspects of the receiver are important to consider, including basic needs (e.g., need theory) and emotions (e.g., Locke's goal-setting theory). Habits or habitual behavior cannot be assumed to be associated with conscious decision processes.

11. The receiver has a number of conscious, psychological attributes that influence receiver behavior, including: expectancies (expectancy theory) regarding effort and performance and performance-outcomes; rationality in that he acts with consistency to given goals, preferences, needs, intentions, and so on [e.g., Barnard (1938) and others, and the needs, rational choice, goal-setting, expectancy, and attitude-behavior theories]; preferences or goals and preference sets [e.g., Barnard (1938) and others, and the needs, rational choice, goal-setting, and expectancy theories]; a history of conditioning, reinforcement, and learning (operant conditioning); perceptions of equity in past rewards for performances (equity theory); levels of affective satisfaction (satisfaction–performance theory); and self-concepts or esteem (self-concept theory).

12. The receivers as individuals can perform a wide variety of behaviors including joining, staying, producing, and so on (e.g., the Barnard tradition).

13. Rewards, effort, performances, and other outcomes affect the receiver's level of satisfaction, which in turn influences receiver behavior and performance (e.g., satisfaction–performance theory, motivation–hygiene theory).

14. Various mechanisms operate within the individual-as-receiver system in converting incentive stimuli to behavior intentions and to actual effort and performance (e.g., rational choice, expectancy, goal-setting, and attitude-behavior theories).

D. *Incentive Relation Setting*

15. A wide variety of factors from the operating or proximal environment may influence the sender, the sender–receiver relation, and the receiver. These include, inter alia, group variables, job design, and organization structure, technology, climate, and environment (e.g., the situational or environment theories).

16.   The approach should be applicable to behavior by actors with varying types of tasks in different organizational settings and at different organizational levels.

The above will generally encompass the strengths of the theories reviewed and eliminate most of the tractable weaknesses. Drawing on the above considerations, we outline in the next section a framework for an incentive system approach to individual behavior in organizations.

A FRAMEWORK FOR AN INCENTIVE SYSTEM THEORY

We have examined in the literature review a number of approaches to the study of incentives and motivation in organizations that are relevant to implementation; we turn now to the specification of the concept "incentive" and the presentation of a conceptual framework or model of incentive systems. The model can be viewed as a kind of mapping/sorting model that allows analysts to sort observed variables (e.g., in an implementation situation) into categories or classes that occupy their position or function in the incentive relation. For the purposes of this paper, we have presented a conceptual framework of the incentive relation at the micro or individual level. The analytical framework is generalizable to other levels, however; it is not tied to specific types of objects, exchanges, or actors.

Definition of the Incentive System

Discussion of the defining properties of the concept "incentive" and the range of its secondary connotations could itself be the subject of a paper, given the many definitions in the literature (for examples, see Rainey, 1977). In the broadest sense, incentives have been defined as stimuli that evoke behavior (e.g., Locke, 1968). Our approach is to narrow the definition of incentive somewhat and to shift its application from an attribute of an isolated entity to a reference to a *relation* between two entities. The relationship between the two entities then defines the *incentive relation* and a system of two or more entities and their relations jointly define the *incentive system.*

Figure 2 presents a simplified model of the basic incentive system, which is a type of control system. The system is defined to include the elements and relations between a sender of incentive information and rewards (positive or negative) and a receiver of the incentive informa-

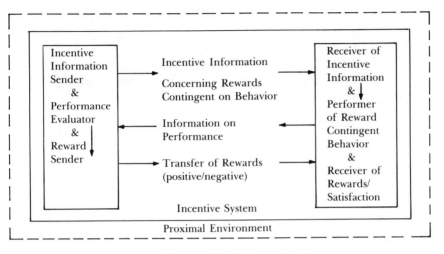

Figure 2. Basic Model of Incentive System.

tion that takes action or behaves to obtain the behavior-contingent rewards. The connecting arrows suggest the basic three-step flow of information or values that would complete a full incentive transaction: the transmission of messages concerning the rewards to be provided contingent upon performing certain behaviors, information to the sender or provider of the rewards that the behavior in question is performed (or not), and the actual transfer or provision of rewards to the behavior performer. Variations on this basic model are possible, e.g., simultaneous flows, incomplete flow, omission of events, and so on.

The five primary defining properties of the incentive relation are listed below:

1. *Exchange assumption*—The stimuli are sent and received by both the sender and the receiver.
2. *Reward assumption*—The stimuli sent by the sender involve or promise direct or indirect positive or negative rewards, i.e., stimuli are directly or indirectly valued, affecting receiver's goals.
3. *Contingent behavior assumption*—The stimuli are linked with given receiver behavior.
4. *Response assumption*—The receiver behaves in response to the stimuli.
5. *Rationality assumption*—The receiver will behave rationally, i.e., to acquire or avoid the positively or negatively valued stimuli.

These five properties not only define the incentive relation; they also exclude various relations. For example, not all exchanges of stimuli and responses between the two acting entities are to be studied, only those involving the promise of reward based on contingent behavior and behavior responses that are purposefully (rationally) selected by the receiver entity (or its subelements).

Definitions of the incentive concept often feature additional properties. Although such definitions usually include the five properties listed above, the added dimensions tend to limit the scope of application of the incentive approach in question. Thus we reserve the five "primary" defining properties for the concept itself and consider the additional dimensions as "secondary" defining properties (see Figure 3 for a composite display of the primary and secondary defining conditions):

6. *Sender goals assumption*—The stimuli sent by the sender are or are not purposefully offered to elicit given receiver behavior.

7. *Agency assumption*—The stimuli sent by the sender do or do not establish (or seek to establish) the receiver as an agent of the sender.

8. *Conscious choice assumption*—The receiver's behavior is or is not consistent with conscious (explicit) goals.

9. *Instrumentality assumption*—The receiver's behavior is consistent with terminal (sought for own sake) or instrumental (sought as means to other goals) goals.

Although we do not intend in this paper to discuss the different subtypes of incentive relations, some brief implications can be drawn from an examination of the secondary properties. Assuming the sender is purposefully offering the stimulus excludes cases where the incentive stimuli are sent without any intention by the sender to elicit the receiver's behavior. One example of this assumption occurs in the management control literature, much of which is concerned with planned incentive offers targeted at evoking worker behavior. The seventh assumption clarifies the relationship between the sender and receiver; it refers to the situation in which the sender attempts to get the receiver to pursue the sender's goals (in addition to the receiver's self-goals). Indeed, a number of approaches have been developed in an attempt to commit organizational members to accept and act toward organizational, subunit, and work group goals, whether the task concerns policy implementation or anything else. Thus assumptions six and seven are obviously likely to be common in implementation studies. The eighth assumption highlights

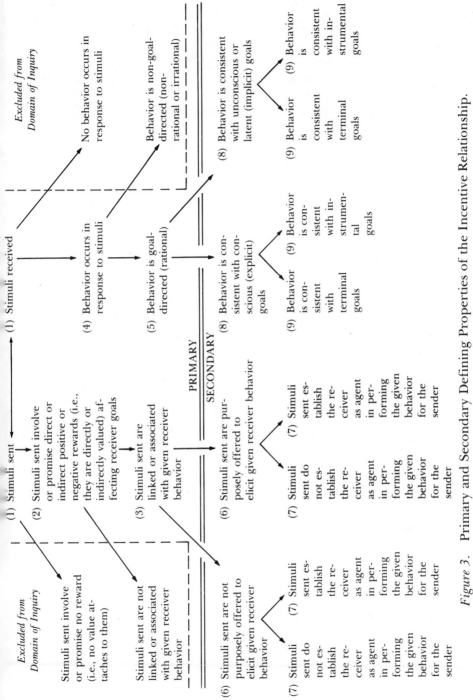

Figure 3. Primary and Secondary Defining Properties of the Incentive Relationship.

89

the importance of the degree to which the receiver is conscious of or explicit in pursuit of his goals. The ninth assumption distinguishes whether the receiver is consistently pursuing terminal (sought for their own sake) or instrumental (sought as means to other goals) goals. Applied distinctions concerning the role of terminal versus instrumental goals in motivating behavior may be important in developing explanations and predictions of implementer performance.

The Incentive System Model

The basic components and relations of the individual-level model of a work organization incentive system are diagrammed in Figure 4. The model extends the more general model of an incentive system presented in Figure 2 and contains seven basic components or elements. The core components, however, are the sender–receiver relations or transactions, the sender, the receiver's dispositional state (labeled receiver system in the diagram), the receiver's behavior, and the consequent outcomes for the receiver, the sender, and the proximal work environment. The model posits multiple senders and receivers and in this way goes beyond the simple model in Figure 2. The senders, sender–receiver relations, receivers, receiver performances, and outcomes are subdivided for analytical purposes into focal and alternative categories. In analyzing incentive situations, normally the analyst will focus on specific senders and receivers and their incentive relations(s); the analysis is enriched, however, if the alternative senders, receivers, and sender–receiver relations are taken into account, e.g., competitive relations are taken into account as sources of potential or actual influence on the focal relation. Figure 5 displays a simplified version of Figure 4 (e.g., only a single sender and receiver are depicted).

Overall, the model portrays the dynamic adaptive properties of the incentive system subsystems (sender, receiver, and transaction relation structure) and assumes various types of feedback paths. Given the adaptive nature of the subsystems, predicting variation in their behavior is conditional on many other properties or variables in the incentive system. Thus our approach can be considered a contingency approach to the study of incentive systems. In the diagram the arrows suggest the basic flow of influence between components. The heavy lines indicate the dynamic flow of influence among the core components; the lighter lines reflect less important or more indirect influences in, to, or from the proximal environment. The arrows within the receiver system are suggestive of the basic influence relations among some frequently noted

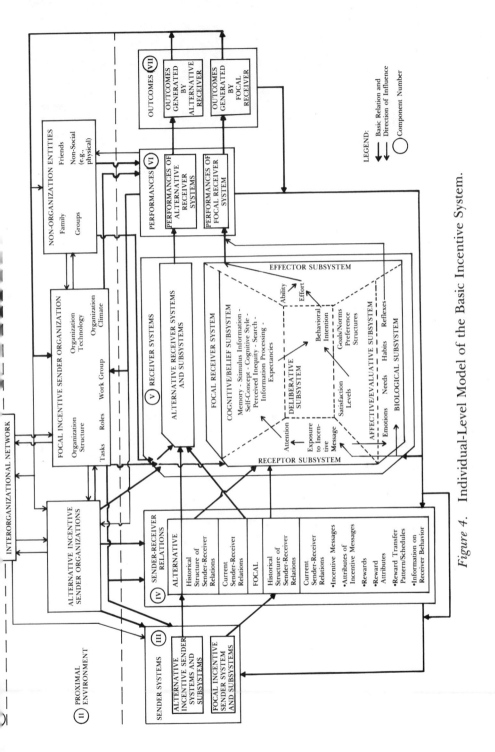

Figure 4. Individual-Level Model of the Basic Incentive System.

91

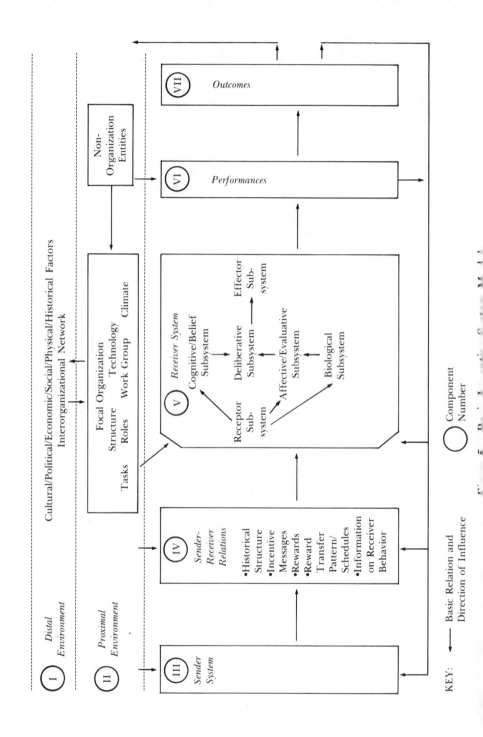

92

psychological or biological properties of individuals. Several of these relations are quite speculative and, based on a reading of the literature, controversial. The receiver system dispositional state is the main case in point (Fishbein and Azjen, 1975). Given the limits of this paper, we shall not discuss this component in great detail. Each component is identified by a circled number, e.g., distal environment (I), proximal environment (II), sender systems (III), sender–receiver relations (IV), and so on.

Although change factors are not explicitly indicated in each component, we shall assume that aspects of change in each variable category are included. For example, "reward attributes" includes reward stability as well as the particular types and amounts of rewards in a given setting.

We shall briefly review the major components and relations identified in the model and, where appropriate, note the location of the theories or approaches identified in the literature review. The *distal component* (I) is composed of the more general structures of the societal system: the cultural, political, economic, social, physical, and historical (events). We assume that these clusters of variables have an indirect antecedent influence on the contemporary, focal incentive system and act through the component named *proximal environment* (II). The literature reviewed earlier does not deal with this component explicitly, although cross-cultural students of individual behavior do utilize it (Triandis, 1972).

The proximal environment includes the work organization and its environment including other incentive senders, technology, structure, tasks, roles, work group, organization climate, and so on. In the diagram, the senders and receivers are shown distinct from the organizations in which they may be located as subcomponents or members; an alternative representation with the senders and receivers as subcomponents of larger units labeled organizations is also tenable but avoided here for clarity. Both the sender and receiver are directly affected by the critical elements and variables in the proximal environment (organization theorists sometimes prefer the term "task environment" here). The immediate work environment provides many stimuli that are perceived and processed by both the sender and receiver. The "moderating" or work context theories and the work environment factors assessed by the two-factor, motivation-hygiene theories reviewed above relate to this component. There is little theory relating the distal environment component to the proximal or task environment component; presumably these relations are less direct and powerful.

The *sender system* (III) may or may not be an individual. If it is, we assume many of the properties associated with the receiver system discussed below apply to the sender as well (the sender has a cognitive belief system, affective/evaluative system, and so on). Sender systems differ in the types of incentive stimuli and associated rewards they actually or potentially transmit to the receivers, and their capacity level for particular stimuli/rewards varies as well. As described below under the discussion of the sender–receiver relation, senders can provide stimuli and rewards on a variety of schedules with diverse contents. The senders possess different expectations or beliefs about the types of incentives that will generate the desired behavior by the receiver, and they can differ in the values they associate with different performance outcomes. They are subject to influence by incentive stimuli provided by other senders, including the focal receiver (e.g., in the work organization context, the worker can provide incentive messages to the managers), and in that case they can be conceptualized as receiver systems themselves. Information on the performance of receivers is evaluated by the senders and may trigger the provision of actual rewards or changes in the incentive messages sent.

The sender has goals, behavioral intentions (dispositions to behave in specific and consistent ways), and beliefs about aspects of his or her proximal environment, the sender–receiver relation, the receiver, the receiver's performance, and the outcomes. The sender system may attempt to establish a relation of agency with the receiver in which the receiver acts on behalf of the sender to achieve sender goals. The sender transmits stimuli called incentive messages in the direction of the receiver, transfers rewards to the receiver, and receives information on the receiver's performance and performance outcomes. The sender may or may not be consistent in rewarding the behaviors suggested in the incentive message; this area of inconsistent contingent rewarding does not appear to be well studied. In addition, the literature does not normally address the various types of senders and their dispositional states.

The relations or transactions between the sender and receiver define the fourth component, the *sender–receiver relation* (IV). In this component, we have distinguished the historical structure of sender–receiver relations from the current. In our view the pattern of historical relations (particularly contractual ones) and their change strongly conditions the nature of current or operating relations and transactions. We make a special point to distinguish the incentive message (promise of reward contingent on specified behaviors/outcomes) from the actual rewards provided. Furthermore, the content of the incentive message and actual rewards is considered multidimensional in nature; rewards or their stimuli may be perceived to be independent of each other, tangible or intangible, substitutable, vary in controllability by the sender, vary in valence for the sender or receiver, satisfy different types of sender and receiver goals, and so on [on these dimensions, see Mitnick (1974, 1975a); a later study that identifies many such dimensions is Zald and Jacobs (1978)]. The information on the receiver's performance and associated outcomes is included since it will influence the provision of rewards, reward scheduling, sender satisfaction, and future sender–receiver relations. Linking the sender and receiver this way provides a basis for determining the extent to which the receiver's behavior is in *conformity* with the sender's incentive message and original intent and the extent to which the sender is actually providing the contingent rewards as promised.

The most critical component for study is, of course, the receiver's dispositional state, which we call the *receiver system* (V) for short (some might want to call it the receiver's personality). Most of the theories we reviewed earlier relate to elements of this component. For the purposes of this discussion we limit ourselves to focal individuals as receivers and exclude reflex-based behaviors. For simplicity, we have noted that the receiver must receive or have exposure to the incentive message for it to activate an incentive relation. In addition, the receiver must attend to the stimulus so that some level of interest is generated. The perceived stimulus is then related to elements of the cognitive/belief subsystem of the receiver and to the affective/evaluative subsystem [some call this the attitudinal substructure; see Fishbein and Ajzen (1975)], which includes goals or preferences, norms, preference structures, decision rules (satisficing, maximizing, and others), satisfaction levels, and so on. The model portrays a biological subsystem in order to indicate that emotions are associated with biological states and that these states influence the satisfactions found in the affective/evaluative component. Basic needs may be included as part of the genetic inheritance of the biological subsystem, although need levels appear to be affected by reinforcement history and seem to influence the affective–evaluative subsystem in such areas as satisfaction levels and goal states.

We have introduced the term "deliberative" subsystem to refer to the internal neural processes that link the other subcomponents in such a way as to produce behavioral intentions that in turn activate the effector subsystem (cf. Kuhn, 1974) to emit effort to act or behave in specific patterns. Behavioral intentions are dispositions to perform specific actions to achieve desired outcomes (some authors refer to this subcomponent as the conative substructure). The formation of the behavioral intention results from the linkage processes in the deliberative subsystem. The linkage processes are not fully understood at the current time; thus, what follows is limited to assertions that linkages are made, without specifying their direction and form. The linkage relations are presumed in the attitude-behavior, goal-setting, rational choice, equity, satisfaction–performance, compliance, and organization "economy of incentive" theories reviewed earlier. Each offers a variant of or highlights specific variables and relations that coproduce the behavioral intentions and presumably the actual performance.

Among the linkage relations that we or others assert to occur in the deliberative process are the following: (1) Affective states of satisfaction–dissatisfaction are felt or perceived and are related to evaluative states such as goals or preferences and norms and to beliefs about the receiver, effort/action, performances, outcomes, incentives/rewards, incentive senders, sender–receiver relations, and other aspects of the proximal or distal environment. (2) Evaluative states such as goals, norms, and preference sets are associated with belief/cognitive components to generate valences (positive and negative) associated with effort/action, performances, and various outcomes [as more differentiated above in (1)]. (3) The cognitive/belief system links internal elements such as memory; cognitive styles; self-concepts; equity perceptions; information processing capacities; expectancies concerning effort, performances, and outcomes; information search procedures; and information associated with the stimulus received from the receptor and/or affective subsystems. (4) The cognitive/belief system is linked with the affective/evaluative system to select potential actions (and sets of actions), form specific behavior intentions, and generate action. As the term "deliberative" suggests, the linkage subprocesses may be quite complex and extended in time prior to the formation of a specific behavioral intention. Figure 4 also notes that the ability of the receiver and the effort expended to produce the performance must be considered in developing a theory of incentive-based individual behavior.

The last components refer to the actual *performances* (VI) and their consequent *outcomes* (VII). Left for future work is development of an extended classification of performance behaviors and of concepts and measures for certain aspects or qualities of performance, such as productivity and production of innovation performance behaviors. The literature reviewed did not provide us with a complete empirical or conceptual classification, even though the performance studies were directed at explaining or predicting variation in individual performance (but see, e.g., Galbraith, 1977). The problem is, of course, relevant to implementation, no matter which principal the implementing agent acts for, i.e., no matter which criteria for implementation "success" are posited.

One of the composite feedback relations to be noted here is that between behavior, outcome, evaluation, and satisfaction. As the brief performance–satisfaction literature review noted, there is some disagreement on the nature of this relationship; the equity literature suggests that it is moderated by perceptions of rewards given to comparable persons in the work environment. Furthermore, the achievement of full understanding of the linkage between outcome and satisfaction would require tracking the effects of outcomes on the sender and of the actual rewards provided to the receiver after the behavior elicited is performed and assessed. For clarity in drawing, Figure 4 does not depict all feedback relationships. We shall assume, for example, that outcomes and performances affect the sender, sender–receiver relation, receiver, and environmental entities in both the focal and alternative components. The full range of outcome effects, i.e., to receiver, sender, and the proximal work environment, are important to specify in greater detail than in the existing literature. In short, a great number of extensions of the current literature and our basic model can be envisaged in the future.

Although we believe that a general incentive system theory within the framework developed in this paper is possible, very significant theoretical benefits may be derived simply from the direct application of the model to sort concepts and propositions for specific cases. Our conceptualization of "incentive" as *incentive relation* directs attention to the relations of elements in control systems of this kind. The model organizes key variables into the sender, sender–receiver, receiver, and other categories (and subcategories such as reward types, incentive message aspects, and so on) and suggests the logic of how explanations should be constructed from this basis. Special case incentive theories built in this framework may indeed contribute to an understanding of important abstract concepts and propositions in a general incentive system theory. Later in this paper we present a seven-stage sorting/mapping model for incentive system analysis and discuss its relevance for implementation.

INCENTIVE SYSTEM CONCEPTS AND IMPLEMENTATION MODELS

If our arguments about the importance of incentive systems in implementation are valid, elements of such systems should appear in leading models of implementation. Indeed, one of the earliest and most widely cited references on the importance of studying implementation devotes several pages to explicit discussion of incentives in the federal government (Hargrove, 1975). An incentive system approach like that we offer requires us to think conceptually about implementation in an explicitly organizational context. It is, at least, apparent that students of implementation have increasingly recognized the need to take organization theoretic approaches to implementation (e.g., Elmore, 1978; Montjoy and O'Toole, 1979; McLanahan, 1980; Jacobs, 1981; Scheirer, 1981). The network aspects of implementation systems have been described (e.g., Hjern and Porter, 1981; Raelin, 1980); some writers have even emphasized, explicitly or implicitly, the relational basis of implementation. Nakamura and Smallwood (1980: Ch. 7), for example, discuss the "implementation linkages" between policymakers and implementers. In the policy literature, incentives themselves are discussed frequently as policy instrumentalities, whether explicitly as components of policy designs [e.g., incentive vs. command-and-control regulation; see, e.g., Schultze (1970); Mitnick (1980a); Brigham and Brown (1980)] or implicitly as part of discussion of incentive-like mechanisms such as intergovernmental grants (e.g., Jacobs, 1981). As yet, however, incentive systems (in "implementation relations") has not been offered as a conceptual focus for a lot of what we know about implementation and a route to more systematic theory in the area.

   In Table 1 we have taken many of the elements of some leading models of implementation and arrayed them in the basic categories of the incentive relation: sender variables (e.g., goals, structure, resources), sender–receiver relation variables (e.g., incentive message and communication aspects, rewards, structure of the relation), receiver variables (e.g., perceptions of messages, goals, capabilities), organizational setting variables (e.g., resources including staff and money, structure, climate, routines), and distal environmental variables (e.g., socioeconomic variables, public opinion, demographics). We have not listed "performances" and "outcomes" categories, although some models do discuss and even typologize these (on performances, see, e.g., Berman and McLaughlin, 1974, 1976; Berman, 1980; Montjoy and O'Toole, 1979; Sorg, 1978, 1983). We do not necessarily list and sort all elements of each model, though most are included. Our decomposition and sorting may make some familiar models seem less so; nevertheless, the pieces do sort into the incentives framework. There are several leading implementation models missing from this chart; it does not seem necessary to sort them all in order to make our point. Readers should find some old friends, however.

   To demonstrate that implementation models can be analyzed for their incentive structure is not the same thing as arguing that the incentive

Table 1. Incentive System Concepts and Implementation Models

			Incentive System Concepts			
Author(s)	*Sender*	*Sender–Receiver Relation*	*Receiver*	*Organizational Setting*	*Distal Environment*
Gross *et al.* (1971) [cf. Sorg's (1978) analysis]	managerial efforts re: overcoming resistance, clarifying understanding, training, provision of materials, provision of rewards and punishments, making organization compatible with innovation	rewards and punishments	resistance to implementation clarity of understanding of innovation knowledge and skills needed for innovation willingness to expend time and effort	materials and other resources compatibility of organization with innovation prior to introduction	
Pressman and Wildavsky (1973)	multiple senders contradictory criteria preferences re leadership	incompatibility with other commitments simultaneous commitments to other projects	multiple receivers (antagonistic) attitudes toward other participants agreement vs. pref-	degree of (lack of) resources/power dependence on others who lack a sense of urgency in project	

(continued)

99

Table 1. (Continued)

Author(s)	Incentive System Concepts				
	Sender	Sender–Receiver Relation	Receiver	Organizational Setting	Distal Environment
		legal/procedural aspects complexity of joint action required	erence for other programs; time priorities in support for a given rather than other programs (differences of) opinion on leadership and propter organizational roles (differences of) opinion on legal and procedural matters intensity of preference on matter		
Berman and McLaughlin (1974, 1976) [see Sorg's (1978) analysis]	project techniques and goals: prior planning and testing specificity of goals and means complexity of	implementation strategy (staff training, frequent and regular meetings, local material development) scope of proposed	innovativeness propensity leadership styles (authoritarian, democratic, etc.) perceived educational objectives, personal conse-	organization status (wealth, budget slack, staff patterns in specialization and differentiation, etc.) locus of decision-	demographic and political conditions in community

100

project
flexibility
selection of
resources
staff develop-
ment aspects
federal and state
policy objectives
federal and state
management
strategies
opportunistic vs.
problem-solving
orientation

change:
project centrality
to educational
objectives in
district
nature and
amount of
change
required
consonance be-
tween project
goals, values,
practices and
those of
schools and
district
project complex-
ity:
structural com-
plexity re
target
aspects
narrow vs.
comprehen-
sive treat-
ment/
coverage in
project
integration re-
quired into
ongoing pro-
cedures

quences and in-
stitutional effects
personal backing of
project
motivations of ad-
ministration and
staff
staff specialization

making
research and devel-
opment capacity
organization's ca-
pacity to
innovate
resource
commitment
organization
climate
support for change-
efforts
critical mass of
project
participants
routinization of
procedures

(continued)

Table 1. (Continued)

Author(s)	Sender	Sender–Receiver Relation	Receiver	Organizational Setting	Distal Environment
		Incentive System Concepts			
Van Meter and Van Horn (1975)	degree of consensus on, clarity or ambiguity in, change required by, and measurability of policy standards and objectives policy resources (e.g., funding) specified in the program	inter-organizational communication and enforcement activities: supply of technical advice use of normative, remunerative, coercive power accuracy of communication of policy standards and objectives consistency of communication of standards and objectives by various sources procedural, planning, and personnel controls	understanding of policy direction of response toward policy intensity of response ability to carry out policy	characteristics of the implementing agencies: staff competence and size political resources vitality hierarchical control in agency openness of communication in implementing agency sufficient economic resources within organization agency's linkages with policymakers	economic, social, political conditions: sufficient economic resources within jurisdiction public opinion elite views partisan support mobilization of interest groups
Baum (1976)	clarity of decisions	accuracy of communication authority attached	favorable attitude to decisions: own interests	selective personnel process	

102

		persuasion	ences perceived authority in decision	
Rein and Rabinovitz (1977)	clarity, instrumentality, consistency, and urgency of goals competing legislative mandates specification re resources	complexity of system	perception of goals (saliency/clarity) loyalty to goals multiple receivers	resources: kind, level, and timing
Montjoy and O'Toole (1979)	specificity of mandates provision of new resources competing mandates		goals and world views held by leadership	routines resources: money, staff, time, authority
Edwards (1980)	vague laws competing, multiple goals complexity of policy making desire to avoid opposition unfamiliarity with area lack of consensus on policy	communication distortion through bureau indirect and ad hoc transmission clarity/consistency of implementation orders discretion permitted implementer poor information	(dis)agreement with policy/favorite policies nature of zone of indifference to policy selective perception unfamiliarity with/lack of understanding in area	public opposition (directed to agency) staff size physical facilities funding parochialism of agency agency rivalries appointments process

(continued)

103

Table 1. (Continued)

| | Incentive System Concepts | | | |
Author(s)	Sender	Sender–Receiver Relation	Receiver	Organizational Setting	Distal Environment
	service vs. regulatory orientation toward implementers alternative principals—e.g., peer group	feedback from low-monitoring staff, reliance on client information, constraints on information collection authority over implementers control of funds to implementers available sanctions; limits on available rewards and reward mechanisms	self-interest agency interest skills knowledge of how to implement career length in agency attitudes reflecting self-recruitment to agency goal displacement	SOPs fragmentation of policy responsibility	
Nakamura and Smallwood (1980)	vagueness of legislation	clarity of policy statements communications procedures administrative distance	norms (e.g., re "keeping the peace") intensity of preferences intermediary status	complexity resources in money, staff, power, time	

104

Mazmanian and Sabatier (1983)	clarity and consistency of objectives adequate causal theory provisions of statute with respect to: funding, hierarchical integration, decision rules of agencies, selection of implementing officials, access by outsiders new and conflicting legal mandates	hierarchical integration among implementing institutions including number of veto/clearance points and inducement/ sanction system oversight from sovereigns	(limited) sanctions of service deliverers multiple actors conducting implementation	choice of implementing official commitment to statutory objectives leadership skill	financial resources decision rules of implementing agencies are biased toward project outsiders who support program can participate tractability of problem: technical difficulties diversity of targeted behavior target group as % of population extent of behavioral change required attitudes and resources of constituency group	socioeconomic conditions and technology public support

system approach is superior to any of them. Incentive systems *is* perhaps one of the few approaches that is largely inclusive of its competitors, a virtue often noted in theory and model comparisons. It is general, systematic, and, we hope, intuitively appealing. We have not argued that the incentive system approach as we describe it subsumes *all* features of implementation; we claim merely that all adequate models must have incentives as a key component. We think Table 1 shows how the variables often offered as parts of implementation models can be consistent with that incentive system core. It remains to be seen whether an explicit incentive system model, with a *full* range of relevant variables, fares better than its implicitly incentive-based competitors in empirical tests. We provide no such tests here.

INCENTIVE SYSTEM ANALYSIS AND IMPLEMENTATION

If implementation processes and settings can be seen as complex networks of incentive relations, we need to know how to identify those relations to permit theory development as well as intervention and design in implementation. We have argued, for example, that an incentive system approach sensitizes us to both the factors that drive behavior and the levers that can potentially be used to manipulate it. In what follows we present a seven-stage model that describes the process of analyzing such incentive systems. The steps include (see Table 2): (1) Frame Selection; (2) Mapping (including relational analysis, element identification, and element sorting); (3) Dependency Analysis; (4) Contingency Analysis; (5) Intervention Strategy Selection; (6) Intervention Implementation; and (7) Intervention Assessment [for a more extended description of the model, see Mitnick and Backoff (1983)]. We shall pay most attention to steps (1)–(4); these are the steps most closely related to the incentive system model itself. Although the other steps are no less important, they bring in analytic perspectives and literatures (e.g., organization development) that could expand the scope of this paper beyond an appropriate limit. Furthermore, our discussion of each step can undoubtedly be expanded and refined; this is an overview of the procedure of analysis. We do expect that what's already here should be useful, however.

Incentive system analysis can be useful both in helping to identify key theoretical components (indeed, the analysis requires us to construct an incentive system theory for the setting in question) and in contributing to the design or planning of, corrective intervention in, or evaluation of,

Table 2.   Stages in Incentive System Analysis

1. *Frame Selection*
   Choosing levels and units of analysis
   Choosing boundaries of analysis
   Choosing constituencies
   Choosing analytic or disciplinary perspective
   Choosing other assumptions about world states and processes

2. *Mapping*
   Relational analysis
   Element identification
   Element sorting

3. *Dependency Analysis*
   Trace relations of effect, making use of groupings/hierarchies of variables
   Identify relations of dependence, including relative scale of dependency
   Map qualities of effect and dependence, including transactional
      dimensions

4. *Contingency Analysis*
   Controllability/noncontrollability analysis
   Static/sensitivity analysis
   Component problem analysis

5. *Intervention Strategy Selection*

6. *Intervention Implementation*

7. *Intervention Assessment*

the implementation situation. To illustrate the model, we shall relate the first few stages to aspects of policy implementation in federal strip mining regulation in 1979. Strip mining regulation will serve more as an example than a case; there is not space here to work out the full details of an incentive system analysis [for other applications, see Mitnick (1979, 1980); Backoff and Mitnick (1981); Backoff and Mitnick (1979)].

The logic of incentive system analysis is simple. The analyst may typically be presented with an undifferentiated group of perceived organizational phenomena. We assume, a priori, that the analyst possesses a rationale for engaging in the exercise, e.g., design of a new organizational system or improvement in organizational functioning in some regard or with respect to some goals. Galbraith (1977:252) identifies five types of potentially desired behaviors: joining and remaining, dependable role performance, effort above minimum levels, spontaneous and innovative behavior, and cooperative behavior. These behaviors may, of course, be instrumental to a variety of other goals. Although we could conceivably create a typology of analyst goals and list choice of such goals as the first stage, we prefer to leave rationale selection as an implicit function at the start of analysis.

Responding to a chosen rationale, the analyst must give meaning to the organizational phenomena, identifying them, grouping them, noting interdependencies, and so on. In this reenactment of the organization from the analyst's perspective (cf. Weick, 1969), certain features are abstracted, organized, and assigned special meanings as part of an incentive system. This suggests the first stage of incentive system analysis: *Frame Selection*. The analyst must enact the frame of analysis. This includes making choices on levels and units of analysis, boundaries of analysis, constituents of the units and their environment that constitute the field for the analysis, analytic or disciplinary perspective and level of abstraction, and a variety of assumptions about the way that the world this organization inhabits functions. Mitroff and Kilmann (see, e.g., Kilmann, 1983) refer to a related process as "assumptional analysis."

Consider implementation of the Surface Mining Control and Reclamation Act of 1977 [on the incentive system in strip mining regulation, see Mitnick (1980b, 1982b)]. The Act regulates coal strip mining through minimum federal standards implemented through a mixture of state bodies and federal inspection activities. States gain "primacy" under the Act through certification of their programs by the federal agency. The unanalyzed perceived field of phenomena in this case includes certain individual and organizational actors (e.g., state and federal inspectors and their agencies, coal companies and officials in them, environmentalist groups, other governmental actors, and so on), behaviors by and goals of those actors, perceived available rewards, and many other factors that may or may not be relevant to an incentive system. Choosing a frame means selecting, say, individual-level actors as representative of their organizations; limiting the analysis to regulators, industry people, and environmentalists in one state; deciding to focus on only certain goals or motivations and a rational choice approach to considering them; and so on. We do have choices here; we could choose the organization level, for example, or exclude certain actors.

With a frame selected, the analyst must turn to organizing the perceived elements of the setting. We have termed this process *Mapping*. It consists of three major subprocesses: relational analysis, element identification, and element sorting.

In *relational analysis* the analyst must locate incentive relations among the perceptual objects resting within the frame. In effect, this means identifying incentive senders and receivers. A kind of figure–ground judgment must be made in that it is likely that the system under study will be filled with exchanges of resources and information. The analyst must isolate relations that satisfy the defining properties given earlier (exchange, reward, contingent behavior, response, and rationality assumptions) and that are relevant to his task. Relevance is determined, of course, by the rationale for undertaking this analytic exercise. If this means failures in performance by some actor, that actor is likely to be identified as among the incentive receivers.

The incentive system can contain a complex of incentive relations, with alternative senders and receivers. Not all relations may be important to the analysis. At this point, however, the analyst may wish to limit his attention to certain relations (at any rate, particular boundaries to the analysis were chosen as part of frame selection).

Having mapped the gross pattern of incentive relations (which can be overlapping and competitive in character), the analyst must perform *element identification*. This involves identification of relevant dimensions, attributes, and other variables that characterize the now-identified incentive relations. There are, of course, potentially an infinite number of such characteristics. In essence, the analyst must perform an inventory of the organizational setting in this regard. Frame selection and relational analysis should put limits on and help suggest the loci of relevant characteristics.

Ideally, one would not want to identify variables that later prove irrelevant to the functioning of the incentive relation. At this point, however, the analyst cannot determine for certain which variables will be relevant. To take account of this and similar problems as one proceeds through an incentive system analysis, stages must be interactive. That is, elements identified early on that prove irrelevant would be dropped; elements suggested later by, for example, consideration of groupings in dependency analysis (see below) would be added.

The third mapping process is simply the *sorting* of the elements into the categories determined by our incentive system model. To the extent to which the model itself can identify elements, the sorting task is eased.

Note that the mapping process can begin anywhere in the system. For example, we can map forward from the initial sender to the ultimate receiver, from the ultimate receiver backward to the initial sender, or both "up" and "down" from some intermediate point in the incentive system [cf. Elmore (1983) on "forward" and "backward" mapping].

Of the possible relations in the strip mining setting, a few stand out. Assume that our objective is to plan (or analyze) state-level implementation of the federal statute. The traditional literature on regulation as

well as the controversy surrounding the Act suggests that we be concerned about the relation of regulators to the regulated industry: will
they somehow be "captured" or unduly influenced by the industry?
Since we are interested in the response of a state agency to federal
controls, the relation between the federal agency [U.S. Office of Surface
Mining (OSM)] and state regulators seems relevant. Of course, the ties
between the state regulators to their own agency as well as to another
possible major participant, environmental groups, seem pertinent as
well.

Elements identified include the historical pattern of relations between
the industry and the state authority (friendly, with minimally restrictive
and often unenforced state controls until a recent state statute); profit
goals in coal companies (which, by the way, may differ in their attitude
toward the regulators depending on such factors as size); career goals of
the state regulators; rewards available to the state regulators in their
present positions and in alternative positions (e.g., in industry, the OSM
or environmental groups); backgrounds and professional development
of the state regulators; aspects of the technology of regulating strip
mining, including sources of information that regulators depend on;
and so on. We sort these factors into the model categories (indeed, the
model categories have suggested what kinds of elements to select).

The third stage in the incentive system analysis is *Dependency Analysis.*
This involves establishing relations of effect, and of dependence, among
the elements. In essence, this means positing a set of propositional relationships among the variables, i.e., an incentive system theory of this
organizational setting. Of course, those propositions can vary in complexity; not all relationships will be simple linear ones of covariance. We
propose, however, to begin the dependency analysis with precisely this
assumption unless we have reason to believe differently. Later analysis
of the system can suggest more complex forms of dependency. The
particular variable relation under consideration can be investigated, if
necessary, through ordinary means (interviews, questionnaries, "expert"
consultation, secondary descriptions, and so on); an instrument like that
of Kerr (n.d.) may be useful here.

The analysis is likely to be informed by the underlying dynamics of the
incentive relation(s). We already know from the element sorting what
the sender's goals, incentive message characteristics, available rewards
and receiver's goals are, for example. It is not "throwing dice" to then
posit certain relationships among these variables. Furthermore, the incentive system model groups certain variables together (e.g., rewards
incentive message characteristics). These are likely to vary in similar or
logically contrasting ways with other system variables.

A key problem will be determining the degree of dependence in any relation. Dependence itself requires several conditions (cf. Emerson, 1962; Pfeffer and Salancik, 1978). We have suggested that relationships of effect be traced through the elements of the system. Of particular importance to design and control, however, are those relationships of effect in which there is significant dependence. These are likely to be the "handles" through which change in the system can be promoted.

A relation of dependence requires more than the existence of some effect. Dependence is a function of the degree of discretion over the process or transaction leading to the effect (e.g., supply of some valued resource) on B possessed by A, the importance of or magnitude of the process or transaction to B, and the status of alternative suppliers or participants in the process or transaction in question. This is most easily understood in the context of resource dependence (e.g., Pfeffer and Salancik, 1978). In other situations, for example, we are in essence dealing with control of variation to produce a given effect, the extent of impact on the dependent entity due to the relation, and the possibility that that impact will be produced by alternative sources.

Thus, after tracing effects, the analyst should chart dependencies. His ability to do this will of course be limited by his knowledge of the system; this, again, is where an instrument like that developed by Kerr (n.d.) can be applied. Ideally, the analyst should seek to identify the relative scale of the dependencies observed.

Besides the existence of effects and dependencies, the analyst may find it useful to map certain *qualities* of the effects/dependencies. For example, one can distinguish the direction of effect or dependence, whether the effect is constraining or facilitative, and whether the effect is neutral or not in creating normative obligation. Related to this are concerns about the nature of any transaction that may occur to produce the effect or dependence. A variety of dimensions of incentives and of incentive offering (Mitnick, 1974, 1975a; cf. Zald and Jacobs, 1978) can be specified. Although these dimensions are features of the sender–receiver relation, some are generalizable to many kinds of transactional relations of effect or dependence (e.g., substitutability, collective good character, target aspects, effect or dependence scheduling, and so on).

Once effects and dependencies in the system are mapped, the analyst can turn to *Contingency Analysis*. This is concerned with assessing the sensitivity of properties of the system or of key components to changes in other parts of the system. The level is shifted from individual relations to system performance. It is at this stage that the bridge is made from incentive system theory to incentive system design and intervention in the implementation setting.

Of particular concern for investigation is the controllability or uncontrollability of certain effects through manipulation of system components as well as the sensitivity of response of key variables to changes in other variables. Relations of high dependence will likely be appropriate foci for the analysis. The analyst must perform a kind of contingent, static analysis in determining the responsiveness of the system to interventions.

The analyst may wish to take a "problem" focus, identifying problems in a tour of each major category or subcategory of the incentive system model (e.g., sender "problems," incentive message "problems," and so on). These "problems" deal with aspects of controllability and sensitivity/responsiveness. In this way, the analyst may isolate regions or components of the incentive system in which intervention efforts should be focused.

In the state strip mining example, we find that the inspector salaries in the state in 1979 are much lower than salaries that could be earned in the coal companies or in the U.S. Office of Surface Mining (OSM). There is little chance for promotion in the state body. The OSM staff has been growing rapidly: 40% of recent departures from the state body have been to coal companies, and 40% have gone to the OSM. State inspectors are heavily dependent on information supplied by coal companies in making decisions on issuing permits. Environmental groups are small, ineffective at the state level, and have few or no full-time members. They cannot and do not offer jobs to inspectors who have state employment.

Dependency analysis thus reveals the existence of an incentive competition between coal companies and the OSM in 1979; contingency analysis reveals the sensitivity of the system to changes. The relation with environmental groups drops out of the analysis. We do not know whether the implicit offer of future jobs in coal companies could have colored the decision making of state regulators in the pre-OSM days; at any rate, the coal companies may be more interested in hiring competent rather than biased employees. The new "promotion" route to the OSM could have both siphoned competent state inspectors from coal company work and reduced the possibility of proindustry bias (indeed, it could have promoted pro-OSM bias).

As a footnote, we observe that severe OSM cuts in the Reagan Administration effectively removed the OSM promotion route, raising the specter again of industry focus. But the state agency, in implementing the federal regulations, doubled in size and extracted salary increases from the legislature. Consequently, the degree of possible dependency on the industry lessened. One method for guarding against any possible excessive sensitivity to the industry would therefore be to boost the regulators' rewards in other incentive relations. The OSM relation represented future rewards (as did the industry); the state agency situation represented, of course, current rewards. If current resources are tight (as was the case in 1979), attention to future-oriented "incentive safety valves" would be especially relevant. We shall end our strip mining regulation example at this point; there are, of course, several more stages in the full model of incentive system analysis.

Once key contingencies are identified, the analyst can move to *Intervention Strategy Selection*. As indicated earlier, this takes us out of the realm of direct incentive system considerations. Analysts must choose strategies to effect change [there is a huge literature on this; see, e.g., Zaltman and Duncan (1977)] that are appropriate, given the controllable, sensitive contingencies, and the resources available to, and constraints on, the analyst and the intervention conductor. Ideally, one has to match a well-defined portfolio of strategies with situational requirements.

Intervention Implementation is concerned with the conduct and management of the actual change or design implementation process. Again there is a huge literature both on management implementation (e.g., Schultz and Slevin, 1975; Doktor, Schultz, and Slevin, 1979) and, of course, on public policy or program implementation; we shall not review the relevant materials here. The contingency analysis should have provided knowledge of some problems to be encountered that deal with the system itself; others stem from the conduct of those who seek the change or new design, including the system of implementation action and structure established to achieve intervention objectives.

The logical last stage in incentive system analysis is *Intervention Assessment*, in which the objectives of intervention or design are used to evaluate the actual achievement. Again, there is a vast literature on evaluation techniques that will not be reviewed in the context of incentive system intervention assessment. The results of the stage may, however, suggest a recycling of this process: reorientation of the frame and alterations in mapping, dependency analysis, contingency analysis, strategy selection, or intervention implementation.

Incentive system analysis could be a valuable tool in implementation studies. Although much more can be done to develop its methodology (see Mitnick and Backoff, 1983), we hope that even at this stage its utility should be apparent. If incentives are at the core of every implementation model, we must learn how to analyze their patterns.

CONCLUSION

We have argued that public policy implementation can be understood as a time-varying system of *implementation relations* between potential principals and implementing agents. Those relations are driven by the *incentive relations* at their cores; the problems observed in implementation can therefore often be analyzed in terms of *incentive failures*. We reviewed some of the incentives-related literature in order to derive some requisites for an adequate conceptualization of the "incentive relation" and of incentive systems. We then produced such a conceptualization, we believe. To show how potentially relevant this was to implementaion, we sorted the variables from some of the leading models of implementation into the basic categories of the incentive system framework. We claim that, implicitly or explicitly, incentive systems are a key component of any adequate model of implementation. Incentive system analysis can therefore be a valuable tool in theory-building as well as intervention and design in implementation. We presented an overview of a model to perform such analysis.

The advantages of taking an incentive system approach are numerous. While it can hardly be offered as a panacea, it grows out of a long and, we feel, insufficiently developed tradition in organization and administrative theory. Ultimately, we must deal with the human element in organizations; it is hard to avoid individuals altogether, though even our incentives model can be used at higher levels of analysis (the definition does not require that the actors be individuals). The approach is consistent with rational choice modeling and enjoys the explanatory and predictive benefits (and, presumably, any debits) often claimed for that perspective. It is sensitive to variations in professional and bureaucratic rewards and motivations; it does not rely on a single substantive factor focus such as bureau structure.

The approach recognizes the key role played by goals in organizational settings. Although a generation of organization theorists made it fashionable to downplay the significance of such goals, the fact is that, as we and a few others are beginning to argue, goals simply will not go away. Even given the change in, ambiguity in, ignorance of, multiplicity of, and overtness/covertness of, goals (as well as many other dimensions), they remain essential analytic (and practical) components of organization systems. They locate baselines, create frames for analysis, and help explain choices of action. They are implicit when reward systems are discussed.

An incentive system approach is transactional in character; it may be valuable, at least as a building block, simply because it focuses on that which actually reaches or affects the actors. In the conceptualization we present, incentives are essentially *relational;* they relate to the linkages and glue in complex systems of acting. It is an approach particularly well-suited for analyzing networks; it brings in structural features (e.g., in sender–receiver relations) automatically. Incentive systems can incorporate the complexity that occurs in real-world organizations and organization-sets. Observation of the "complexity of joint action" (Pressman and Wildavsky, 1973) is a natural derivation in a model based on a network of incentive relations.

The incentive system approach reflects the complexity of the real world in the approach's own complexity. Although certainly a drawback for human modelers, this feature is not necessarily crippling for theoretical and prescriptive/design purposes. As Bunge (1961) makes clear, parsimony should *not* be a primary criterion in the evaluation of scientific theories and models; a theory is not better on basic grounds because it is simpler. Parsimony provides convenience and little else. Furthermore, the literature on human information processing makes clear that methods for handling complexity are routinely employed.

Incentive systems are particularly meaningful in understanding the possibility of, and isolating the levers of, change in organizational systems (cf. Jacobs, 1981). The approach has a natural affinity for considerations of manipulability; it is related to control system approaches in implementation and elsewhere, but does not necessarily suffer from the rigidity of some of such approaches (cf. Bardach, 1977; Mazmanian and Sabatier, 1983). It does not require centralized control and does not presume system-level intentionality. It can be a tool in explaining the structure of systems that produce emergent behavior. In the sense that it frequently concerns contests over control of resources, it is an approach that should be useful in depicting politics. It may, furthermore, be useful in providing the prescriptive designs that may be needed to ensure public responsiveness to democratic controls (see Kaufman, 1973; Rein and Rabinovitz, 1977).

The incentive system approach is not tied to particular institutions or, again, to certain levels of analysis (cf. Hargrove, 1975). It is not a theory of the American federal government or system or of the implementation of a particular program. It is an approach that can produce such special-purpose theories, and, conceivably, could itself be developed into a general theory of behavior in and among organizations. It has a dynamic element—it can tell us why certain relationships and behaviors, and not others, develop. It takes account of real, not merely formal, systems, even if those real systems must be analytically identified (see Kerr, 1975, n.d.).

Finally, the incentive system approach is explicitly, and intentionally, systematic in at least two senses. The model permits systematic analysis of incentive phenomena; we can sort the variables into a meaningful, inclusive framework and construct incentive system theories of the observed behavior. And the model deals with systems, not disjoint "games" or atomistically listed inventories of factors. It is peculiarly suited to provide understanding of complex systems of relationships by permitting us to map those relationships.

In the end, we cannot say, following Edmund Spenser in *The Faerie Queen,* that our analytic world of incentive relations performs "all for love, and nothing for reward." Indeed, both love and material rewards are among the infinite array of benefits that incentive messages can promise.

ACKNOWLEDGMENT

The authors wish to acknowledge the contribution of Hal G. Rainey, now of Florida State University; some of his work on models in the incentives literature from Mitnick, Backoff, and Rainey (1977) appears in the relevant section in this paper. Our 1977 paper was the initial exposition in detail of the incentive relation and system model featured in this paper. George Edwards and James D. Sorg provided a number of suggestions for improving the presentation of our arguments. Mitnick also wishes to thank the Business, Government, and Society Research Institute in the Graduate School of Business, University of Pittsburgh, for its partial support of work on incentives under a grant from the General Electric Foundation. The authors are grateful for the assistance of a number of research assistants over the years of the Incentive Systems Project.

REFERENCES

Adams, J. S. (1965) "Injustice in social exchange." In L. Berkowitz (ed.), Advances in Experimental Social Psychology, Vol. 2. New York: Academic Press.
——— (1976) "The structure and dynamics of behavior in organizational boundary roles." In Marvin D. Dunnette (ed.), Handbook of Industrial and Organizational Psychology. Chicago: Rand McNally.
Alderfer, C. P. (1969) "An empirical test of a new theory of human needs." Organizational Behavior and Human Performance 4:142–175.
Aldrich, H. E. (1979) Organizations and Environments. Englewood Cliffs, N.J.: Prentice-Hall.
——— and D. Herker (1977) "Boundary spanning roles and organization structure." Academy of Management Review 2(2):217–30.
Anderson, J. E. (1979) Public Policy-making, 2nd ed. New York: Holt, Rinehart and Winston.
Backoff, R. W. and B. M. Mitnick (1979) "Overcoming barriers to efficient implementation of innovation in provision of urban fire services." Graduate School of Business Working Paper Series, WP-331, University of Pittsburgh, January 1979. Paper presented at the 1982 Annual Meeting of the Midwest Political Science Association, Milwaukee.
——— (1981) "The systems approach, incentives, and university management." New Directions for Higher Education (symposium edited by James A. Wilson), No. 35. San Francisco: Jossey-Bass (September).

Baiman, S. (1982) "Agency research in managerial accounting: a survey." Journal of Accounting Literature 1:154–213.

Bardach, E. (1977) The Implementation Game: What Happens After a Bill Becomes a Law. Cambridge, Mass.: MIT Press.

Barnard, C. I. (1938) The Functions of the Executive. Cambridge, Mass.: Harvard University Press.

Baum, L. (1976) "Implementation of judicial decisions: an organizational analysis." American Politics Quarterly 4(1):86–114.

Behling, O., C. Schriesheim, and J. Tolliver (1973) "Present trends and new directions in theories of work effort." Journal Supplement Abstract Service of the American Psychological Association.

Berman, P. (1978) "The study of macro and micro-implementation." Public Policy 26(2):157–84.

—— (1980) "Thinking about programmed and adaptive implementation: matching strategies to situations." Pp. 205–27 in H. M. Ingram and D. E. Mann (eds.), Why Policies Succeed or Fail. Beverly Hills, Cal.: Sage Publications.

—— and M. W. McLaughlin (1974) Federal Programs Supporting Educational Change, Vol. 1: A Model of Educational Change. R-1589/1-HEW (September).

—— and —— (1976) "Implementation of educational innovation." The Educational Forum 40 (March):345–70.

Blau, P. M. (1964) Exchange and Power in Social Life. New York: Wiley.

Brigham, J. and D. W. Brown (eds.) (1980) Policy Implementation: Penalties or Incentives? Beverly Hills, Cal.: Sage Publications.

Bunge, M. (1961) "The weight of simplicity in the construction and assaying of scientific theories." Philosophy of Science 28(April):120–49.

Campbell, J. P. and J. D. Pritchard (1976) "Motivation theory in industrial and organizational psychology." Pp. 63–130 in M. D. Dunnette (ed.), Handbook of Industrial and Organizational Psychology. Chicago: Rand McNally.

Clark, P. B. and J. O. Wilson (1961) "Incentive systems: a theory of organizations." Administrative Science Quarterly 6:129–66.

Cohen, M. D., J. G. March, and J. P. Olsen (1972) "A garbage can model of organizational choice." Administrative Science Quarterly 17(1):1–25.

Conway, M. M. and F. B. Feigart (1968) "Motivation, incentive systems, and the political party organization." American Political Science Review 62:1159–73.

Cook, K. S. (1977) "Exchange and power in networks of interorganizational relations." Sociological Quarterly 18(Winter):62–82.

Coombs, F. S. (1980) "The bases of noncompliance with a policy." Policy Studies Journal 8(6):885–92.

Diver, C. S. (1980) "A theory of regulatory enforcement." Public Policy 28(3):257–99.

Doktor, R., R. L. Schultz, and D. P. Slevin (eds.) (1979) The Implementation of Management Science. TIMS Studies in the Management Sciences, Vol. 13. Amsterdam: North-Holland Publs.

Downs, A. (1967) Inside Bureaucracy. Boston: Little, Brown.

Edwards, III, G. C. (1980) Implementing Public Policy. Washington, D.C.: Congressional Quarterly Press.

Elmore, R. F. (1978) "Organizational models of social program implementation." Public Policy 26(2):185–228.

—— (1983) "Forward and backward mapping: reversible logic in the analysis of public policy." Paper presented to the International Workshop on Interorganizational Implementation Systems, Erasmus University, Rotterdam, The Netherlands, June 27–30, 1983.

Emerson, R. M. (1962) "Power–dependence relations." American Sociological Review 27:31–40.

—— (1972) "Exchange theory (parts I & II)." Pp. 38–87 in J. Berger, M. Zelditch, Jr., and B. Anderson (eds.), Sociological Theories in Progress, Vol. 2. Boston: Houghton Mifflin.

—— (1976) "Social exchange theory." Pp. 335–62 in A. Inkeles (ed.), Annual Review of Sociology, Vol. 2. Palo Alto, Cal.: Annual Reviews, Inc.

Etzioni, A. (1961) A Comparative Analysis of Complex Organization: On Power, Involvement, and Their Correlates. New York: Free Press.

Evan, W. M. (1976) Organization Theory: Structures, Systems, and Environments. New York: Wiley (Interscience).

Fishbein, M., and I. Ajzen (1975) Belief, Attitude, Intention, and Behavior: An Introduction to Theory and Research. Reading, Mass.: Addison-Wesley.

Galbraith, J. (1977) Organization Design. Reading, Mass.: Addison-Wesley.

Georgiou, P. (1973) "The goal paradigm and notes towards a counter paradigm." Administrative Science Quarterly 18(September):291–310.

Gross, N., J. B. Giacquinta, and M. Bernstein (1971) Implementing Organizational Innovations: A Sociological Analysis of Planned Educational Change. New York: Basic Books.

Guetzkow, H. (1966) "Relations among organizations." In R. V. Bowers (ed.), Studies On Behavior in Organizations. Athens: University of Georgia Press.

Halperin, M., with P. Clapp and A. Kanter (1974) Bureaucratic Politics and Foreign Policy. Washington, D.C.: Brookings Institution.

Hardin, R. (1976) "Hollow victory: the minimum winning coalition." American Political Science Review 70(December):1202–14.

Hargrove, E. C. (1975) The Missing Link: The Study of Implementation of Social Policy. Washington, D.C.: Urban Institute (July).

Herzberg, F., B. Mausner, and B. Snyderman (1959) The Motivation to Work, 2nd ed. New York: Wiley.

Hjern, B. and D. Porter (1981) "Implementation structures: a new unit of administrative analysis." Paper presented at the International Conference on the Analysis of Intergovernmental and Interorganizational Arrangements in Public Administration, Indiana University, Bloomington, May 11–14. (Forthcoming in Organization Studies.)

Hofstetter, C. R. (1971) "The amateur politician: a problem in construct validation." Midwest Journal of Political Science 15:31–56.

—— (1973) "Organizational activists: the bases of participation in amateur and professional groups." American Politics Quarterly 1:244–76.

Homans, G. C. (1961) Social Behavior: Its Elementary Forms. New York: Harcourt, Brace Jovanovich.

Jacobs, B. (1981) The Political Economy of Organizational Change: Urban Institutional Response to the War on Poverty. New York: Academic Press.

Jensen, M. C. and W. H. Meckling (1976) "Theory of the firm: managerial behavior, agency costs and ownership." Journal of Financial Economics 3:305–60.

Johnson, R. W. and R. E. O'Connor (1979) "Intraagency limitations on policy implementation: you can't always get what you want, but sometimes you get what you need." Administration and Society 11(2):193–215.

Kaufman, H., with M. Couzens (1973) Administrative Feedback: Monitoring Subordinates' Behavior. Washington, D.C.: Brookings Institution.

Kerr, D. (1976) "The logic of 'policy' and successful policies." Policy Sciences 7 (September):351–63.

Kerr, S. (1975) "On the folly of rewarding A, while hoping for B." Academy of Management Journal 18:769–83.

Kilmann, R. H. (1983) "A dialectical approach to formulating and testing social science theories: assumptional analysis." Human Relations 36:1–22.

Knoke, D. and C. Wright-Isak (1982) "Individual motives and organizational incentive systems." Research in the Sociology of Organizations, Vol. 1. Greenwich, Conn.: JAI Press, 209–254.

Korman, A. K. (1966) "Self-esteem variable in vocational choice." Journal of Applied Psychology 50:479–86.

Kuhn, A. (1974) Logic of Social Systems. San Francisco: Jossey-Bass.

Laumann, E. O. and F. U. Pappi (1976) Networks of Collective Action: A Perspective on Community Influence Systems. New York: Academic Press.

Lawler, E. E. (1971) Pay and Organizational Effectiveness. New York: McGraw-Hill.

——— (1973) Motivation in Work Organizations. Belmont, Cal.: Brooks/Cole.

Leifer, R. and A. Delbecq (1978) "Organization/environmental interchange: a model of boundary spanning activity." Academy of Management Review 3(1):40–50.

Levine, C. H., R. W. Backoff, A. R. Cahoon, and W. J. Siffin (1975) "Organizational design: a post-Minnowbrook perspective for the 'new' public administration." Public Administration Review 35(July/August):425–35.

Levine, S. and P. E. White (1961) "Exchange as a conceptual framework for the study of interorganizational relationships." Administrative Science Quarterly 5:583–601.

Litwak, E., with J. Rothman (1970) "Towards the theory and practice of coordination between formal organizations." Pp. 137–86 in W. R. Rosengren and M. Lefton (eds.), Organizations and Clients: Essays in the Sociology of Service. Columbus, Ohio: Merrill.

Locke, E. A. (1968) "Toward a theory of task motivation and incentives." Organizational Behavior and Human Performance 3:157–89.

McClelland, D. C. (1961) The Achieving Society. Princeton: Van Nostrand Reinhold.

McKean, R. N. (1980) "Enforcement costs in environmental and safety regulation." Policy Analysis 6(3):269–89.

McLanahan, S. S. (1980) "Organizational issues in U.S. health policy implementation: participation, discretion, and accountability." Journal of Applied Behavioral Science 16(3):354–69.

Majone, G. and A. Wildavsky (1978) "Implementation as evolution." Pp. 103–17 in Policy Studies Review Annual, Vol. 2. Beverly Hills, Cal.: Sage Publications.

March, J. G. and H. A. Simon. (1958) Organizations. New York: Wiley.

Marsden, P. V. and N. Lin, eds. (1982) Social Structure and Network Analysis. Beverly Hills, Cal.: Sage Publications.

Maslow, A. H. (1954) Motivation and Personality. New York: Harper & Row.

Mazmanian, D. A. and P. A. Sabatier (1983) Implementation and Public Policy. Glenview, Ill.: Scott, Foresman.

Migue, J. -L. and G. Belanger (1974) "Toward a general theory of managerial discretion." Public Choice 17(Spring):27–47.

Miles, R. (1980) Macro Organizational Behavior. Glenview, Ill.: Scott, Foresman.

Mitchell, T. R. and D. M. Nebeker (1973) "Expectancy theory predictions of academic effort and performance." Journal of Applied Psychology 57:61–7.

Mitnick, B. M. (1973) "Fiduciary rationality and public policy: the theory of agency and some consequences." Paper presented at the 1973 Annual Meeting of the American Political Science Association, September 4–8, New Orleans.

——— (1974) "The theory of agency: the concept of fiduciary rationality and some consequences." Ph.D dissertation, Department of Political Science, University of Pennsylvania.

—— (1975a) "A typology of goals for positive theories: the theory of agency and the incentive systems approach to organizations." Paper presented at the Organizations Workshop, Fels Center of Government, University of Pennsylvania, October 24, 1974. College of Administrative Science Working Paper Series No. 75–45, Ohio State University, October.

—— (1975b) "The theory of agency: the policing 'paradox' and regulatory behavior." Public Choice 24(Winter):27–42.

—— (1979) "An incentive systems model of organizations and the regulatory environment." Paper presented at the Symposium on Regulatory Policy: The Analysis of Regulatory Policy, University of Houston, November 19–20. Graduate School of Business Working Paper Series, WP-368, University of Pittsburgh, November.

—— (1980a) The Political Economy of Regulation: Creating, Designing, and Removing Regulatory Forms. New York: Columbia University Press.

—— (1980b) "Incentive systems in environmental regulation." Policy Studies Journal 9(Winter):379–94.

—— (1982a) "Agents in the environment: managing in boundary spanning roles." Paper presented at the 42nd Annual Meeting of the Academy of Management, New York.

—— (1982b) "The two-part problem of regulatory compliance: compliance reform and strip mining." Pp. 215–42 in L. E. Preston (ed.), Research in Corporate Social Performance and Policy, Vol. 4. Greenwich, Conn.: JAI Press.

—— and R. W. Backoff (1983) "Incentive system analysis and organization design." Paper presented in the Second Annual International Prize Competition for the Most Original New Contribution to the Field of Organizational Analysis and Design, TIMS College on Organization, TIMS/ORSA Joint National Meeting, The Palmer House, Chicago, April 24–27.

——, ——, and H. G. Rainey (1977) "The incentive systems approach to the study of public organizations." Paper presented at the 1977 Annual Meeting of the American Political Science Association, Washington, D.C.

Moe, T. M. (1980) The Organization of Interests: Incentives and the Internal Dynamics of Political Interest Groups. Chicago: University of Chicago Press.

Montjoy, R. S. and L. J. O'Toole, Jr. (1979) "Toward a theory of policy implementation: an organizational perspective." Public Administration Review, 39(5):465–76.

Nakamura, R. T. and F. Smallwood (1980) The Politics of Policy Implementation. New York: St. Martin's Press.

Niskanen, W. A. (1971) Bureaucracy and Representative Government. Chicago: Aldine.

Pfeffer, J. and G. R. Salancik (1978) The External Control of Organizations: A Resource Dependence Perspective. New York: Harper & Row.

Pressman, J. L. and A. B. Wildavsky (1973) Implementation. Berkeley: University of California Press.

Raelin, J. A. (1980) "A mandated basis of interorganizational relations: the legal-political network." Human Relations 33(1):57–68.

Rainey, H. G. (1977) "Comparing public and private: conceptual and empirical analysis of incentives and motivation among government and business managers." Ph.D. dissertation, School of Public Administration, Ohio State University.

Rainey, H. G., R. W. Backoff, and C. H. Levine (1976) "Comparing public and private organizations." Public Administration Review 36(March/April):233–44.

Rein, M. and F. F. Rabinovitz (1977) "Implementation: a theoretical perspective." Working Paper No. 43, Joint Center for Urban Studies of MIT and Harvard University, March.

Riker, W. H. and P. C. Ordeshook (1973) An Introduction to Positive Political Theory. Englewood Cliffs, N.J.: Prentice-Hall.

Rosenbaum, N. (1980) "Statutory structure and policy implementation: the case of wetlands regulation." Policy Studies Journal 8(4), Special issue No.2:575–96.

Ross, S. A. (1973) "The economic theory of agency: the principal's problem." American Economic Review 63:134–39.

Salisbury, R. H. (1969) "An exchange theory of interest groups." Midwest Journal of Political Science 13(February):1–32.

Scheirer, M. A. (1981) Program Implementation: The Organizational Context. Beverly Hills, Cal.: Sage Publications.

Schultz, R. L. and D. P. Slevin (eds.) (1975) Implementing Operations Research/Management Science. New York: American Elsevier.

Schultze, C. L. (1970) "The role of incentives, penalties, and rewards in attaining effective policy." Pp. 145–72 in R. Haveman and J. Margolis (eds.), Public Expenditures and Policy Analysis. Chicago: Markham.

Schwab, D. P. and L. L. Cummings (1970) "Theories of performance and satisfaction: a review." Industrial Relations 9:408–30.

Simon, H. A. (1945, 1947) Administrative Behavior. New York: The Free Press.

Simon, H. A., D. W. Smithburg, and V. A. Thompson (1950) Public Administration. New York: Knopf.

Sorg, J. D. (1978) "A theory of individual behavior in the implementation of policy innovations." Ph.D dissertation, School of Public Administration, Ohio State University.

——— (1983) "A typology of implementation behaviors of street-level bureaucrats." Policy Studies Review 2(3):391–406.

Thibaut, J. W. and H. H. Kelley (1959) The Social Psychology of Groups. New York: Wiley.

Thompson, F. J. (1981) Health Policy and the Bureaucracy. Cambridge, Mass.: MIT Press.

Triandis, H. C. (1972) The Analysis of Subjective Culture. New York: Wiley.

Tullock, G. (1965) The Politics of Bureaucracy. Washington, D.C.: Public Affairs Press.

Van de Ven, A. H. (1976) "On the nature, formation, and maintenance of relations among organizations." Academy of Management Review 1(4):24–36.

Van Meter, D. S. and C. E. Van Horn (1975) "The policy implementation process: a conceptual framework." Administration and Society 6(4):445–88.

Vroom, V. H. (1964) Work and Motivation. New York: Wiley.

Walster, E., E. Berscheid, and G. W. Walster (1978) Equity: Theory and Research. Boston: Allyn & Bacon.

Wamsley, G. L. and M. N. Zald (1973) The Political Economy of Organizations. Bloomington, Ind.: Indiana University Press.

Weick, K. E. (1969, 1979) The Social Psychology of Organizing, 2nd ed. Reading, Mass.: Addison-Wesley.

White, H. C., S. A. Boorman, and R. L. Breiger (1976) "Social structure from multiple networks. I. Blockmodels of roles and positions." American Journal of Sociology 81(4):730–80.

Williamson, O. E. (1964) The Economics of Discretionary Behavior: Managerial Objectives in a Theory of the Firm. Englewood Cliffs, N.J.: Prentice-Hall.

——— (1975) Markets and Hierarchies: An Analysis and Antitrust Implications. New York: Free Press.

——— (1979) "Transaction-Cost Economics: The Governance of Contractual Relations." Journal of Law and Economics 22(October):233–61.

——— (1981) "The economics of organization: the transaction cost approach." American Journal of Sociology 87:548–77.

Wilson, J. Q. (1966) "Innovation in organization: notes toward a theory." Pp. 195–218 in J. D. Thompson (ed.), Approaches to Organizational Design. Pittsburgh: University of Pittsburgh Press.

—— (1973) Political Organizations. New York: Basic Books.

Wolf, C., Jr. (1979) "A theory of nonmarket failure: framework for implementation analysis." Journal of Law and Economics 22 (April):107–39.

Zald, M. N. (1970) "Political economy: a framework for comparative analysis." Pp. 221–269 in M. N. Zald, ed. Power in Organizations. Nashville, TN: Vanderbilt University Press.

Zald, M. N. and D. Jacobs (1978) "Compliance/incentive classifications of organizations: underlying dimensions." Administration and Society 9(February):403–24.

Zaltman, G. and R. Duncan (1977) Strategies for Planned Change. New York: Wiley (Interscience).

PART III

GOVERNMENT STRUCTURE AND COMPLIANCE

POLICY IMPLEMENTATION IN THE FEDERAL AID SYSTEM:
THE CASE OF GRANT POLICY

Robert M. Stein

INTRODUCTION

Research on domestic policy implementation is strongly tied to the federal character of American public policy. Pressman and Wildavsky's (1973) seminal study of the federal government's Economic Development Administration may have told us more about the status of American federalism (ca. 1974) than the process of policy implementation in Oakland, California. An examination of any bibliography on implementation (Edwards, 1980; Nakamura and Smallwood, 1980; Ripley and Franklin, 1980; and Mazmanian and Sabatier, 1983) shows that an overwhelming number of entries address the implementation of intergovernmental policies (i.e., policies enacted, administered, or financed by two or more levels of government) rather than intragovernmental policy. This condition is not altogether surprising. Since the 1930s American public policy has moved steadily toward a system characterized by extreme dependencies among levels of government. No public good or service is solely produced and implemented by one level of government. Moreover, this condition is not limited to the United States and has grown with similar speed in a number of European federal systems (ACIR, 1981).

Given the intergovernmental character of American public policy, surprisingly only a handful of studies on implementation have specifically addressed federalism as a force shaping the nature of policy implementation [the exceptions to this are Ripley and Franklin (1980) and Ingram (1977)]. Although many researchers have studied the implementation of federal policies, they have overlooked the importance of a federal setting to the explanation of policy implementation.

This chapter will review and expand upon the literature on intergovernmental policy implementation. We proceed first with a generic definition of implementation, distinguishing it from other stages in the policy/making process (i.e., impact, evaluation, and compliance). Next, we define the specific content and scope of intergovernmental policy implementation and review its empirical literature. This review identifies a number of ambiguities in the literature that require our attention.

A bargaining model of implementation resolves a number of the ambiguities and limitations of previous models of implementation. In this model negotiations between relevant actors are the object of implementation and the outcome of these negotiations defines the content of the policy activity. Over time, policies go through various stages/types of negotiations that define and redefine the program's content. The bargaining model focuses attention on the role of subnational actors in the implementation process.

A GENERIC DEFINITION OF IMPLEMENTATION

Policy implementation is comprised of two elements: compliance and impact. The former addresses the actions of individuals directed at the achievement of specific policy objectives. Impact concerns the long-run effects of enacted policies, focusing on nonstatutory variables. Mazmanian and Sabatier (1983) combine both elements of implementation, impact and congruence, in a sequential definition of implementation. The authors suggest that implementation develops through a number of stages, beginning with:

> the passage of the basic statute, followed by the policy outputs (decisions) of the implementing agencies, the compliance of the targeted groups with those decisions, the actual impacts—both intended and unintended of those outputs, and the perceived impacts of agency decisions and finally, important revisions or (attempted revisions) in the basic statute (Sabatier and Mazmanian, 1982:6).

Mazmanian and Sabatier do not suggest that either question (compliance vs. impact) subsumes the other. Rather, their sequential definition of implementation places compliance logically prior to the issue of impact.

Administrative action to fulfill the goals and objectives of a public law must occur before the legislative enactment can have any impact, either intended or unintended. These actions may still lead to policy failure, either because of poor implementation or an ill-conceived policy. Not until the implementation process is set in place, however, can one determine the success or failure of the policy, and if the latter, its causes. Our analysis of implementation will examine the issue of congruence between legislative intent and the administrative actions taken to fulfill the intent of the law.

IMPLEMENTATION AS AN INTERGOVERNMENTAL ACTIVITY

Intergovernmental relations encompass interactions between federal, state, and local governments (Wright, 1982). These relationships are directed at a variety of policy activities, often centering either on defining, financing, or administering various public policies. As we noted earlier, there are few if any public policies that are not in some way affected by the actions of two or more levels of government. The dominant mechanism for promoting intergovernmental relations is the grant-in-aid. The federal government, and to a lesser extent state governments, has used the transfer of aid monies from one level of government to another as a means of promoting a wide range of public policies through the cooperation of lower-level governments.

The fiscal size of federal aid transfers has grown dramatically over the last 50 years, increasing an average of 5% each year between 1929 and 1978 (ACIR, 1978). More importantly, the scope of federal aid has broadened to include virtually every aspect of lower-level public policy. Not surprisingly, the degree of municipal and state participation in the federal aid system has grown over the last four decades, with every state extensively involved in a wide range of federal grant programs. Participation in the federal aid system among general purpose governments over 25,000 in size has grown from 50% participation in 1967 to 100% in 1977 (Stein, 1981).

The use of the grant mechanism is historically associated with a wide range of policy objectives. Generally, however, federal aid represents a means of promoting national public policies through the cooperative actions of aid recipients. Thus, the successful implementation of grant policies is dependent upon the cooperation of aid recipients in implementing the goals and purposes of grant legislation. This task is made significantly more complicated by the fact that implementation of intergovernmental policies involves not only two or more levels of government, but also hundreds of potential recipients whose behavior must be coordinated in order to achieve the desired policy effect.

Though it would be naive to consider the purposes of any grant program as unambiguous, there is a consensus on the universe of goals applicable to most federal aid programs (Mushkin and Cotton, 1969; Wagner, 1976; Break, 1967). We can identify at least three broad goals associated with federal aid transfers:

1. *Fiscal support*—to relieve fiscal strain on state or local governments caused by unequal revenue capacity
2. *Fiscal stimulation and innovation*—to help states and local governments accomplish policy goals/activities that they are unable or unwilling for political or institutional reasons to do for themselves
3. *Redress inequality*—to compensate with respect to the nation as a whole for the fact that some of the benefits produced by a program conducted in one subnational government inevitably "spill over" to other jurisdictions, providing a windfall to the latter and inequitable strain on the former.

The Grant Delivery Mechanism

Associated with federal aid programs are different methods for delivering and administering the federal largess. In his review of the grant impact literature Gramlich (1977) identifies three methods for distributing federal assistance that he labels A, B, and C type grants. Type A grants [e.g., Medicaid and Aid for Dependent Children (AFDC)] are intended to adjust benefit spillovers by reducing the price associated with the production of a good or service from which the producing community is unable to recoup all costs. By matching state or local expenditures on the specific good or service, the federal government enables the producing community to recover their costs. The open-ended nature of the matching grant allows the producing community to continue production until optimality is reached. Type A grants are normally distributed on a formula basis.

Type B grants (e.g., general revenue sharing and some block grants) address the income and fiscal inequality problem by providing a lump sum nonrestrictive grant to recipient governments. The purpose here is merely one of income redistribution by the most direct means available.

Type C grants, the most widely employed aid mechanism, are intended to extract some form of compliant policy behavior from the recipient. These closed-ended, conditional grants enable the federal government to stimulate programmatic expenditures, innovations, or the achievement of minimum service levels and operate as "devices by which local governments are acting as the agents or contractors for the central government in carrying out specific tasks" (Gramlich, 1977:222). Type C grants are distinguishable from A and B grants by their terminal nature. Type C grants are awarded for a fixed period of time, and although renewal is possible, it is not certain. Moreover, these grants are competitively awarded so that the number of applicants always exceeds the number of recipients.

Grant Implementation: A Macro Perspective

The desired policy effect and therefore effective implementation of types A and C grant programs is an increase in recipient spending on the funded activity in excess of the amount of the grant: stimulation. More specifically, stimulation of recipient spending occurs when the provision of a federal grant increases the recipient's expenditures on the funded activity above what would have been spent on the aided activity had the grant not been awarded. Innovation and the adoption of new policy responsibilities are also stimulative effects since the net fiscal impact of these functional adoptions is an increase in municipal spending in excess of the federal grant award.

Stimulation, however, is not always the test of effective policy implementation. In order to correct for severe fiscal imbalances between cities, it might be necessary to allocate grant monies in a manner that minimizes additional fiscal strain on the recipient's revenue system. In this case aid monies would have either a neutral fiscal effect on recipient spending or actually relieve the recipient's fiscal burden by substituting federal grant monies for municipal taxes (i.e., substitution). This is the expected effect for type B grants (i.e., revenue sharing and block grants).

Presumably, Congress or its agents employ one of these aid mechanisms in order to maximize the achievement of programmatic goals. Gramlich's (1977) review of the aid impact literature suggests that this effect is not always achieved. Though there is ample evidence that each mechanism is associated with a specific fiscal and policy impact, it is not altogether clear which mechanisms are best at achieving the desired policy impact. Gramlich notes that the fiscal impact of grants (i.e., their ability to increase or decrease recipient spending) should be greatest for type A grants, next greatest for type C grants, and least effective for type B grants that might be expected to produce a substitution effect.

The empirical findings, however, do not fully confirm this hypothesis. In the case of type A grants recipient spending is somewhat "less than the size of the grant, indicating that the price elasticity of demand for most services is probably less than unity" (Gramlich, 1977:234). Moreover, type B grants stimulate much more recipient spending than expected. Finally, type C grants actually stimulate higher levels of recipient spending than either type B or A grants, usually equal to the size of the grant. Probably the most significant finding in Gramlich's review is the absence of a significant degree of fiscal stimulation. When discounting for those studies that are either methodologically or substantively flawed, Gramlich finds a surprisingly low level of fiscal stimulation attributable to federal aid offerings.

This condition does not go unexplained by Gramlich and other researchers (Miller, 1974). The greater stimulative effect of type C grants relative to A and B grants may be due to the fact that demand is more price elastic for those goods and services funded by type C grants. Thus, the functional character (i.e., price elasticity, economies of scale, etc.) and not the closed-ended nature of type C grants may account for the strong stimulative effect on the expenditures of recipient governments.

The fact that type B grants actually stimulate recipient expenditures suggests a need for some revision in theories that assume a harmony of interests between city officials and voters. The median voter thesis suggests that the average voter prefers to use each additional dollar of federal aid to reduce their taxes rather than increase spending. Where aid recipients are unconstrained by federal regulations (i.e., lump sum unconditional grants), aid monies are used to either reduce local tax burdens or do the same indirectly by substituting federal monies for own source revenues. The empirical findings, however, do not support the median voter hypothesis; rather, they support a "flypaper" effect. The flypaper thesis maintains that all federal aid monies have a tendency to stick where they hit "because of the inability of voters to perceive the true marginal price of public expenditures when nonmatching grants are present" (Courant et al., 1980). The fact that aid recipients increase spending rather than reduce taxes suggests a disharmony between the interests of the public and government officials and a possible sharing of values between local and federal officials concerning the utilization of federal aid monies.

The unexpectedly high stimulative effect of type B grants is explained in terms of local officials who do not perceive any incentive (due to public ignorance) to use federal aid transfers as a means of reducing local taxes. Others (Niskanen, 1971, and Romer and Rosenthal, 1978) have expanded on this argument to show that individual decision makers are budget maximizers, seeking to increase their agency's budgets rather than pursuing reductions in taxes. As noted earlier, the behavioral motivation of the local budget maximizer may be consistent with the goals of the federal aid program. This suggests that the behavioral orientations of administrative personnel play a major role in the success of implementing federal grant legislation. Revenue sharing and other lump sum aid transfers may produce significant fiscal stimulation because of a behavioral orientation among local budget officials that is at variance with the utility of the median voter.

McGuire (1976) maintains that aid recipients possess a host of ways to avoid the stimulative effects of federal aid programs, thus accounting for the nonstimulative effect of many federal grants:

> [T]he grant-in-aid system is embedded in a political process with a large element of bargaining and negotiation; hence there are built-in incentives for striking mutually beneficial bargains. In particular, key provisions for grant programs such as matching ratios and budget allotments to states and other jurisdictions are not determined arbitrarily (McGuire, 1976:35).

Employing these bargaining devices, aid recipients effectively transform contingent grant awards into a complicated income transfer (McGuire, 1976:49). Rather than increasing the recipient's own spending on the aided activity, these conditional matching grants (type A) actually have the same effect as an increase in own-source revenues, leaving the recipient to convert these new revenues into fungible resources.

McGuire explains the fungability of federal grant monies by recipient governments in behavioral terms. Either local officials are more effective in their negotiations with federal aid administrators and thus able to extract greater concessions from federal officials or federal enforcement of aid guidelines and regulations has declined. This explanation minimizes the effect the delivery mechanism has on the recipient's fiscal response to a grant award. McGuire's explanation suggests that the fiscal impact of a grant is mediated by the existence of a bargaining process between the federal grant donor and the state or local aid recipient. The bargaining process is directed at two distinct stages in the grant process: the allocation of aid monies and compliance with the conditions of the grant legislation. Within the constraints of the political arena, federal grant officials will seek to distribute federal grant monies in a manner that maximizes program implementation, "so that by implication the federal–local negotiation process involves some type of price discrimination or some type of budget supplementing discrimination among localities" (McGuire, 1976:41). When federal bureaucrats are allowed some discretion in the allocation of federal aid monies, a utility-maximizing model is operative in which the "grantor discriminates between communities on the basis of local willingness to pay for federal aid" in order to maximize program compliance (Chernick, 1979:103).

Price discrimination practices on the part of federal aid administrators may explain the significantly high stimulative effect of type C grants. Moreover, it also provides some clue as to the variable price effect of type A grants. Allocated on a formula basis, type A grants provide federal administrators little discretion in the allocation of federal monies. The successful implementation of type A grants thus centers on another subject of donor–recipient negotiations: the specific conditions of the grant. Gramlich suggests that an examination of grant legislation may help in identifying the source of variation in the implementation of federal grants, especially type A grants.

> Each existing or prospective grant program is obviously unique and the response of local governments to it will depend on underlying elasticities, the size of the grant, the homogeneity of local expenditures, restrictions on the grant and any other political factors. . . . If econometric research pretends to be relevant it must extend beyond the broad and general and get into these more specific questions of individual programs (Gramlich, 1977:234).

Essentially, Gramlich is suggesting that there are other dimensions to the grant system that have not yet been examined. Besides the delivery mechanism, there are a host of program-specific and nonprogram- specific traits associated with federal grants (e.g., environmental impact statements, affirmative action requirements). Each of these traits can enhance or weaken the attainment of specific program goals and may become the subject of donor–recipient negotiations. The potential recipient of a grant approaches participation in the federal aid system with an awareness of these traits, and their potential impact.

Theoretically, the relations between different delivery mechanisms and other traits represents a constraint on the operation of the delivery mechanism and thus might account for some of the indeterminacy in the econometric literature on grant impacts. For instance, requiring recipients of open-ended matching grants to fulfill National Environmental Protection Act standards imposes a direct and fixed cost on the aid recipient that increases rather than decreases the price of the aided function. These costs need not always be fiscal in nature. Many aid programs impose significant political costs on aid recipients. The grant notification and clearinghouse function (A-95) and mandated state plans require aid recipients at one level of government (e.g., cities) to obtain approval or conform to state or regional plans in order to qualify for federal funding. These conditions do more than distort the fiscal decisions of aid recipients. They also transfer a significant portion of local autonomy to other units/levels of government, indirectly affecting the cooperation of local aid recipients in the implementation process.

When controlling for the effect of various nominal legal provisions, Stein (1982) found that types A, B, and C grants had fiscal impacts consistent with the expectations outlined by Gramlich. This finding confirms that specific provisions of individual grant programs operate to alter and in some cases (i.e., types A and B grants) mute the implementation of federal grant legislation. Consistent with Gramlich's hypothesis, various conditions of grant legislation do work against the goals associated with a grant program's delivery mechanism (e.g., stimulation, innovation, or redressing inequality).

This research raises an obvious yet unanswered question. Why are grant programs, especially types A and B grants, associated with nominal legal provisions that work against effective implementation of program goals? Is this condition the result of a haphazard and illogical legislative process or could it be a product of a bargaining process between the federal donor and aid recipients occurring over the life of the aid program? Existing aid legislation is often the product of successive changes in the original enabling legislation. It is possible that conflicting traits in a grant program are produced by the political realities of building legislative coalitions to adopt the aid program. Successive reauthorizations of the program may work to iron out these inconsistencies, producing a more effective piece of grant legislation, or they may further weaken the program's chances for successful implementation with additional and inconsistent aid provisions. This scenario would suggest that policy implementation is a dynamic process, unfolding over the life of a federal aid program (5–25 years). The modus operandi for this process is donor–recipient negotiations in which actors arrive at short- and long-term agreements on the implementation of federal aid legislation. This explanation of intergovernmental policy implementation shifts our attention from the price and income effects of federal grants to the political and behavioral arena of the aid recipient.

Grant Implementation: A Micro Perspective

Political scientists have not been surprised by the indeterminant findings obtained from econometric studies of fiscal impacts of aid transfers (Wright, 1982:192). To the contrary, many have in fact hypothesized that aid programs are likely to provide recipients with a set of confusing and often contradictory cues and incentives for compliant behavior. Aware of the vicissitudes of the legislative process, many political scientists expect that the outputs of Congress will reflect the competing interests vying for control over the content of different public policies.

Ingram (1977) suggests that the grant-in-aid is a less-than-efficient legislative tool for promoting public policy because of its potential for political exploitation:

> Subsidy techniques such as grants are sometimes chosen less for their supposed effectiveness than for their acceptability. Because participation is voluntary, state governments need not accept grants unless it is to their advantage to do so. Congressmen see to it that for state governments the ratio of benefits to costs in the grant program is high enough to be attractive (Ingram, 1977:506).

It is often the case that "subsidy programs are legislatively packaged with other more coercive programs to make controversial provisions more palatable" (Ingram, 1977:506). Legislative adoption of the Pollution Control Act of 1972 (Mann, 1975) and the Secondary Education Act of 1965 (Murphy, 1973) were both facilitated by the inclusion of lucrative grant provisions. One of the obvious consequences of this practice is the inclusion of ineffectual and even conflicting program traits in the same grant package. This condition manifests itself in two ways. Less restrictive aid conditions are matched with legislatively controversial issues (Ingram, 1977; Murphy, 1973; and Mann, 1975). Policies that have difficulty garnering congressional majorities often are matched with nonrestrictive grant mechanisms (type B block grants). It is hardly coincidental that federal assistance for law enforcement, community development, health care, and job training and employment are packaged as block grants. Local aid recipients are reluctant to share authority over these functional responsibilities with federal officials (Stein, 1982; Thomas, 1978; Williams, 1967). The promise of unencumbered federal assistance provides an effective means of building legislative coalitions by muting objections to otherwise controversial federal policies. However weak, this strategy still provides some fiscal incentives for the performance of the funded activity.

The Recipient's Perspective on Grant Implementation

One approach to the study of grant implementation has been to examine this topic from the recipient's perspective, focusing on the structure of the recipient's bureaucracy and the predispositions of local actors. Elmore (1978) notes that the systems model ignores the basic element common to all cases of social program implementation—federalism. Regardless of how well organized an agency may be its ability to implement programs successfully depends to some degree on its ability to influence agencies at other levels of government (Elmore, 1978:195).

Rather than concentrating on the donor's organizational capacity to induce recipient compliance, Elmore suggests we begin with the assumption that "the process of initiating and implementating new policy actually begins at the bottom and ends at the top" (1978:215). The recipient's administrative structure is a more appropriate focus for the study of implementation than actions taken by federal officials to hold recipients accountable for standards and performances.

The factors shaping successful implementation of national public policies are internal to the recipient's own organization. Studies by Rand (1975) and Berman et al. (1975) demonstrate that the motivation and general disposition of local administrators to federally initiated innovations in education are critical in the successful adoption of these innovations by local school systems. These findings effectively

> turn the entire implementation process on its head. It reverses what we instinctively regard as the normal flow of policy, from top to bottom. The message of the model is quite bluntly, that the capacity to implement originates at the bottom of organizations, not at the top (Elmore, 1978:215).

The idea that the recipient's perspective is relevant to successful program implementation is neither new nor controversial. Others (Chernick, 1979; McGuire, 1976) have recognized the receptivity of aid recipients to federal aid initiatives as a major factor structuring implementation. What is novel about Elmore's approach is that recipient-level conditions are posited as the dominant determinant of implementation. The structure, size, and policy content of federal aid offerings are the driving force behind program compliance, reinforcing local predispositions to support federal aid initiatives.

Research on the sources of innovations among state administrators provides some evidence for Elmore's thesis. Light (1978) hypothesized that the sources of policy innovations (i.e., the production or performance of new goods or services) included professional associations, other states, and the federal government. Light found, however, that the type of agency and its functional responsibility "seems to offer a potentially fruitful avenue to explaining the differences among administrators in their ranking of the three sources of innovation" (Light, 1978:150). Federal influence, in the form of fiscal assistance, was ranked highest by state administrators for social services and environmental and natural resource policies. Federal authorities, however, were never ranked as most influential at inducing adoptions of innovations by a majority of the respondents for any state function. These findings provide limited confirmation of Elmore's thesis. Federally controlled factors are not sufficient for effective implementation. More importantly, the federal government's ability to induce states to adopt policy innovations varies with the content of the policy. This suggests that either federal monies are skewed toward specific and homogeneous functions (e.g., welfare) or that state receptivity varies with some yet undefined policy dimension(s).

Research on municipal functional assignment patterns explores this specific question (Liebert, 1975; Stein, 1982). A minimal condition for successful policy implementation is that the aid recipient perform the aided service. Stein sought to determine the extent to which the scope of municipal functional responsibility (i.e., the number of functions performed) and, more specifically, changes in the scope of municipal functional responsibility were related to federal, state, and municipal factors. Stein suggests that local officials prefer to perform functions that afford them maximum returns to scale in their production (i.e., economies of scale) and generate a narrow, homogeneous set of preferences for service delivery (e.g., highways, water, and sanitation):

> under normal conditions cities should avoid responsibility for costly, inefficient, and controversial services. The incentives or coercive actions of federal and state governments force municipal officials to deviate from their preferred assignment patterns and assume responsibility for economically and politically costly functions (Stein, 1982:234).

Stein finds support for this thesis. Federal aid eclipses the influence of both state (e.g., home-rule, direct expenditures) and local factors (e.g., demand and local resources) in structuring the assumption of economically and politically costly functions (e.g., welfare, urban renewal, and corrections). Conversely, local and to a lesser extent, state, factors structure the number of politically and economically inexpensive functions that are provided by city governments. This particular finding may reflect the efforts of federal officials to leverage policy implementation by varying the costs associated with different aid programs. By matching a nonrestrictive aid mechanism (e.g., block grants and revenue sharing) with controversial programs (e.g., welfare, urban renewal, law enforcement), federal officials have been able to reduce the political and economic costs associated with municipal participation in and compliance with federal aid programs. Interestingly, where the economic and political costs of program participation are minimal (e.g., highways), federal aid offerings tend to be more restrictive. This would suggest that the effect of current federal aid policy has been to impose the fewest costs and program requirements on recipients of aid that is designed to stimulate the adoption of politically and economically costly functions (Stein, 1982:545).

Stein and Light question the dominance of the recipient's perspective in explaining the implementation of intergovernmental policy. Stein and, to a lesser extent, Light are suggesting a revision of the recipient model of implementation along a policy dimension. Federal vs. state/local influence over policy implementation will vary with the diversity of preferences and economy of scale associated with the specific functional activity. Moreover, Stein clearly demonstrates that no one level of government dominates municipal functional assignment to the exclusion of actors at other levels of government. At the micro level this condition implies a complex set of interrelationships among actors at different levels of government.

A Bargaining Model of Implementation

Recognizing the interdependencies between the donor and aid recipient, a number of researchers have proposed a model that characterizes implementation in a federal system as a game in which the donor and recipient bargain over specific conditions of the grant program (Pressman, 1975; Bardach, 1977; Ingram, 1977; Derthick, 1970, 1972; Nathan, 1983; and Ripley and Franklin, 1980). Each have characterized implementation as involving the politics of bargaining rather than coercion by any one level of government or set of actors.

The bargaining process entails two or more actors, each seeking to maximize a set of goals. No one actor dominates all outcomes:

> A bargaining framework fits more accurately than a superior subordinate model the complex intergovernmental relations involved in grants-in-aid. Instead of a federal master dangling a carrot in front of a state donkey, the more apt image reveals a rich merchant haggling on equal terms with a sly, bargain-hunting consumer (Ingram, 1977:501).

As with any collective activity, there must be a reason or motivation for the various actors to engage in negotiations. Ingram in fact defines bargaining as a decision-making process "used when participants share a common interest in coming to a decision but have divergent values and objectives" (1977:502).

Each actor has specific resources with which to influence the outcome of the bargaining process and thus optimize his individual values and objectives. The federal donor maintains a strong hold over aid negotiations by controlling the fiscal incentives associated with the grant offer-ing. Moreover, the legal authority of the federal government to enforce the contractual agreements it enters into with aid recipients greatly en-hances the donor's bargaining position (ACIR, 1980).

Aid recipients, however, are not without significant resources them-selves. Ingram identifies three important resources available to aid re-cipients: (1) the recipient's prior experience with the federal aid system, (2) the diversity of grant offerings, and (3) state and local representation in Congress.

Prior Experience with Federal Aid System. Ingram suggests the relative bargaining advantages of recipients increases as they learn from prior aid negotiations. Studies of the Community Development Block Grant (Nathan and Dommel, 1978; Nathan et al., 1977) show that recipients with prior aid experience were more likely to prevail in their negotia-tions with federal officials on matters of program compliance than those lacking this experience.

Different actors tend to dominate negotiations on different aspects of program implementation. Local aid recipients prevailed on issues in-volving the distribution of aid monies within the city. Federal officials tended to dominate on administrative, technical, and compliance issues (Nathan and Dommel, 1978:442). This finding actually corroborates Ingram's hypothesis that through negotiations federal officials are more likely to win improvements in state organizational infrastructure than to change the state's substantive policy activity. Derthick's (1972) work fur-ther indicates that changes in the infrastructure of recipient govern-ments at least precedes substantive program compliance. This might suggest that recipient compliance is an acquired condition of program implementation, occurring over the life of the federal aid program and not just at the initiation of the program. This finding has been substanti-ated by researchers studying other aid programs including the Compre-hensive Employment Training Act (Ripley and associates, 1977; 1978; 1979; Van Meter and Van Horn, 1979) and the Economic Development Administration's public works program (Pressman and Wildavsky, 1979).

A historical analysis of grant utilization further shows that the pattern of aid use works against the recipient's pursuit of its own interests (Stein, 1981). Initially, new aid participants use those aid programs that afford them maximum freedom in the spending of federal monies (e.g., block grants and revenue sharing). However, once in the federal aid system there is a strong tendency for governments to develop a fiscal dependen-cy on federal assistance, resulting in extensive use of less desirable and more costly project grants (type C). Loucks (1978) maintains that general revenue sharing and block grants were used as bait to stimulate wide municipal participation in the federal aid system. Unable to extract themselves from the aid system for political and fiscal reasons, these new participants found it increasingly difficult to expand their use of federal assistance without using restrictive and costly project grants.

These findings should not be interpreted to mean that aid recipients trapped by more restrictive aid programs are unable to resist complying with the requirements of these programs. Ingram's view that state and local governments are free to choose from a diverse set of aid programs is not completely accurate. There is evidence to suggest that this advantage is operational only during the recipient's initial foray into the federal aid system. Subsequent participation expands to include more numerous and restrictive project grants, possibly resulting in more competetive bargaining between federal officials and aid recipients.

The Diversity of Grant Offerings. Ingram maintains the comparative bargaining advantage of aid recipients is further enhanced by the large number and diversity of grant offerings. Participation in the federal aid system remains a voluntary association. The fiscal incentives attached to each grant are not the only criteria on which potential aid recipients base their decision to participate in the federal aid system. There is a wide degree of variation in the program requirements, and there are crosscutting aid obligations associated with each aid program (Ingram, 1977:504).

The diversity of grant offerings may work work against the interests of the potential aid recipient. The application process associated with certain aid programs has operated to screen out certain willing and needy aid recipients because they were unable to bear the costs associated with seeking and receiving federal assistance (Stein, 1979, 1981). Moreover, there is evidence to suggest that when the costs associated with seeking and receiving federal assistance are minimal (e.g., block grants and revenue sharing), participation in these federal aid programs increases. Effective program implementation as well as recipient needs can remain unfulfilled due to the economic and political costs associated with participation in the federal aid system.

State and Local Representation in Congress. Once a state or city enters into an aid agreement with the federal government, it becomes a client of the administering agency. The federal agency in turn develops a dependency on the aid recipient not only for achieving program compliance, but also for legislative support in Congress as the agency seeks

to protect and expand its funding levels. This client relationship is reinforced by the recipient's lobbying of congressional representatives, who
presumably will be more responsive to their electoral constituents than
the bureaucrats of the implementing agency. This condition results in a
patterned response to aid recipients on the part of the federal
bureaucracy:

> The tendency of federal granting agencies is to pursue grant allocation practices
> that gain broad support, even if this means refusing to terminate funds for reasons
> of noncompliance or poor performance, or failing to reward states that excel in
> program objectives (Ingram, 1977:525).

Attention to allocation patterns as a means of generating support for
the aid program is supported by Anagnoson (1979). He found evidence
to suggest that implementing agencies distribute grant monies in a manner that treats every recipient equally rather than distributing aid
monies based on the strength of the recipient's congressional representation in Congress or other political factors. Studying the highly pol-
iticized Economic Development Administration's (EDA) public works
aid program, Anagnoson found that EDA sought to distribute its aid
monies in a manner that maximized equity and not necessarily federal
program goals. The spreading effect of a universal distribution of
federal aid also has the effect of trivializing individual allocations so that
they are too small to produce much change.

An Extension of the Bargaining Model

The bargaining model outlined by Ingram and others has clear advantages over the previously discussed approaches. There are, however,
some missed theoretical opportunities with a bargaining model as it is
applied to the study of implementation. Ingram's own application of the
model to the study of water resource policy is not fully integrated into
the dynamics of the policy process. Specifically, there is a tendency in
this and other research on implementation to employ a short time horizon. Implementation is often defined in terms of immediate conditions
(i.e., one year lags between legislative enactment) rather than examining
the evolutionary consequences of the bargaining model of implementation. For example, what, if any, relationship exists between the product
(output) of recipient–donor negotiations and changes in federal aid
legislation? This question can only be addressed by adopting a dynamic
perspective on implementation, where outputs from implementation activities are studied as inputs to the legislative formulation (or reformula-

tion) stage of the policy process. The product of donor–recipient nego-tiations may spill over to the legislative process in the form of changes in the program's enabling legislation. Nathan (1983) suggests just such a linkage between implementation and policy formulation. He posits two complementary bargaining processes, vertical and horizontal, operating to structure the implementation of a federal aid program:

> The best way to think about this process is that there is a horizontal policy bargain-ing process that consists of decision-making about policy goals and instruments for the country as a whole, and a vertical dimension, involving the way in which a particular grant is defined and executed by individual recipient jurisdictions. Federal grants, especially larger ones, need to be viewed as involving both a horizon-tal and vertical political bargaining process. The vertical policy bargaining process— the ways grants are treated by the recipient state and local government—has a great deal to do with the way grants work (Nathan, 1983:31).

Nathan's predictive theory of federal grants adopts a dynamic ap-proach to the execution of intergovernmental aid policy. The bargaining between the federal government and a specific recipient is but one point in this process that eventually loops back to the agenda and policy for-mulation (reformulation) stages in the form of revisions in the original enabling legislation.

AN EVOLUTIONARY MODEL OF GRANT IMPLEMENTATION

Expanding on the work of Ingram, Nathan, and economists Chernick and McGuire, I will outline a process model of grant implementation. Like Mazmanian and Sabatier (1983), I conceive of implementation in a federal system as a multistaged process that occurs over an extended period of time (i.e., the life of the grant program). During this time effects from one stage structure or restructure successive steps in the implementation process. Also like Mazmanian and Sabatier, I adopt a relatively long time horizon (5–25 years) in order to analyze the feed-back component.

Assuming that the implementation process begins with an enacted law, we are concerned with four specific steps in the implementation of intergovernmental aid policy: (1) utilization/participation in the federal aid system, (2) allocation of aid monies to recipients, (3) donor–recipient negotiations, and (4) feedback to the legislative process (i.e., policy refor-mulation). The feedback or legislative reformulation stage is the topic of a more detailed discussion in the concluding section of this paper.

Application and Utilization

The first and possibly the most important step toward achieving compliance is the participation of intended beneficiaries in the federal aid
program. In this regard utilization is a necessary though not sufficient
condition for program compliance. This condition of grant implementation is viewed by Ingram and others (Derthick, 1972) as a weak link in
the implementation of federal grant programs. In order to maximize
participation in the federal aid program by those intended to benefit
from the federal largess, it is necessary to ensure that eligibility standards are appropriately defined and that the relative costs of seeking
and receiving federal assistance do not outweigh the recipient's perception of the benefits associated with participation.

Eligibility defines the population of potential recipients, those who
may apply for assistance. Eligibility may be defined broadly or narrowly,
depending on the goals and purposes of the program and the political
costs associated with achieving legislative adoption. Narrow eligibility
standards tend to produce a homogeneous set of recipients, increasing
the chances for uniform program compliance. A larger and more diverse population of eligible recipients increases the variation in responses to aid offerings among eventual participants and potentially
reduces the probability of uniform program compliance. Limiting the
universe of eligible recipients to a small and homogeneous set of communities should enable federal administrators to standardize their negotiations with all aid recipients, thus increasing the chances of successful
implementation. Specifically, federal officials can avoid the costly procedure of individualized negotiations with each recipient by seeking to
standardize their rules for program implementation.

There is circumstantial evidence to suggest that federal officials structure their aid offerings with specific cost-benefit behavior in mind. Minimal entry costs are associated with formula, block, and revenue sharing
grants. These devices have been used to promote aid policies where
donor–recipient consensus on program goals is thought to be low (i.e.,
community development, law enforcement, public health, and public
employment and training). Conversely, where goal consensus is expected to be high (e.g., sewer treatment, roads, and general public
works) the delivery mechanisms for federal assistance have imposed
greater entry costs on the prospective applicant.

It remains empirically undetermined whether utilization of more controversial aid programs can be extended by use of broad eligibility standards and entitlement grants (type A) rather than more costly project
grants (type C). It is possible that federal officials use nonrestrictive aid

mechanisms to entice reluctant participants into a dialogue on the aid program where a negotiated settlement to the implementation issue can be achieved. This would suggest that the product of aid negotiations serves as the basis for a more permanent donor–recipient relationship.

As noted earlier, experience with the federal aid system strengthens the bargaining position of the aid recipient. Older aid recipients are expected to be more successful in their negotiations with federal officials than less experienced aid recipients. Their inability to obtain satisfactory concessions from federal aid officials forces new aid recipients to seek program exemptions from congressional representatives in the form of revisions in the grant legislation.

Allocation/Distribution

An obvious means for promoting policy compliance is through the distribution of aid monies in a targeted fashion (Mazmanian and Sabatier, 1983:189; Cucitti, 1978). Targeted aid allocations allow for the identification of a specific population of recipients whose participation in the aid program will promote the goals and purposes of the program more effectively and efficiently than other recipients. The need of recipients or their willingness to fulfill program goals are the criteria most often used to target aid monies. The mechanism used for distributing aid monies provides a second opportunity to deliver monies where they will maximize program implementation. This is particularly relevant where eligibility is broadly defined and entry costs are minimal. In order to obtain legislative support for an aid program it may be necessary to provide supporters of the bill a share of the program's benefits. Broad eligibility and minimal entry costs are effective means for achieving this goal. A targeted delivery mechanism, however, still allows all eligible recipients to receive some monies (keeping the legislative coalition intact) while still providing a disproportionate amount of money to those with the greatest need or potential for achieving program objectives.

Efforts to target aid monies have met with limited success. Gist and Hill (1981) have shown that targeted allocations of Urban Development Action Grants (UDAG) to fiscally stressed cities was related to the program's main goal of increasing private sector investment in fiscally stressed cities. However, when aid monies were targeted to those recipients most supportive of the urban renewal program, there were only marginal increases in program compliance. Gilbert and Specht (1974) found that cities awarded Model Cities monies were no more likely to achieve the desired level of performance than nonrecipients. [For a further discussion of this literature, see Kelly and Frankel (1978).]

The allocation device associated with a project grant (type C) allows federal aid administrators to review each grant request against their own criteria for successful implementation. Entitlements and other formula-based allocation devices (types A and B) place the responsibility for distributing aid monies with Congress. Here a legislatively agreed-upon formula is used to allocate monies to a predefined population of recipients, with little chance for deviation from the statutorily set procedure. A project-by-project review of each application strengthens the bargaining position of the federal officials and enhances their ability to obtain program compliance. Entitlement formulas remove this power and discretion from federal administrators, depositing it with Congress, whose susceptibility to interest group lobbying on these issues is well documented (ACIR, 1982; Dommel, 1975; Stanfield, 1979).

Negotiations and Bargaining

The application and allocation stages effectively define the nature and scope of participation in the federal aid system. Moreover, the agenda for aid negotiations is established at these earlier stages of implementation. Recipients shop among various aid programs, seeking those that maximize their needs and objectives relative to the costs imposed on them by the grant. Since the application and allocation stages precede donor–recipient negotiations, recipients can only reduce some of the uncertainty concerning cost calculations (i.e., compliance with federal aid standards). Chernick (1979) demonstrated that potential aid recipients may actually bargain with federal officials during the application stage, seeking to obtain a reduction in costs (e.g., matching rates) in return for concessions on substantive policy issues.

Once entry costs have been minimized and allocations maximized, participants may be less aggressive in their negotiations with federal aid officials over issues of program compliance. If, however, recipients perceive they have not been treated fairly in these first two stages, their willingness to acquiesce to federal negotiators will be minimal. Aid recipients will seek ways to avoid complying with costly aid requirements, preferring to substitute own-source revenues with federal aid.

Negotiations between aid recipients and federal officials do not take place in a vacuum. Explanations of aid recipient behavior based solely on the flexibility or distribution mechanism of the grant can be misleading (Nathan, 1983). The social, political, and most importantly, economic climate of the recipient jurisdiction heavily influences the recipient's cost–benefit calculations and thus indirectly defines the bargaining behavior of the aid recipient. Fiscally stressed, dependent, and politically crossed–pressured (i.e., socially heterogeneous) cities may find it necesary to pursue their own policy objectives rather than federal guidelines when executing federal aid programs. These communities may be expected to use aid negotiations as a means of achieving independence from federal regulation of their spending decisions.

Continuing to assume that each actor in the bargaining process is a utility maximizer, there should develop a point in donor–recipient negotiations where specific agreements regarding program execution are the product of an inefficient activity. From the donor's perspective implementation of an aid program involves a large number of state or local jurisdictions and actors. It is not efficient in terms of overall implementation to arrive at dozens or even hundreds of separately negotiated aid agreements. The cost in time and personnel as well as the potential for fragmented implementation should make the federal administrator seek a more efficient means of executing aid policy. The aid recipient is similarly disserviced by individualized aid negotiations. Foremost on the recipient's agenda is establishing some certainty and regularity regarding the availability of federal assistance (Nathan et al., 1975:204). Cyclical negotiations (i.e., yearly or biannually) do little to secure this type of fiscal stability. It is difficult to prepare long-term budgets if a jurisdiction is not certain as to the amount and condition of intergovernmental revenues. Moreover, as specific actors change the stability and relevance of previously negotiated agreements may be brought into question. For these reasons, both the donor and recipient have a strong incentive to shift the arena of their negotiations from the local recipient level to a setting where (1) more efficient negotiations can take place, and (2) a degree of stability or even permanence can be attached to the negotiated agreements.

Legislative Feedback

These goals can best be achieved by elevating the results of individual aid negotiations to the national level (i.e., Congress) where similar aid agreements can be incorporated into the program's original enabling legislation. Changes in grant legislation provide the recipient with the security that recently negotiated aid agreements will be effective for a relatively long period of time. As suggested by Ingram (1977) and Nathan's (1983) horizontal bargaining process, aid recipients have strong congressional ties. Representation of recipient interests by national public interest groups (e.g., National Association of Counties, National League of Cities, and National Governors Association) provides the recipient an effective and efficient lobbying mechanism with which to favorably alter federal aid legislation.

Federal administrators are also advantaged, though not so obviously,

by this shift to the congressional arena. National-level negotiations ca
take place between federal aid officials and representatives of nationa
recipient associations. This minimally reduces the bargaining costs fo
federal officials while still stylizing their aid programs to different classe
of recipients (e.g., cities, counties, states, nonprofits). The influence c
public interest groups provides the federal agency a strong and effectiv
advocate for seeking budget increases and other favorable legislativ
enactments from Congress. [See Haider (1974) and Wright (1982) for
further discussion of public interest groups and congressional lobbying

This view of intergovernmental policy implementation implies tha
the nature of program compliance cannot be studied cross-sectionally
but requires a time-series analysis in order to capture the dynamics c
the bargaining process. Since the product of aid negotiations change
the expectations for program compliance, the dependent variable in an
study of intergovernmental policy implementation will vary over time
Initial aid legislation merely establishes the basis for recipient–dono
discussions over the nature of compliance. Unless researchers are pre
pared to study intergovernmental policy implementation as a cyclica
process, they will miss much of what is actually happening in the polic
process. Moreover, revision in federal aid legislation is not idiosyncrati
to the program. Rather, change is a condition common to all aid legisla
tion and associated with a specific evolutionary pattern.

THE CHANGING CHARACTER OF FEDERAL AID: CONSEQUENCES FOR IMPLEMENTATION

Studies of governmental growth have provided some useful models fo
understanding change in the structure of federal aid programs. Olso
(1971) and Buchanan and Tullock (1962) emphasize the role of specia
interests and the process of logrolling in the formation and subsequer
passage of intergovernmental aid proposals. A group of individuals wit
special interests in an aid program will form legislative coalitions wit
other groups advocating approval of similarly narrow-purpose aid pack
ages. The members of the coalition benefit as the costs of their progran
are borne by the general tax-paying public. Issues are voted on sepa
rately and a particular coalition does not take account of the fact tha
other coalitions benefit at its expense. This free-riding legislative behav
ior tends to produce an oversupply of particularized public ai
expenditures.

Monypenny (1960) has noted that narrow aid legislation is more prev
alent at the federal than at the state level. He argues that most state an

local governments are not sufficiently diverse to support a system of logrolling. Groups that are too small at the state and local level achieve a critical mass at the national level, enabling them to participate in the process of congressional logrolling. Without strong legislative cooperation between various interest groups, little if any grant legislation would pass, since no single interest group is large enough to sustain a successful legislative battle for its pet aid program. The exchange of votes between supporters of different aid programs provides the means for legislative enactment of numerous narrow-purpose aid programs.

The aid programs produced by this legislative quid pro quo are associated with a specific structure that influences implementation. Authorization for a new aid program requires clearing significant legislative hurdles. Supporters of the program much compete for scarce monies, already appropriated to previously authorized aid programs. The most likely structure to emerge for a new aid program is a competitively awarded project grant with specific program and matching requirements. First-time aid proposals will be fiscally modest, especially in comparison to the reappropriation for ongoing aid programs. Program eligibility is made broad in order to maximize on legislative support. The number and scope of actual aid recipients, however, will be considerably smaller and more homogeneous than the population of eligible recipients. The extension of aid benefits to a universe of eligible recipients (e.g., all cities) rather than a smaller subset of the universe would risk producing trivial aid allocations, thus undermining the strength of legislative support that could be generated for these aid packages. Promising a larger number of congressmen that their districts (or communities or individuals within their district) will be eligible to apply for federal assistance is an effective means for gaining legislative support without committing the program's sponsors to a broad (and fiscally trivial) allocation of assistance. Sponsors of the aid program are willing to extend eligibility since they are confident that only those directly affected by the program and supportive of its goals and purposes will seek, and eventually receive, assistance. As Anagnoson (1979:26) has shown, this implicit targeting of assistance is not the result of pork barrel politics.

Demand for assistance effectively skews the population of actual applicants and recipients to those units of government most knowledgeable and supportive of the program (Hebert and Bingham, 1972). The ability to cut through this legislative maze and eventually receive federal assistance, according to Hebert and Bingham, is related to the recipient's employment of an intergovernmental lobbyist, either individually or through a consortium of recipients (i.e., public interest group). Under this scenario we would expect the population of initial aid recipients to be dominated by the governmental and nongovernmental units mo: heavily involved in lobbying for the creation of the aid program.

Though this is almost trivial hypothesis, confirmation is necessary t establish the next cycle in our model of policy implementation. New ai programs will initially achieve high levels of program compliance, du mostly to a supportive clientele group. Problems arise, however, whe eligible applicants outside the population of initial supporters (and ai recipients) seek and receive funding from these newly enacted aid pro grams. The infusion of new aid recipients (Stein, 1981) creates signif cant tensions in the implementation of aid programs. Unlike their pred ecessors, new entrants to a narrow-purpose aid program are not likely t share the high level of support for the program's goals and purpose: Consequently, aid requirements, matching ratios, and other condition of the aid program will prove burdensome and costly to second genera tion participants. This dissatisfaction with the conditions of the gran program leads second generation participants to negotiate with federa administrators for exemptions from aid requirements. Like all othe forms of legislation, aid programs are authorized for a finite period o time. Their reauthorization often requires some formal review and thu sets the stage for a reevaluation of the aid programs' purposes and struc tures.

It is at this point in the implementation process that donor–recipien negotiations affect the content of the federal aid programs. Dissatisfie recipients or those able to extract concessions from federal admin istrators seek to revise the program's enabling legislation. These pro posed changes are not idiosyncratic. Rather, they take on a predictabl pattern, reflective of the growing number of aid recipients and the di versity of this population. With time and effective grantsmenship ever the narrowest grant programs attract broader legislative attention. Dis satisfied with the narrowness of aid beneficiaries, the size of aid alloca tions, and program restrictions, the newly enlarged population of recip ients lobby for: (1) increased aid appropriations. This increases th number of potential aid recipients without limiting the aid allocations t trivial amounts. (2) The replacement of a project-grant mechanism with a congressionally controlled formula grant. And (3) the removal of aic requirements and restrictions on the use of federal aid monies.

These changes are not adopted simultaneously, and their incorpora tion into the aid program's enabling legislation may occur over suc cessive reauthorizations. Initially aid appropriations expand to accom modate increased demand for the specific program. This, however, doe: not address the problem of a low level of support for the program's goal and purposes, a condition that is negatively related to the increased umber and diversity of new aid recipients. Once appropriations and ιdividual aid allocations have reached a nontrivial level, recipient lobby-ιg efforts shift to the issue of replacing bureaucratic discretion over aid ιlocations to a congressionally controlled distribution mechanism. This ς followed by a final move to purge the aid program of costly require-ιents and restrictions. With each successive reauthorization of an aid ·rogram, its character will shift closer to a nonrestrictive block grant ιith minimum program, matching, and administrative requirements. ∶ligibility will be universal and funding levels will continue to grow in ·rder to meet the demands of an increased population of aid users.

A CASE STUDY

·ederal aid policy in the area of community development and urban ·enewal provides an excellent illustration of this evolutionary process. Γhe main vehicle for current federal policy in the area of community ιevelopment and urban renewal is the Community Development Block ɔrant (CDBG), established by the Housing and Development Act of .974 and subsequent amendments in 1978. Consistent with the traits of ·ther lump sum aid transfers, CDBG provides for a formula-based dis-ribution of monies to a large population of aid recipients. Under the :urrent provisions of the block grant all states, counties, and cities over ;0,000 are automatically allocated community development monies ·ased on their population size and other relevant characterisitcs. Cities ınd counties below 50,000 in size are eligible to apply for community ιevelopment monies under a project grant program. Program require-ιents are minimal, and restrictions on the expenditure of CDBG ιonies are confined only to vague statements certifying that recipients ιave given "maximum feasible priority" to the national goals of prevent-ng or eliminating slums and urban blight. Although amendments to the 1974 act have tightened the restrictions on recipient expenditures (e.g., imit on social service spending), the current grant program remains ·ssentially a nonrestrictive lump sum transfer.

The 1974 act was the product of a consolidation of eight project ɟrants, many of which had undergone significant changes since their ɔriginal passage. In all but a few instances program requirements were ·educed rather than increased over the life of the project grant. As ·xpected, authorizations and appropriations increased significantly over :ime.

Changes in eligibility and subsequent grant utilization are less obvious. A number of grants expanded eligibility by establishing special provi-sions and funds for targeted aid recipients. Amendments to the Open-

Space program established funding for both urban and low-incom
communities without reducing outlays for other eligible recipients. Sim
ilar amendments in 1966 to the 1949 Housing Act extended the Urba
Renewal aid program to "smaller cities." Program use was extended i
the case of the Model Cities program by limiting the amount of ai
money any one state could receive.

Table 1 reports the participation rates and average size of aid award
for the years preceding and following passage of the 1974 CDBG. Prio
to the 1974 enactment, the distribution of community development an
housing assistance was decidedly skewed toward larger central cities, th
original sponsors of these aid programs. Though eligibility was broadl
defined in all eight project grants, participation rates among cities belo
100,000 did not exceed one-third of the population. Conversely, par
ticipation among cities over 100,000 was well in excess of 50%. By 1977
three years after enactment of the CDBG, participation rates increase
150% for cities between 25,000 and 49,999 and 53% for cities betwee
50,000 and 99,999. Participation rates among cities over 100,000 re
mained stable after enactment of the 1974 block grant. Though man
factors contributed to the changing level of municipal participation i
federally funded community development aid programs, the shift to

Table I.   Municipal Participation in Federally Funded Community
Development Programs

	Population Size				
Variable/Year	25,000– 49,999	50,000– 99,999	100,000– 249,999	250,000– 499,999	500,000+
1967					
Percent participating	10.6	25.9	50.0	67.7	67.9
Mean grant award[a]	15.82	11.91	9.18	8.08	8.40
1972					
Percent participating	14.3	28.0	52.0	64.5	80.0
Mean grant award	15.03	13.38	18.88	15.61	14.37
1977					
Percent participating	22.9	38.0	51.0	64.5	76.2
Mean grant award	38.44	39.15	36.17	45.74	54.00
Percent change in awards	+142.9	+228.7.0	+294.0	+466.0	+542

[a]Average per capita aid award in constant 1972 dollars.

formula-based block grant was a major factor in expanding municipal participation.

Average per capita aid awards in constant 1972 dollars for community development programs increased steadily between 1967 and 1977. Interestingly, the average size of 1967 community development grant awards was largest for smaller-sized cities (25,000–49,999) while cities over 500,000 received the second smallest average award. This trend changed in 1972 and was reversed by 1977. In fact the average 1977 grant award for cities over 500,000 was more than three times the award to cities between 25,000 and 49,999 in size. Limited participation by smaller size cities early in the life of community development assistance netted these participants higher than average grant awards. As participation increased, however, the average award for smaller cities increased at a much slower rate (142%) than for larger-sized cities (228–542%).

This pattern is consistent with earlier hypotheses. Sponsors of pre-block grant community development aid legislation sought support for their programs from suburban and rural interests. Expanding eligibility by adding special funding provisions for these communities ensured the support of these interest groups throughout the life of the aid program. The extension of benefits to other recipients did not come at the expense of the original sponsors. To the contrary, grant awards for larger cities increased dramatically between 1967 and 1977, allowing the promoters of community development aid programs to maximize legislative support for their program and individual aid allocations.

This case study partially confirms our main thesis: federal aid legislation changes over time. The change is directed at lessening program requirements and other costs associated with participation in the federal aid program. Participation rates increase by expanding the population of eligible recipients. These aggregate conditions, however, are not sufficient to confirm an evolutionary explanation of grant implementation. It remains to be demonstrated that these conditions are the product of recipient–donor interactions elevated to legislative action (i.e., lobbying by aid recipients). The behavioral component of this research question requires a different type of analysis than we have employed. Given the historical character of this research, it is not possible to interview relevant actors, donors, or recipients. Rather, we need to examine committee hearings, reports, and floor action in order to reconstruct the history associated with changes in the enabling legislation for individual grant programs. A reconstruction of the legislative histories for each grant program will provide both the dynamic and behavioral components lacking in our aggregate-level analysis of community development aid programs.

CONCLUSION

Policy implementation in a federal system with specific emphasis on grants-in-aid has become the dominant setting for the study of domestic public policy. We have endeavored to show that within a federal system policy implementation is best understood as part of a dynamic process in which the character and content of individual programs change over time. This view is not novel to policy literature and has been well documented by others. What is not fully understood is whether change, at least in federal grant policy, is idiosyncratic or patterned. Our own thesis and subsequent case study argues for the nonidiosyncratic explanation.

Compliance with federal assistance programs is dependent upon the content of the program and recipient support for program goals and purposes. Compliance and therefore effective implementation are retarded when there is significant variance between aid program goals and the preferences of aid recipients. Congruence between program goals and recipient preferences is an obvious but critical precondition for achieving grant compliance. This apparently trivial precondition, however, is not itself easily explained. Programs not only grow fiscally, they also change structurally to accommodate recipient preferences and the federal government's desire to achieve greater program compliance. The evolutionary character of federal aid programs is not one in which the donor is pitted against the recipient. Rather, grant implementation is the product of a dynamic process in which each actor seeks to achieve different goals through a common mechanism, the federal grant.

REFERENCES

Anagnoson, T. (1979) "Policies in the distribution of federal grants: the case of the economic development administration." In B. S. Rundquist ed. Political Benefits, Lexington: Heath.
Bardach, E. (1977) The Implementation Game: What Happens After a Bill Becomes a Law. Cambridge, Mass.: MIT Press.
Berman, P., et al. (1975) Federal Programs Supporting Educational Change. Santa Monica, Cal.: Rand Corp.
Break, G. (1967) Intergovernmental Fiscal Relations In the United States. Washington, D.C.: Brookings Institution.
Buchanan, J. M. and G. Tullock (1962) The Calculus of Consent. Ann Arbor: University of Michigan Press.
Chernick, H. (1979) "An economic model of the distribution of project grants." In P. Miewskowski and W. H. Oakland (eds.), Fiscal Federalism and Grants-in-Aid. Washington, D.C.: Urban Institute.
Courant, P., E. Gramlich, and D. Rubinfeld (1980) "Why voters support tax limitation amendments: the Michigan case." National Tax Journal 33:1–20.

Cucitti, P. (1978) The Role of Equalization in Federal Grants. Washington, D.C.: U.S. Government Printing Office.

Derthick, M. (1972) New Towns In-Town. Washington, D.C.: Urban Institute.

—— (1970) The Influence of Federal Grants: Public Assistance in Massachusetts, Cambridge: Harvard Univ. Press.

—— (1974) Between State and Nation: Regional Organizations in the United States, Washington, D.C.: Brookings.

Dommel, P. (1975) "Urban policy and federal aid: redistributive issues." In L. Masotti and R. Lineberry (eds.) New Urban Politics. Lexington, Mass.: Heath.

Edwards, III, G. C. (1980) Implementing Public Policy. Washington, D.C.: Congressional Quarterly Press.

Elmore, R. F. (1978) "Organizational models of social program implementation." Public Policy 26:185–228.

Gilbert, N. and H. Specht. (1974) "Picking winners: federal discretion and local experience as bases for planning grant allocations." Public Administration Review 35:565–74.

Gist, J. and R. Hill. (1981) "The allocation of Urban Public Development Action Grants." Public Choice 36:121–34.

Gramlich, E. (1977) "Intergovernmental grants: a review of empirical literature," in W. Oates (ed.) The Political Economy of Fiscal Federalism, Lexington: D. C. Heath.

Haider, D. (1974) When Governments Come to Washington: Governors, Mayors, and Intergovernmental Lobbying. New York: Free Press.

Hebert, R. T. and R. Bingham. (1972) "The city manager's knowledge of grants-in-aid: some personal and environmental influences." Urban Affairs Quarterly 7:303–06.

Ingram, H. (1977) "Policy implementation through bargaining." Public Policy 25:449–501.

Kelly, R. M. and B. Frankel (1978) "The Federal Decision to Fund Local Programs: Utilizing Evaluation Research." In J. May and A. Wildavsky (eds.), The Policy Cycle, Beverly Hills, Cal.: Sage Publications.

Liebert, R. J. (1975) Disintegration and Political Action. New York: Academic Press.

Light, A. F. (1978) "Intergovernmental sources of innovation in state administration." American Politics Quarterly 6:147–68.

Loucks, E. (1978) "The new federalism and the suburbs." Growth and Change 9:2–7.

McGuire, R. (1976) "The analysis of federal grants into price and income components." In P. Miewszkowski and W. H. Oakland (eds.), Fiscal Federalism and Grants-in-Aid. Washington, D.C.: Urban Institute.

Mann, D. E. (1975) "The political incentive of U. S. water policy: the relationships between distributive and regulatory policies." In M. Holden, Jr., and D. L. Dresang (eds.), What Government Does. Beverly Hills, Cal.: Sage Publications.

Mazmanian, D. A. and P. A. Sabatier (1983) Implementation and Public Policy. Glenview, Ill.: Scott Foresman.

Miller, E. (1974) "The economics of matching grants: the ABC highway program." National Tax Journal 44:221–30.

Monypenny, R. (1960) "Federal grants-in-aid to state government: a political analysis." National Tax Journal 13:1–15.

Murphy, J. T. (1973) Grease the Squeaky Wheel. Cambridge, Mass.: Harvard Research Center for Educational Policy.

Mushkin, S. and J. F. Cotton (1969) Sharing Federal Funds for State and Local Needs. New York: Praeger.

Nakamura, R. T. and F. Smallwood (1980) The Politics of Policy Implementation. New York: St. Martin's Press.

Nathan, R. P. (1983) "The behavior of state and local governments under federal grants: toward a predictive theory." Political Science Quarterly 99:102–18.

—— and Paul Dommel (1978) "Federal–local relations under block grants." Political Science Quarterly 93:424–43.

—— et al. (1977) "Monitoring the block grant program for community development," Political Science Quarterly 92:219–44.

—— et al. (1975) Monitoring Revenue Sharing. Washington, D.C.: Brookings Institution.

Niskanen, R. (1971) Bureaucracy and Representative Government. Chicago: Aldine-Atherton.

Olson, M. (1971) The Logic of Collective Action: Public Goods and the Theory of Groups. Cambridge, Mass.: Harvard University Press.

Pressman, J. G. and A. Wildavsky (1973) Implementation, 2nd ed. Berkeley: University of California Press.

—— (1975) Federal Program and City Politics: The Dynamics of The Aid Process in Oakland. Berkley: University of California Press.

Ripley, R. B. and G. A. Franklin (1980) Bureaucracy and Policy Implementation. Homewood: Dorsey Press.

—— and associates (1977) The Implementation of CETA in Ohio, Washington, D.C.: U.S. Government Printing Office.

—— (1978) CETA Prime Sponsor Management Decisions and Program Goal Achievement. Washington, D.C.: U.S. Government Printing Office.

—— (1979) Areawide Planning in CETA. Washington, D.C.: U.S. Government Printing Office.

Romer, T. and H. Rosenthal (1978) "Political resource allocation, controlled agendas and the status quo." Public Choice 33:27–43.

Sabatier, P. A. and D. A. Mazmanian (1982) "Implementation of public policy: a framework for analysis." In D. A. Mazmanian and P. A. Sabatier (eds.), Effective Policy Implementation. Lexington, Mass.: Heath.

Stanfield, R. (1979) "Playing computer politics with local aid formulas." National Journal (Dec. 9):1977–81.

Stein, R. M. (1983) "The structural character of federal aid: an examination of fiscal impact." In R. D. Ebel, Research on Urban Economics: The Changing Economic and Fiscal Climate. Greenwich, Conn.: JAI Press.

—— (1982) "The political economy of municipal functional responsibility." Social Science Quarterly 63:530–48.

—— (1981) "The allocation of federal aid monies: the synthesis of demand-side and supply-side explanations." American Political Science Review 75:334–43.

—— (1979) "Federal categorical aid: equalization and the application process." Western Political Quarterly 32:396–409.

Thomas, R. D. (1978) "Policy issues and intergovernmental responsibility: A state legislative perspective on change." State and Local Government Review 9:54–59.

U.S. Advisory Commission on Intergovernmental Relations (1978) Significant Features of Fiscal Federalism: 1978–1979. Washington, D.C.: U.S. Government Printing Office.

—— (1981) Studies in Comparative Federalism. Washington, D.C.: U.S. Government Printing Office.

—— (1982) The Condition of Contemporary Federalism: Conflicting Theories and Collapsing Constraints. Washington, D.C.: U.S. Government Printing Office.

—— (1980) Awakening the Slumbering Giant: Intergovernmental Relations Grant Law. Washington, D.C.: U.S. Government Printing Office.

Van Horn, C. E. (1970) Policy Implementation in the Federal System: National Goals and Local Implementators. Lexington, Mass.: Heath.

Wagner, R. E. (1976) Revenue Structure, Fiscal Illusion and Budgetary Choice. Public Choice 25:45–61.

Williams, O. (1967) "Lifestyle values and political decentralization in metropolitan areas." Social Science Quarterly 48:299–310.

Wright, D. (1982) Understanding Intergovernmental Relations, 2nd ed. Monterey, Cal.: Brooks/Cole.

GAMES FEDERAL OFFICIALS PLAY:

THE CASE OF THE HOUSING ASSISTANCE PLANS

Frederick A. Lazin and Samuel Aroni

INTRODUCTION

Many housing experts and elected officials hoped that the Housing and Community Development Act of 1974 would end the divorce of "responsibility for overall community development from the responsibility of providing housing" (*Daily Congressional Record,* September 5, 1973:168). The legislation integrated into a single Community Development Block Grant (CDBG) previously separate grant-in-aid programs, including model cities, urban renewal, neighborhood development rehabilitiation loans, water and sewer grants, public and neightborhood facility loans, and grants for open space, urban beautification, and historic preservation. The U.S. Department of Housing and Urban Development (HUD) administered the new program.

Coordination with housing was to be achieved through the submission of a Housing Assistance Plan (HAP) as part of the annual CDBG application. The HAP measures housing conditions and needs of lower-income persons residing or expected to reside in the city, specifies annual and three-year housing goals by unit size and type to best serve the needs of lower-income persons, and indicates the housing location with "a view to furthering revitalization, promoting greater housing choice and avoiding undue concentration of low income persons" (U.S. Subcommittee of House Committee on Banking and Currency, 1974:2). Accordingly, then-HUD Secretary Carla Hills stated in July 1975 that the amount and mix of types of Section 8 Housing Assistance Programs for a particular community "should respond to local needs as expressed through the housing assistance plans of local communities" (U.S. Subcommittee on Housing and Community Development, 1975:11–15).[1] With the second year CDBG application the municipality had to present to HUD a Grantee Performance Report (GPR) citing progress toward achieving HAP goals (Polikoff, 1978:74).

This paper examines the implementation of the HAP component of the Housing and Community Development Act of 1974. It is based on an in-depth study of the annual submissions by the city of Los Angeles, California, and the subsequent review and approval process by HUD from 1975 through 1980 (Lazin and Aroni, 1983). The analysis focuses on the character and status of HUD regulations, the accuracy of the data submitted, and federal monitoring practices.

Although the paper focuses on the utility of the HAP as a basis for the coordination of federal urban policy and the allocation of federal housing assistance, it also deals with the issue of federal monitoring and control of the activities of local governmental units that administer federal programs. The success of the 1974 Act in coordinating community development and housing rests on the submission and quality of the HAP, prepared by local authorities and approved by HUD. Failure to submit or approval of an inaccurate or unrealistic document limits the achievement of the goals of the legislation.

The study is important for several reasons. It provides a rare glimpse at the actual implementation of planning theory and administrative reforms, logical in principle and problematic in practice. Moreover, the analysis of the HAP procedures and the relationship between the HAP, the CDGB application, and the HUD allocation of Section 8 adds to a sparse body of literature about a crucial component of contemporary federal urban policy.

Despite limitations, a case study has its advantages when compared to research based on national or regional samples. Although not necessarily typical, the case study illustrates in great depth and detail the problems of implementation and action of policies and practices introduced to overcome obstacles created by social, economic, and political conditions at the local level. Los Angeles, moreover, is representative of many major American cities in terms of its dealings with HUD and serves to illustrate many of the important issues and problems facing federal urban policies today.

THE HAP PROCESS

The city of Los Angeles submitted its HAP each year to the area HUD office, located in Los Angeles. The area HUD staff, in turn, conducted an in-house review of the CDBG application and HAP. HUD approval was forthcoming unless "the description of community development and housing needs and objectives is plainly inconsistent with generally available information, and activities proposed are plainly inappropriate to meeting stated needs and objectives, or the application does not comply with the requirements of the title or other applicable laws or proposed ineligible activities" (U.S. Subcommittee of House Committee on Banking and Currency, 1974:3).

During the period of submission and review of the first five HAPs, the city followed standard HUD procedure.[2] Similarly, HUD reviewed the applications, sometimes requesting revisions and clarifications, and then approved them. With the exception of the first year, the city, prior to formal submission, consulted extensively with HUD in preparing its HAP. For example, by the final year it gave HUD a draft for comments at least six months before formal submission. The following analysis focuses on (1) the HUD regulations, (2) the accuracy of data submitted by the city, and (3) HUD monitoring practices.

REGULATIONS

Several aspects of HUD regulations significantly affected the implementation process, the value of the HAPs for planning, coordination, and allocation of federal housing resources, and the ability of the federal agency to monitor local government activity. Many HUD regulations, for example, including those governing preparation of the HAPs and acceptability of data, changed continuously from year to year, contributing to confusion on the local level and uncertainty in the HUD area offices. The requirement that the city estimate the number of additional low-income persons expected to move into its jurisdiction during the coming year, the "expected to reside" (ETR) figure, illustrates the problem. This figure was essential for determining both housing needs and goals in the HAP. Initially HUD permitted a "zero" figure, that is, it accepted an estimate that no additional lower-income residents would reside in the city. Later, HUD found this unacceptable but then re-adopted its original position. Importantly, the decisions to submit and to approve a zero figure were based more on the formal HUD position than the actual number of additional families either the city or HUD expected to reside in the city in the coming year.

In addition, HUD regulations left undefined important terms like "high-" and "low-vacancy" rates and "substandard housing" that influenced the description of housing conditions and needs and the calculation of proper programs to meet them. The lack of clear definition meant that the city and HUD often referred to different phenomena when discussing substandard housing. In the case of housing needs for low-income persons, for example, HUD regulations left open the issue of whether or not to include all low-income persons or to exclude low-income residents of public housing and recipients of federal housing subsidies. Similarly, at times it was unclear to all whether to include as housing goals units to be inspected and upgraded by the landlords.

This uncertainty maximized the discretionary character of determining the city's needs and goals and made it more difficult for HUD to supervise and monitor local efforts. Undefined terms and unclear regulations opened for negotiation plans and figures submitted by the city. Rather than determine acceptability according to well-defined criteria, HUD area staff consulted confusing and often unclear guidelines. Much was left open to different interpretations, thus undercutting its authority. Consequently, much of what was submitted and then accepted or rejected was arbitrary. In the 1976/77 HAP, for example, the difference between HUD and city estimates of needs was 93,400 units.[3]

A related problem concerned the "realistic" nature of certain key elements of HUD regulations. Most significant was the HUD requirement that the city have a goal to supply 15% of its housing needs over three years.[4] Before the major housing slowdown in the later 1970s, the city and its private sector achieved less than one-third of the stated and approved HAP goal! Neither HUD, the state, the city, nor the private sector had the resources to reasonably accomplish this goal. For example, according to a City Council report in 1980, Los Angeles needed between 60,000 and 70,000 annual housing starts over the next five years to cope adequately with the needs of low- and moderate-income persons. But the city could be expected to muster at most a total of 15,000 units over the next five years, if it used all available federal, state, and municipal programs (*Los Angeles Times*, April 1, 1980). The ludicrous nature of these regulations is also seen in the response by HUD to revised and scaled-down figures in 1978. Although the HUD reviewers raised doubts about the accuracy of the match between needs and goals, they wrote: "goals are much *more reasonable,* although they still exceed potential funding level by ten times."[5]

Finally, HUD violated its own regulations and criteria for the HAP. This occurred with the Loan Management Set Aside, by which HUD allocated Section 8 subsidies to bail out previously insured FHA projects in serious financial difficulties. In Los Angeles many of the projects for which subsidies were used were located in areas that conflicted with HAP-designated and HUD-approved locations for low- and moderate-income housing (U.S. Department of Housing and Urban Development, 1977:71, 65).

THE DATA

An inquiry into the subject of data raises serious questions about the validity and worth of the entire HAP process. HUD is concerned essentially that data sources be "recent," as required by law, but fails to emphasize accuracy. For example, during the first- and second-year HAPs, the city used the 1970 Census to determine housing needs and vacancy rates. In the third year it supplemented its continued use of the 1970 Census with the 1974 Annual Housing Survey of HUD, the Postal Vacancy Survey (PVS), and the City Housing Environmental Study. On the latter source one HUD area analyst responsible for monitoring market conditions commented: it "is not accurate but meets our minimum criteria." Thereafter HUD persuaded the city to use figures from the Southern California Area Government's (SCAG) HUD-approved Area-Wide Housing Opportunities Allocation Plan (AHOP). Although a HUD official deemed the SCAG AHOP an aggregation of HAPs within its jurisdiction, not more accurate than the city of Los Angeles data but uniform within the region, another commented that the SCAG model was inaccurate but consistent, that is "consistently inaccurate in all communities."

Equally important for the issue of the validity of the data is that HUD was unable to determine the accuracy of the figures submitted by the city. There is no basis to claim that HUD estimates were any more accurate than those of the city. The Los Angeles area office Economic and Market Analysis Division (EMAD) admitted to its inability to determine accurately vacancy rates, Fair Market Rents (FMR), and housing needs in the city of Los Angeles. It also questioned the accuracy of the annual computation of FMRs done by HUD's central office (Washington, D.C.) for each county in the United States as well as the Annual Housing Survey (1976) on which it is based.[6] According to one area office official, the FMR is basically realistic or functional only in areas impacted with racial minorities. Others argue that the FMR "is out of date before you print it" because of inflation. In other words, it is unrealistic from the moment it is issued.

MONITORING

During the first year HUD seemed determined to approve the city's HAP regardless of shortcomings. For example, the HUD area office overruled its Economic and Market Analysis Division's decision that the first-year goals were unacceptable and should be revised downward. In approving the CDBG application, the area office requested that the city "give more thought" in the future to the matter of Hap goals, but ruled that the original goals were acceptable.[7] A year later HUD supported EMAD's reservations about the second-year HAP and forced the city to make revisions. EMAD had found the HAP unacceptable on grounds that identified needs are "plainly inconsistent with generally available facts and data" and "programs and activities are plainly inappropriate to the needs and objectives identified in HAP."[8] HUD had also noted that the goal of providing assistance for 263,000 units (25% of need) was "laudable but totally unrealistic" when the city only provided an additional 9000 units of its goal of 29,000 the previous year.[9] During the third, fourth, and fifth years HUD continued to require revision of goals and other aspects of the HAP application.[10]

Before concluding effective monitoring by HUD, it is necessary to weigh HUD's response to the city's failure to implement the previously approved HAPs. The requirement that the city submit an Annual Grantee Performance Report beginning with its second-year HAP supplied HUD with evidence of the city's progress or lack of it.

With the submittal of the city's first Grantee Performance Report in April 1976, HUD became concerned about the lack of progress in implementing housing goals as set down in the first-year HAP. The city failed to construct or rehabilitate a single housing unit toward the proposed first-year goals of 8180 and 1000 units for Section 8 new construction and substantial rehabilitation, respectively. Of the 7500-unit Section 8 goal for existing housing, the city rented only 431 units of the 4000-unit allocation it received from HUD. Reports of poor results continued to follow through the next four years. While HUD's policy became one of consistently forcing the city to reduce its objectives, as described above, it continued to approve goals that could not possibly be implemented. In effect, this process of revising and scaling down goals was a charade by which HUD forced the city to change numbers that had virtually no relation to reality. Neither the city not its private sector could provide new, rehabilitated, or existing units for low-income persons in accordance with HAP goals, nor could HUD fund its programs at the level set down in the HAP. For example, HUD approved figures for Section 8 goals in the second-year HAP that exceeded HUD's funding for the entire Los Angeles County.[11] The most important concern of all parties was conformity to formal regulations, regardless of the accuracy of the figures, the potential to fund, or the feasibility to implement.

Regardless of the inflated goals and the city's poor record in implementing its HAP, HUD refused to hold up the CDGB funding. Each year HUD approved the HAPs after review and chastisement. Those in the area office who objected to inflated goals and dismal results in providing housing eventually yielded to pressures from their superiors to approve a revised HAP and to urge the city to improve its housing record. Typical is HUD's letter to the city, informing it of the approval of the fourth-year CDBG: "It is thus the city's responsibility to demonstrate to this Department's satisfaction that . . . the lack of progress toward meeting goals is due to factors beyond the city's control."[12]

Perhaps most illustrative of the meaning of HUD monitoring is its response to an administrative complaint that was filed in May 1979 against the city of Los Angeles's fifth-year CDBG application.[13] The complaint charged that the CDBG application and its HAP were inconsistent with generally available data and that proposed programs, especially housing, did not meet stated needs of low-income as well as moderate-income persons and created displacement without a strategy to help those displaced. The major objection was that the HAP failed to address the critical shortage of low-income housing. Part of the problem, the complainants argued, was that the use of SCAG data and plans allowed the city to provide less housing for low-income persons on the grounds that within the region the suburbs should provide more to make up for past imbalances in low-income construction between the central city and suburbs. Orange County and other suburban communities, it held, would not build subsidized housing, thus hurting the poor of Los Angeles.

After receiving the revised figures, HUD decided to approve the HAP and CDBG application, thus rejecting the complaint. In a letter approving the CDBG application HUD criticized the city's housing record:

> The record indicates that the city has had only limited success in implementing its goals. The city achieved only 30 percent of all housing proposed in its 1976 three year goals through December 31, 1978. Most housing went to senior citizens, and the least amount to family units where the greatest need exists. . . .[14]

Hud called on the city to commit itself to developing homes for families and to "take positive steps" and aggressive action to encourage private builders to get involved in HUD programs and to utilize Section 8 certificates.

Although the above letter lends support to the charges brought against the city in the complaint, the area HUD office justified the city's housing record both publicly and to its Washington office. Its Economic and Market Analysis Division, for example, defended the city's statement of housing needs in the revised fifth-year HAP of May 1979 as being consistent with SCAG guidelines for setting three-year goals at 9% of needs and annual goals at 3%. In a report to its superiors in Washington, area HUD noted that the city's use of CDBG monies had more than adequately served low- and moderate-income persons and that revised goals corresponded with needs. While repeating its statement that the city had to make greater efforts, it noted that the overly ambitious statement of goals had made the city's accomplishment appear to be "even worse than it is."[16]

CONCLUSION

Polikoff (1978:74–76) argues convincingly that the link between community development and the HAP is illusory because the city is not required to implement the HAP. The findings here suggest an additional explanation for the failure to achieve this goal, namely, the tendency of HUD to approve HAPs containing incorrect and unrealistic data about housing conditions, needs, and goals. The practice contradicts the very foundation of the HAP to provide an accurate picture of housing conditions and needs of lower-income persons in order to serve as the basis for coordinating community development and housing. Moreover, the approval of unrealistic goals that neither HUD could fund nor the city and its private sector provide ensures further shortcomings in implementing the HAP.

During the five years reviewed here HUD received HAPs submitted by the city of Los Angeles that HUD professionals knew to be inaccurate and unrealistic. Although it consistently questioned and criticized the city's figures, goals, and performances, HUD approved each HAP. When a significant challenge was made against the city's fifth-year plan, HUD chose to defend the city. In pursuing this policy HUD foreclosed on its potential option to obtain a more accurate and meaningful HAP to serve as the basis for coordination of federal community development and housing assistance programs. Equally important, it undercut its own influence and ability to monitor and control the actions of the lower governmental unit.

In traditional terms this can be seen as a case of "constituency relation" whereby the local authority coopts the federal agency to serve rather than regulate local operation of a federal program (Selznick, 1966:147, 148; Lazin, 1973;264). In Edwards's terms federal officials often exhibit:

> a service rather than a regulatory orientation toward officials of lower level jurisdictions, who actually implement many programs. In other words, officials of higher level jurisdictions approach implementation from the standpoint of asking officials of lower level jurisdictions for assistance rather than from the standpoint of imposing the will of a higher level jurisdiction upon them. The hope is that through such an approach lower level officials will give them at least some of what they want (Edwards, 1980:74).

Why was HUD either unable or reluctant to influence or alter the efforts of the city of Los Angeles? Several reasons explain HUD's position. First HUD did not issue "clear, accurate, and consistent" regulations (Edwards, 1980:9–11). Thus, HUD monitoring centered on an element of arbitrary discretion rather than enforcement of clear rules. As noted in a previous study of the failure of HUD to enforce civil rights regulations, when "there is no explicit regulation or binding rule to enforce," then bargaining rather than regulation occurs (Lazin, 1973:267). For example, in many of the HAPs the city initially included as units to be rehabilitated those that would rent out of the range of low-income persons. Rather than be excluded automatically, this became a subject of negotiation between the city and HUD. To ensure the possibility of effective regulation, therefore, there is a need for explicit and clear regulations in which key terms are defined.

Second, HUD lacked the resources to monitor the city's implementation of the HAP. More important than the lack of sufficient manpower was the absence of skills (Edwards, 1980:61). The value of the HAP was based on the assumption that data could be obtained about housing conditions and needs of a particular community. Evidence here suggests that HUD had no accurate empirical knowledge of the conditions of the housing market, vacancy rates, and housing needs for Los Angeles. According to HUD personnel responsible for obtaining such information, the figures and data supplied by municipal, federal and SCAG officials were either inaccurate or out of date. HUD lacked, moreover, a methodology to obtain the information. Economic and Market Analysis Division staff were unable to determine vacancy rates, FMR, and other essential aspects of the HUD HAP. Consequently, HUD could not judge the accuracy of criteria and figures submitted by the city. This situation also contributed to a tendency to stick to formal regulations regardless of actual market conditions and made most decisions on figures arbitrary. In effect, HUD was unable to determine or obtain information necessary to properly monitor the compliance with federal regulations by a local authority implementing a federal program.

If the situation in Los Angeles is typical, then HUD operates a program designed to coordinate community development and housing assistance without accurate knowledge of the housing needs and conditions of the environments to be served. Evidently the use of computers and advanced technology does not guarantee a more correct empirical picture of the environment. It is still very difficult to determine the numbers of people in our cities, their housing needs, vacancy rates, and housing conditions. If the Economic and Market Analysis Division of the Los Angeles area HUD office is to be believed, then we seriously underestimate the inaccuracy of federal surveys and samples that HUD and cities use. Much more attention should be given to this serious phenomenon of not being able to determine and compute empirically housing conditions of urban America. This shortcoming must be addressed by HUD and others if we intend to adapt models of planning to actual practices in hopes of coordinating community development and housing subsidies in a meaningful way.

Finally, a lack of commitment by HUD to enforce HAP requirements and objectives contributed to the manner in which the city implemented the federal program. Staff of several divisions of the area office seemed concerned about the accuracy of the application. Changing and unclear regulations and inadequate skills and resources to verify market conditions, however, hindered their ability to perform its statutory functions. In the final analysis they exercised flexibility and accepted decisions from their superiors restricting their reservations and objections to the HAP.

In contrast, the orientation of senior area HUD personnel was toward serving rather than regulating. They wanted to avoid controversy or a showdown with the city (Edwards, 1980:67). Too much money and activity were at stake in the CDBG to be overly concerned with details of the HAP. They insisted, therefore, on formal compliance with regulations and procedures regardless of the accuracy of the data or actual performance by the city in achieving its approved goals. Their position thus ensured that important aspects of the HAP intended to coordinate housing and community development became a farce.

In order for HUD to monitor more effectively the activities of local authorities implementing federal programs, the attitude of HUD senior officials must change. Unless they are committed to compliance it is unlikely that their subordinates will act to enforce regulations that may conflict with local interests. The problem is political. The federal character of the American political system in which local authorities and interests are represented in national political and legislative institutions having oversight over federal departments, including HUD, accounts for many of the failings of federal monitoring practices. No change in the status quo should be anticipated as the service ideology probably reflects the political balance of power between local and national interests in the United States.

In the meantime it is interesting to ask whether hundreds of municipalities throughout the United States have submitted inaccurate figures and documents that have been approved by HUD and serve as the basis for coordination of federal community development and housing assistance programs.

NOTES

1. The Section 8 Housing Assistance Program was also enacted by the Housing and Community Development Act of 1974. Funding was not, however, part of the CDBG. Section 8 provided rent subsidies for new construction, existing housing, and substandard rehabilitation.

2. The first five HAPs were for the years 1975/6, 1976/7, 1977/8, 1978/9, and 1979/80.

3. Memo, Bricker to Franco (May 3, 1976). HUD claimed that the city overestimated small family needs by 125%. All memos and letters cited here are from the HUD area office files in Los Angeles, California.

4. HUD area office allowed the city to adopt Southern California Area Government policy of providing 9% of its housing need over three years or 3% in one year. The housing could also be provided within the SCAG area rather than being restricted to city limits.

5. HUD area office memo (June 2, 1978) (emphasis added). These figures were later scaled down.

6. HUD's central office computes annually the FMR for units by bedroom size and for elevator and nonelevator buildings for all counties in the United States. Through March 29, 1979 HUD used the 1970 Census tape of recent movers, updated by the Consumer Price Index (CPI). Thereafter, it used the Annual Housing Survey (1976), also updated by the CPI.

7. Letters, Camfield to Mayor Bradley (May 9, 1975) and Roberts to Camfield (May 20, 1975).

8. EMAD memo (May 3, 1976).

9. Letter, Crisp to Mayor Bradley (May 12, 1976).

10. Nevertheless, in the fifth-year review two senior staff members overruled objections of subordinates and recommended approval "because of time constraints" [Letter, Zellhart to Crisp (June 18, 1979)].

11. EMAD memo (June 14, 1976).

12. Letter, Roberts to Mayor Bradley (June 28, 1978).

13. Attorney Joel S. Aronson filed the complaint (Comments on City of Los Angeles

5th year CDBG Application before the U.S. Dept. of HUD) with HUD on behalf of the California Public Policy Center, the Central City Tenant Action Center, the Coalition for Economic Survival, the Concerned Citizens of the Chicano Community of Canoga Park, the Greater University Parish, the Little Tokyo's People's Rights Organization, the People's Housing and Community Development Corporation, the Venice Town Council, and the Westside Action Center.

14. Letter, HUD area office to Mayor Bradley (June 29, 1979).
15. Letter, Bricker to Sabella (June 15, 1979).
16. Letter, Sabella to HUD Washington (October 1, 1979).

REFERENCES

Cole, R. (1977) "The politics of housing and community development in America: The Housing and Community Development Act of 1974." In D. Caputo (ed.), The Politics of Policy Making in America. San Francisco: Freeman.
Daily Congressional Record (September 5, 1973). Washington, D.C.: U.S. Government Printing Office.
Edwards, III, G. C. (1980) Implementing Public Policy. Washington, D.C.: Congressional Quarterly Press.
Larzin, F. (1973) "The failure of federal enforcement of civil rights regulations in public housing, 1963–1971: the co-optation of a federal agency by its local constituency." Policy Sciences 4:263–73.
Larzin, F., and S. Aroni (1983) The Existing Section 8 Program and the Housing Assistance Plans: A Case Study of Los Angeles and HUD, 1975–1980. Los Angeles: Graduate School of Architecture and Urban Planning (UCLA).
Los Angeles Times (April 1, 1980).
Polikoff, A. (1978) Housing the Poor: The Case for Heroism. Cambridge, Mass.: Ballinger.
Selznick, P. (1966) TVA and the Grass Roots. New York: Harper & Row.
U.S. Department of Housing and Urban Development, Office of Policy Development and Program Evaluation (1977) Section 8 Housing Assistance Payments Program: The Loan Management Set Aside. A Field Study. Washington D.C.: HUD.
U.S. Subcommittee on Housing and Community Development of the House Committee on Banking and Currency (1974) Directory of Recipients of Housing and Community Development Act of 1974. 93rd Congress, 2nd Session. Washington, D.C.: U.S. Government Printing Office.
U.S. Subcommittee on Housing and Community Development of the House Committee on Banking, Currency and Housing (1975) Hearings on Implementation of Section 8 and Other Housing Programs. 94th Congress, 1st Session. Washington, D.C.: U.S. Government Printing Office.

PART IV

SERVICE DELIVERY AND EQUITY

IMPLEMENTING URBAN SERVICES

Kenneth R. Mladenka

INTRODUCTION

Urban public services are essential to the safety, health, and well-being of citizens. Life could not proceed in any civilized way without them. These services are so routine that we seldom consider how vital they really are: police and fire protection, education, transportation, water, sewerage, refuse collection, recreation, flood control, sanitation, and health. One of the myths about these services is that they have little to do with politics. What is political about picking up the garbage, patrolling the streets, educating students, providing an adequate water supply, or maintaining a fire protection system?

In fact, the implementation of routine public services is fraught with opportunities for political conflict. The political issues and choices inherent in service delivery decisions are significant. Which services should be provided? How much of a particular service should be delivered? Which services should be assigned priority? Who should pay for the service? How should burdens and benefits be distributed among the population? Who will win and who will lose?

I will consider a variety of issues relevant to the implementation of urban public services. First, I will examine those factors that complicate

171

effective implementation. Second, I will evaluate competing conceptions of equity in service distribution and emphasize the value judgments implicit in each equity standard. Third, I will examine the research evidence from a variety of cities with respect to distributional patterns and comment on the role played by decision rules, professional norms, technical-rational criteria, and the bureaucrat-elected official conflict over service delivery.

THE ENVIRONMENT OF SERVICE DELIVERY

Municipal governments are severely limited in terms of their ability to manage their environments. They are acted upon by a variety of forces over which they have little or no control. Many cities are unable to generate sufficient revenues because of state limitations on their ability to levy taxes. Frequently, cities are required to provide expensive, state-mandated programs in the absence of adequate state aid and financing. State limitations on the city's annexation authority further restrict its capacity to respond to change.

The role played by the federal government also illustrates the city's dependency. Many cities rely heavily upon federal aid. Their fiscal health is closely tied to the structure and funding of federal aid programs. Federal intervention in a variety of local activities and institutions further impinges upon the ability of the city to conduct and manage its own affairs. Examples range from court involvement in the local educational system to federal rulings that dictate changes in the city's electoral system. There are few areas of local government that are immune from the control or direct influence of state and federal authorities.

The city is also particularly susceptible to the play of private sector forces. The circulation of jobs, money, and credit within the city and between the central city and suburbs exerts dramatic impacts upon the behavior of metropolitan areas. Private investment decisions determine whether the city will grow or decay. The strength and vitality of the city are also heavily dependent upon the personal choices and preferences of individual citizens. The massive exodus of middle- and upper-class families to the suburbs (and the continuing threat of further population erosion) has had a major impact upon urban development.

Urban political authorities are highly sensitive to business and upper-class goals because they perceive that propertied interests are in the best interests of the city as a whole. They identify with the wealthy rather than the poor because the former are associated with economic growth, jobs, low taxes, reasonable expenditure levels, and social stability. The underclass is synonymous with white flight, high unemployment, rising taxes, increasing service demands, and social disorganization. The already limited capacity of local public officials to deal with their problems is further restricted by the need to placate powerful economic interests. To antagonize a major employer is to run the risk of weakening the tax base of the city. To pursue policies that will anger middle- and upper-class neighborhoods is foolhardy when wealthy citizens can simply relocate to a nearby suburb if they become sufficiently disenchanted with public programs.

I have argued that cities are severely limited in terms of their ability to shape and control their own destinies. Constitutionally, they are creations of their respective state governments. As such, they are heavily dependent upon the state for grants of power and resources. The reliance of cities upon federal aid further restricts their capacity to realize their policy agendas. Finally, the advantageous bargaining position of economic interests and of upper-class citizens greatly reduces the extent to which local public officials can pursue an independent course of action.

The only arena in which urban political authorities still maintain significant control is the service delivery one. Essential public services such as police and fire protection and education remain the responsibility of local government. Although many city governments are virtually powerless in major policy areas such as the regulation of business, income redistribution, and social welfare programs, they retain program authority for vital urban services.

The effective implementation of these services is not an easy task. Several factors complicate the implementation process. First, many of these services, such as education and police protection, are capable of generating intense conflict. Many parents, for example, look to the public schools as an avenue of upward mobility for their children. The perception that certain policy changes will operate to weaken the educational system may stimulate significant citizen involvement and conflict. Many people believe that they have a large, personal stake in public services. Consequently, their expectations for the service, as well as their propensity to express their grievances and discontents, are exceedingly high. When services are essential to citizen safety, well-being, and hopes for the future, whether and how they are delivered can arouse widespread public concern and involvement.

Citizen involvement complicates the implementation process because public officials have less freedom to deliver services according to established decision rules and routines when citizens impose multiple and conflicting demands. Differing public preferences require the bureaucrat to balance competing expectations.

Another factor that complicates implementation is the divisible nature of many services. More and better qualified policemen, firemen, garbage collectors, dogcatchers, and teachers can be assigned to some neighborhoods than to others. Some neighborhoods can have better schools, parks, libraries, and streets than others. The public perception that some receive more and others receive less increases the possibility for conflict over who does and who should get what. Of course, these perceptions may simply be wrong. What is significant, however, is that implementation is more difficult when some groups of citizens consistently complain that they are receiving less than others. If the expression of such grievances is sufficiently intense (in the form of legal action, for example), public officials may be required to actually redistribute service resources. The divisible nature of public services introduces another element of risk and uncertainty into the bureaucrat's environment. Citizen demands for redistribution complicate implementation because the public official is forced to pay more attention to political factors. Professional values such as service efficiency, effectiveness, and impact are accorded a lower priority.

Implementation is also made more difficult by the considerable variation in need and preferences for services. For example, poor people may well prefer more parks and fewer libraries. Differences in preference extend to the same service as well. Wealthy parents are likely to expect the public schools to serve as a college preparatory institution. Minority parents may well prefer that more vocational training programs be offered and that the neighborhood be given more control over the way its schools are run—control that extends to the hiring, firing, and promotion of teachers and staff. Similarly, some neighborhoods expect the police to devote the bulk of their time and resources to the enforcement of the criminal law and the apprehension of criminal suspects. Other citizens expect that the police should perform a service as well as a criminal-enforcement function.

These conflicting needs, preferences, and expectations are difficult to satisfy. As a result, it is frequently impossible for local governments to please all, most, or even some of its constituents. For example, the police cannot be all things to all people. Many citizens expect them to spend most of their time enforcing the law and catching criminals. One study found, however, that 90% of the police effort was devoted to functions other than the traditional law enforcement one (Wilson, 1968). Even the same citizen may expect a particular service to pursue a variety of goals and achieve a number of different and even conflicting objectives. We want the police to regulate traffic, perform community relations, apprehend suspects, investigate crimes, come when we call (even though the call may have little to do with a criminal act or violation of a criminal law), and provide information. These conflicting expectations immensely complicate effective implementation because the same service is required to perform a variety of functions and achieve contradictory goals. Since the service delivery system is simply incapable of satisfying conflicting needs, preferences, and expectations, the public official makes service delivery choices in an atmosphere characterized by confusion and uncertainty. Effective implementation is difficult when service goals are unclear because citizens demand the accomplishment of conflicting objectives.

The conflict between elected officials and bureaucrats adds another layer of complexity to the implementation process. Bureaucrats are a powerful force in local government. In many departments they enjoy a virtual monopoly over information, experience, and expertise. Elected officials come and go. Bureaucrats are career administrators. They develop expertise in a narrow area of governmental operations. Frequently, elected officials are simply unequipped by virtue of training, information, and inclination to challenge bureaucratic choices. There are too many services to provide and too many decisions to make to permit elected political authorities to exercise effective direction and control over dozens of separate agencies.

This observation is particularly accurate in those instances where the issues under consideration involve complex technical matters. Decisions that appear to involve only routine, technical choices may actually have significant political implications and consequences. Because of bureaucratic power, elected officials are often forced to rely upon the bureaucrats themselves for an evaluation of whether policy change should be initiated. If they do order that a new policy be implemented, public officials must trust the bureaucrats to put the change into effect. Their powers to force compliance are severely limited.

Implementation is further complicated by the fact that lower-level bureaucrats are often immune from control by top-level administrators. How can the police chief know if the officer on the street is enforcing all laws rigorously and fairly? How can the department head determine if the building inspector is performing his duty in compliance with the provisions of the building code? Establishing and maintaining control over the "street-level" bureaucrat is immensely difficult and probably impossible. There are never enough supervisors to monitor performance. The problem is particularly acute for vital services such as police protection and education since the policeman on the beat and the teacher in the classroom *is* the service. Directives from agency and bureau chiefs may be carefully followed by some street-level bureaucrats, partially implemented by others, and completely ignored by still others. If elected political authorities often cannot get the bureaucracy to do what they would like, it is also frequently the case that the heads of city agencies find it exceedingly difficult to modify the behavior of workers at the level at which tangible services are actually delivered to clients (Nivola, 1978; Lipsky, 1976).

Control of the street-level bureaucrat is made even more difficult by the fact that organizational goals are frequently unclear. They are generally implicit rather than explicit, conflicting rather than compatible. In the absence of clearly defined and expressed goals, however, the street-level bureaucrat is *forced* to exercise personal discretion and pursue his own vision of the appropriate organizational mission. Upper-echelon control of employees requires that there exist a shared set of expectations with respect to task performance. Objectives must be clearly stated. In fact, however, service delivery goals are frequently vague or unexpressed. Is the street cop to enforce all the laws? If not, which violations should be ignored? How rigorously should laws be enforced? Should different standards be employed in some neighborhoods and for some groups? Should the law be uniformly applied even if such consistent application appears to violate widely shared norms and values in some neighborhoods? Should the police officer concentrate on the most serious crimes or should he devote his effort to those offenses most likely to be solved? Should he respond to all citizen requests for service even if many of these requests are so-called nuisance calls and have nothing to do with violations of the criminal law?

Generally, police departments provide little or no guidance to the street officer with respect to these and other major issues. Consequently, the cop on the beat is required to make his own determination and apply his own interpretations with respect to departmental priorities and organizational goals. As a result, street-level discretion is encouraged rather than restricted and controlled.

It should be noted that some public services are easier to implement than others. For example, park and library services involve the delivery of tangible facilities and resources at fixed sites and locations. The use of the services is discretionary. While the public employees who staff these facilities are not irrelevant to client utilization, they are certainly far less crucial than is the case for police, education, and building inspection services. Implementation is much easier to accomplish for these services that do not require control of the street-level bureaucrat (Mladenka, 1980).

Still another factor that complicates effective implementation of basic public services revolves around the multiple-dimension nature of service delivery systems. We can think of the service process in terms of at least three distinct stages: resources, activities, and results. For police, personnel and equipment are examples of resources while patrolling, responding to calls for service, and investigating crimes are all examples of police activities. Examples of results include crime rates, number of crimes solved, citizen satisfaction with police services, and public fear of crime.

These various levels of the service delivery system make implementation more difficult because of the confusion that exists with respect to the uniqueness of the different stages and relationship between them. For example, demands for more and better police protection generally center upon additional manpower and equipment. However, significantly greater numbers of police may have only a marginal impact upon activities and no discernible effect at all upon results. In fact, the relationship between resources and results is very poorly understood. What is known is that a variety of factors other than service resources exert significant impacts upon service outcomes. More police, for example, may have no effect upon crime rates. Instead, crime levels may reflect a much higher association with poverty, unemployment, and density.

The public, however, frequently misunderstands the relationship between the various stages. For example, citizens expect that more police officers will translate into better police protection and lower crime rates. The failure on the part of the typical citizen to recognize the highly tenuous linkage between resources and outcomes accounts in large part for public frustration and dissatisfaction with government services. When more policemen (particularly when they are accompanied by a tax increase) do not automatically translate into quicker response times, more visible neighborhood patrols, lower crime rates, and more crimes solved, the result is apt to be public disenchantment. Citizen expectations for dramatic improvements in service outcomes are easily heightened by enhanced levels of service resources. They are just as easily dashed when such results do not automatically materialize.

The degree of difficulty involved in implementing public services also varies from city to city as well as from neighborhood to neighborhood within cities. One significant factor is the level of resources available to different governments. Cities with substantial resources are better able to effectively implement services than those experiencing fiscal strain. For example, governments with slack resources are capable of responding to conflicting expectations for the same service. I have previously discussed how different groups may expect the police to perform different functions: fight crime, provide routine, noncrime-related services on an individual basis, maintain order, enforce the laws, or regulate traffic.

Cities with high resource levels are in a much better position than other
to employ sufficient police to fulfill most or even all of these expecta
tions. Cities with inadequate public funds are forced to make choice
among conflicting demands and goals. When they do so, they will likel
antagonize some groups of citizens. If citizens become sufficiently dis
gruntled, they will express their grievances and discontents throug
participation in decision-making processes such as attendance at publi
hearings and law suits. Enhanced citizen involvement complicates imple
mentation because it forces public officials to balance competing politica
demands.

It is also significant that the element of street-level discretion on th
part of the bureaucrat assumes greater importance in heterogeneou
cities. When citizen values and preferences clash, the street-level em
ployee is forced to choose among conflicting public expectations in th
discharge of his duties. The individual policeman, teacher, and buildin
inspector cannot satisfy all preferences when preferences conflict. Th
biases of some citizens are implemented in decisions about service deliv
ery while the preferences of others are excluded.

Whether the governmental jurisdiction represents a central city loca
tion or a suburban area also makes a difference with respect to the eas
with which public services are implemented. Central city jurisdiction
are more likely to contain heterogeneous populations than suburbar
areas. In addition, central city governments are generally subject t
greater financial strain than suburban governments. For reasons alread
mentioned, both factors complicate the implementation process.

The concept of coproduction is also relevant to implementation. Cit
izens share in the production of services by contributing to or detractin
from efficiency and effectiveness in delivery. For example, some citizen
carefully package their garbage and place it in the appropriate locatior
for collection. Others simply toss it out at the curb. Some citizens take
pains to keep their neighborhood parks clean while others misuse the
equipment, discard their trash, and even commit acts of vandalism
Some neighborhood residents play a very active role in their publi
schools by contributing time, money, and effort as well as disciplinec
and well-prepared students. Other parents do nothing. The quality o
services delivered is determined, in large part, by the citizen's contribu
tion to the production of these services.

I have discussed a variety of factors that complicate the effective im
plementation of basic local services. They include the fact that appar
ently mundane services actually involve basic human values, conflicting
needs and demands for service, the divisible nature of municipal ser
vices, insulation of the bureaucracy from political control, the tremen

ous discretion enjoyed by the street-level bureaucrat, the multiple ages of the service delivery process, varying levels of wealth and heterogeneity, and citizen coproduction of services.

IMPLEMENTATION AND EQUITY

We now turn to a discussion of how competing conceptions of equity further hamper successful implementation. Equity involves justice and fairness. The immense problem from an implementation perspective is that what constitutes fairness is open to a variety of differing interpretations. What appears to be indisputably fair to the public official and a majority of citizens may well strike a substantial minority of the population as eminently unjust. The public official is forced to grapple with these distinctly normative concerns during the process of implementing public services.

Conceptions of Equity

Every service delivery decision involves an explicit or implicit standard of equity. The equity dimension is particularly relevant at the distributional stage. How should service benefits be distributed across neighborhoods and groups? Should some receive more than others? Under what conditions? We can identify at least five competing conceptions of equity: equality, need, demand, preference, and willingness and ability to pay. Each will produce a distinctly different distributional pattern.

Equality in distribution implies only an approximation of strict equality. What is really indicated is that differences in the distribution of benefits will be limited to some permissible or acceptable range of variation. The differences that are tolerated will be unrelated to the characteristics of the population and the conditions of neighborhoods. Dissimilar clients and environments will be treated similarly. It should also be noted that equality in distribution is relevant at each stage of the process: resources, activities, and results. For police services, equality in distribution would mean an equal number of patrolmen per 1000 population (resources), equality of response times to citizen calls originating in different parts of the city (activities), and equality of crime rates across neighborhoods (results). Of course, equality of results would imply a highly unequal distribution of resources because many more policemen would be required in high crime areas.

Need as equity assumes that some citizens have a greater need for services than others and that these needs are entitled to preferential consideration in distributional choices. One of the difficulties associated

with implementing need as equity is that it is the equity standard that i
most likely to generate intense political controversy and conflict. Dis
tribution based on need obviously implies a highly unequal distribution
of service resources and benefits. Since many urban services exhibit a
potential for high divisibility, need as equity frequently enters delibera
tions at the local level about appropriate equity standards.

Demand as equity indicates that public services should be distributed
according to variations in citizen demand. Demand can be expressed in a
variety of ways. Use of services and service facilities implies demand
Requests for and complaints about services also express demand. The
communication of demand to political authorities is apt to vary widely
across groups and neighborhoods (Verba and Nie, 1972; Eisinger
1972). Therefore, distribution of service resources and benefits on the
basis of demand will produce a highly unequal distributional pattern

Another equity concept is preference. Services could be distributed
according to the variation in citizen preferences for public programs and
facilities. Differences in service preferences are closely associated with
differences in personal incomes. Poor people are likely to have a greater
preference than wealthier citizens for public recreational programs and
facilities because their access to private recreational opportunities is lim
ited. Rich persons are apt to have a greater preference for library ser
vices and other publicly supported cultural activities. Responsiveness to
the variation in consumer preference will produce a highly uneven and
involved pattern of public benefits.

A final standard of equity is willingness and ability to pay. Many local
services are currently provided on that basis: garbage collection, water
sewerage, recreational facilities. All could be. No citizen would be al
lowed to consume a service unless he was willing and able to pay for it at
the time of consumption. The individual assessment of specific costs
rather than reliance upon tax and grant revenue, would be employed to
finance service delivery. The intent would be to duplicate the operation
of the private sector as closely as possible. Citizen preference would
become susceptible to precise measurement.

Implications of Equity Standards

The requirement that public officials resolve the equity issue im
mensely complicates implementation because it increases the choice
available. Each equity concept produces a distinct set of winners and
losers. Equality as equity enjoys the virtue of simplicity because it ignore
the variation in need. It is unlikely to generate substantial political con
flict because poor persons are not singled out for preferential treatment

Under some conditions, however, equality in distribution is absurd. For example, neighborhoods with extraordinarily high crime and fire hazard rates would not be allocated more resources than areas that seldom experience a crime or fire. Consequently, equality is most apt to be employed for those services for which dramatic spillover effects are *not* perceived. That is, it is more likely to be used as a guide to distributional policy for recreational services than for so-called protective services such as police and fire.

Need as equity implies an array of difficulties with respect to implementation. For example, measurement of need is more complicated than it appears at first glance. How should need for public recreation services be determined? Variations in income levels may be too gross an indicator of differences in need. More precise and appropriate measures might include age, mobility, crime and delinquency rates, differences in access to private recreational facilities, and unemployment, welfare, and poverty levels.

Another problem with need as equity revolves around the issue of how great a share of resources to provide to different need categories. Let us assume that need is measured according to income levels. How many more service resources should low-income neighborhoods receive than are provided in wealthy areas? Should middle-income citizens receive more than upper-income clients? How much more? Why? Should need as equity apply only to the distribution of resources or should it extend to service activities and results as well? Under what conditions? Who should control the operationalization and measurement of need, bureaucrats or elected officials?

Demand and ability to pay also ensure that some citizens will receive higher service levels than others. However, these equity standards are less likely to stimulate opposition because the differential distribution that results from their use will disproportionately benefit the better-off. Need is unique in that it tends to confer greater service benefits on the disadvantaged. Consequently, arousal of the politically active segment of the population is most apt to occur in response to need as equity.

Demand is frequently used in American cities to determine the distribution of service benefits. It enjoys several advantages from the perspective of the urban administrator. Unlike need as equity, demand does not require public officials to develop allegedly objective indicators. Instead, they gather data on user rates and the number of complaints/requests, and distribution occurs on that basis. They rely upon the number of citizen calls for police service, circulation rates at branch libraries, user levels at neighborhood recreation facilities, and complaints about the condition of neighborhood streets to distribute service resources. The higher the user and complaint/request level, the large the share of available resources. The local official is not required t undertake elaborate measurements of consumer need or preferenc Resource distribution simply coincides with the variation in clien demand.

Another virtue of demand as equity is that it appears to emphasiz rationality in the allocation of public resources. The administrator ca easily defend demand by pointing out to critics that the most efficien and effective use of available resources is to distribute them to areas o high consumption. It is unreasonable to provide services to citizens wh have not used them or asked for them. It is wasteful to distribute re sources on the basis of equality or need since demand alone allows th administrator to determine if the service will actually be consumed b the potential client. All citizens have the opportunity to express deman through use of existing services or through communications with polit cal authorities. If they fail to express such demand, it would represent gross misuse of scarce resources to provide those citizens with high se vice levels.

Another advantage of demand as equity from the perspective of th government official is that it entails responsiveness to citizen grievances Local political authorities are keenly sensitive to the argument that thei primary function as officeholders is to respond to and solve the person problems of their constituents. To ignore citizen demands and impos one's own value judgments with respect to the appropriate division o resources is to violate a canon of local government. Equality and need a equity tamper with the sanctity of that pervasive and powerful premise Demand does not.

However, demand as equity may impose severe penalties on som citizens. There is some evidence to suggest that blacks and other low income persons are less likely to communicate complaints and request to public officials than wealthier citizens. In addition, depressed use o existing service facilities may be attributed to factors other than lack o client interest. That is, some groups of citizens may use services less tha other groups because the facilities available in their neighborhoods ar of poor quality. Since some people are less likely to express demand tha others, demand as equity will produce a differential pattern of distribu tion. Frequently, that pattern operates to the disadvantage of the poo

Preference as equity also presents a variety of problems with respect t implementation. It certainly appears rational to elicit and consult con sumer preferences about public services. Service facilities and program that go unused because citizens are not interested in them represent highly inefficient use of resources. However, preferences are exceed ngly difficult to measure and respond to. First, preferences vary widely across groups on the basis of income, education, race, and age. Second, the intensity-of-preference issue is difficult to resolve. Some citizens feel very strongly about a particular service while others are lukewarm in their expression of preference. Attempts to assign values to differing intensities of preference would enormously complicate the implementation process. Third, public preferences are highly volatile and subject to change. Since many public services frequently involve the heavy investment of resources at fixed sites, adaptation to shifting preference as a result of population movement or changing consumer taste is difficult to accomplish. Consequently, preference as equity is apt to violate established notions of efficiency in public sector allocations.

Conflicting preferences, differing intensities, and the volatility of preference complicate effective implementation. This does not mean, however, that service administrators never consult citizen preferences in their deliberations about the appropriate division of resources. In fact, responsiveness to demand ensures that some types of public preference will be incorporated into the distributional formula. What is significant is that public officials do not attempt to *elicit* citizen preferences except in the most rudimentary and haphazard of ways. Consequently, these preferences are highly unrepresentative of the general population. Since officials heavily rely upon complaints and requests as a guide to opinions about services, their knowledge about actual citizen preferences is limited. Rather than undertake the elaborate effort that would be required to accurately assess public preference, local officials are content to accept the expressed demands of the upper strata as a guide to what different groups prefer.

Ability to pay is a final standard of equity. According to this notion of equity, no citizen would be required to pay for any service that he did not want. People would pay only for those services that they used. Government officials would not have to make efforts to measure the variation in public demand and preference. Willingness and ability to pay incorporate precise measures of consumer demand and preference. Specific costs are assessed at the time of consumption. Use is voluntary. The service needs, demands, and preferences of some are not imposed upon others.

Ability to pay attempts to duplicate as closely as possible the operation of the private sector. The citizen-consumer shops and chooses from among a variety of service options. The extraordinary service needs of some groups are ignored by government. Although it is likely that ability to pay enhances efficiency in service delivery, it is also the case that it is the least redistributive of the standards considered here. Public sector

delivery systems would make no effort to counteract the disparities produced by the operation of the private sector. In fact, ability to pay mir-
rors those disparities.

Ability to pay presents some unique problems for implementation.
Although some services (refuse collection, public transportation, water,
utilities) are highly amenable to delivery on this basis, others are not.
Services for which unit costs and consumption can be easily measured
and calculated are frequently provided according to ability to pay. A
government employee simply reads a meter, counts a delivery, imposes a
toll, or assesses a fee. For some services, however, such ease of measurement and assessment is simply not feasible or possible. For example, who
should bear the costs of a police response to investigate a family distur-
bance? The neighbor who complained? The participants? All citizens
who derived benefit? Should more be charged for a police investigation
of a prowler report than for a residential burglary? How should relative
costs be assigned for time involved as opposed to risks encountered?
Because of the problems involved in measuring use and assigning costs
to individual citizen consumers, ability to pay is much more likely to be
used for some services than for others.

Implementation and the Bureaucracy

Every urban public service incorporates a particular conception of
equity. Each standard of equity imposes a different set of distributional
consequences. The choice of equity standards represents a significant
decision because it determines the winners and losers of service benefits.
These equity choices are frequently implicit rather than explicit. There
are good reasons for this. The provision and delivery of public services is
the major task of city government. Distributing these service benefits to
citizens implies immense opportunity for political controversy and conflict. When city budgets total billions of dollars, decisions about which
neighborhoods and groups will receive these services and at what levels
assume vital significance. Will police, fire, education, sanitation, recreation, and other services be delivered on the basis of equality, need,
demand, ability to pay, or some other standard? Since each equity notion
will produce a distinct pattern of winners and losers, decisions about
equity standards become the most significant political choices made by
local government.

Generally, elected political authorities have little to gain and much to
lose by participating in deliberations about the appropriate distribution
of public service benefits. The choice of one equity standard and the
rejection of others will inevitably antagonize some groups. The decision

to deny selected neighborhoods another recreational facility, a new school, more police patrols, or an additional branch library is guaranteed to stimulate citizen opposition. Elected officials would prefer to avoid such conflict. Consequently, mayors and councilmen seldom participate in routine decisions about service distribution. That task is left to the bureaucrats.

The bureaucrats control decisions about who gets what by default. The perspective they bring to the resolution of distributional issues reflects their organizational background and experience. Rather than recognizing and addressing the explicitly political nature of the distributional task, they attempt to reduce it to the level of an administrative chore. The powerful drive within organizations to simplify reality and ensure the predictability of routine decisions reinforces this tendency. Once the dimensions of the distributional problem have been redefined and transformed from a political to an administrative task, the bureaucracy can employ decision rules to guide the search for solutions. The organization rather than individual public officials now makes decisions about who will get what. As a result, personal political liabilities are reduced and the risks associated with selecting one standard of equity over another are, in large part, eliminated.

The following propositions describe the role of decision rules:

Proposition A: *Rules serve as the memory of the organization, transfer past learning, and reduce uncertainty.*

Allison (1971:76–77) writes that:

> Uncertainty is a critical factor of the environment in which organizations live. Organizations seek to avoid uncertainty. The first rule is: solve pressing problems rather than developing long-run strategies. The requirement that events in the distant future be anticipated is avoided by using decision rules that emphasize short-run feedback.

Proposition B: *Rules simplify decision making by eliminating the need to consider a variety of alternative solutions to the performance task.*

Simon (1961:88–89) observes that "a matter has become part of the organizational routine when it is settled by reference to accepted or approved practices rather than by consideration of the alternatives on their merits." Perrow (1972:31) notes that "frequently, there is no clear ground for doing A instead of B; both will have unpleasant outcomes. Rather than agonize over a decision, a rule cuts the knot." Rules provide a guide to decision making when several choices are equally appropriate.

Proposition C: *Rules are resistant to change.*

Perrow (1972:20) observes that:

> Rules are like an invisible skin which bundles together all the technological and
> social aspects of organizations. As such, rules stem from past adjustments and seek
> to stabilize the present and the future. When things are different in the future, an
> attempt to change the tough invisible threads means that all kinds of practices,
> bargains, agreements, and payoffs will tumble out of the web and must be stuffed
> back in again. As a result of these kinds of interdependencies, changes in organiza-
> tional rules are generally incremental.

Proposition D: *Rules are influenced by the records maintained by the
organization.*

That is because "the records that are kept determine in large part what
aspects of the environment will be observed and what alternatives of
action will be considered" (Cyert and March, 1963:106). However, much
information is unreliable and there is more information than can be
efficiently processed and analyzed. Therefore, Cyert and March
(1963:110) maintain that:

> One of the ways in which the organization adapts to the unreliability of information
> is by devising procedures for making decisions without attending to apparently
> relevant information. Thus, the internal biases in the organization increase the
> pressure (from external uncertainty) to develop decision-methods that do not re-
> quire reliable information (other than the simplist, most easily checked
> information).

Proposition E: *The origin of decision rules can be traced to organizational
experience and the impact of extraorganizational norms.*

These rules are maintained by recruitment, training, and socialization.
Perrow (1972:27) observes that one way "of reducing the number of
written rules is to 'buy' personnel who have complex rules built into
them." These professionals "are trained on the outside, usually at the
public expense, and a large number of rules are inculcated into them.
They bring these into the organization and are expected to act from
them without reference to their skills."

Proposition F: *Because rules are objectively applied, they appear to be fair*
(Levy et al., 1974); *however, every rule has distributional consequences*
(Simon, 1961:178).

Because specific standards of equity (equality, need, demand, preference, ability to pay) may generate controversy, considerations of equity will not be made explicit in the decision rule selected. Rules will tend to avoid conflict over who should get what by emphasizing technical-rational rather than political criteria. Conventional and quantifiable rather than controversial solutions to the performance task will be incorporated in the rule. Consequently, certain values about who should get what will be systematically excluded.

Proposition G: *Because organizational rules tend to be defined in technical terms, their distributional implications are little understood; therefore, rules are seldom subjected to challenge by either elected officials or citizens.*

As Simon (1975:44) observes, policy questions where "technical complexity hides the value issues" are less likely to become political "than matters readily accessible to common sense."

Each decision rule represents a choice about competing conceptions of equity. Instead of directly confronting the equity issue, however, bureaucrats make distributional decisions on the basis of technical-rational criteria. The political choice is reduced to an administrative task. Equity is accomplished according to formula. It becomes a by-product rather than an intended consequence of the distributional process.

The bureaucrat vigorously resists the inclusion of political factors into deliberations about the division of service resources. Far from simplifying solutions to the distributional puzzle, politics introduces an endless variety of possible solutions. Who should win and who should lose? Answers to that enduring question based on distinctly political considerations involve immense and unacceptable risk. We know that rationality in decision making is limited by the inability to predict the consequences of decisions, by the lack of information on alternative courses of action available, and by the inability of the participants to rank-order preferences and priorities. To avoid the consequences of these various limitations, decisions are sought according to a scenario that tends to reduce, simplify, distort, and even omit parts of reality. The goal is a workable solution, one that "satisfices." The search for solutions is controlled by indoctrination and training, standard operating procedures (which reflect the organization's experience with past, workable decisions), and specialized vocabularies and channels of communication.

For bureaucrats, political factors do not provide the basis for a workable solution. The risks are unacceptable. The debate would be rancorous, the feuding bitter and unending. The inadequacy of political considerations as a guide to the successful resolution of the resource distribution issue is enhanced by the inability to rank-order priorities. Which goals should be maximized? Does government have a responsibility to address the disproportionate service needs of the poor? Should it respond to those who demand services? There is little to be gained and much to be lost by employing politics as a basis for choosing winners and losers. Ironically, control over who gets what with respect to essential public services proves to be an asset of dubious value and a liability of major proportions. At first glance it would appear as if the ability to reward friends and punish enemies by offering or withholding vital services would confer a significant political advantage on those who make such decisions. Surprisingly, this is not the case. The use of political criteria in delivering services is fraught with risk. The services to be delivered are so fundamental to the health, safety, and well-being of citizens that the only acceptable, workable solution to the distributional task is to transfer decisions about them from the political to the administrative realm.

As a result, distributional issues tend to be defined in technical-rational rather than political terms. Police resources are allocated on the basis of crime rates and calls for service while recreation services are distributed according to demand and user levels. Sanitation resources are assigned on the basis of tons of refuse generated and number of miles traveled on collection routes. The division of resources in the municipal library system coincides with the variation in branch circulation rates while bureaucrats implement fire protection systems according to the standards established by professional fire fighting associations. The great virtue in using technical-rational criteria as a basis for making distributional choices is that these criteria defuse conflict, routinize decision making, and ensure predictable, workable solutions to the distributional problem. Bureaucrats simplify the decision-making process by invoking criteria that are least likely to generate intense political conflict and that are compatible with the need for large-scale organizations to establish routine, predictable patterns of behavior.

Administrative control of the distributional process is reinforced by the bureaucratic monopoly over information, experience, and expertise. These organizational strengths confer a disproportionate advantage in interactions with both politicians and citizens. The strong professional values and orientations of administrators serve as an effective defense against attempts to politically interfere with the distributional process. Bureaucrats identify with norms of efficiency, effectiveness, economy, and fairness. They rely upon appeals to professional standards. They emphasize the benefits to be realized from the rational application of sophisticated technology. They are able to marshall a wide array of complex, technical evidence in support of their policy choices.

Politics provides a poor basis for resolving distributional issues. Political solutions to the distributional puzzle are not workable solutions. It is exceedingly difficult to rank-order political goals and priorities. Little consensus exists with respect to which objectives should be maximized. Politics introduces conflict and risk into the distributional arena. Citizens argue for a particular distributional scenario from the perspective of selfish, narrow interests. To distribute resources in response to a multiplicity of these fragmented, particularistic demands would satisfy only a few and outrage many. The subsequent feuding over who should get what according to the variation in political power would significantly impair the predictability of service delivery. Therefore, distributional policy is fashioned in a way that ensures predictable, workable, and noncontroversial solutions. The policy process becomes routinized and is structured according to technical-rational criteria.

Equity and Political Conflict

Demand is the standard of equity most frequently employed in American cities to guide the distribution of local public services (Jones, 1978; Mladenka, 1978; Lineberry, 1977; Levy et al., 1974). It provides a workable solution to the distributional problem. Demand possesses several compelling virtues from the perspective of political authorities. First, it appears reasonable and rational. Government provides services to those who use them or ask for them. Efficiency in resource allocation is enhanced. Second, it appears fair. Bureaucrats can deliver services on the basis of citizen requests/complaints and use patterns and thereby avoid or defend against the allegation that they discriminate on the basis of race, income, or class. Demands are treated equally.

Third, demand as equity emphasizes responsiveness to the citizen. Government does not impose its own version of the appropriate division of public resources upon the consumer. Instead, the initiative rests with the citizen. The role of government in equity choices is simply to react to the expression of citizen demands. Fourth, demand is easily measured. Unlike preference, citizen demands and user patterns can be incorporated into decision rules with a minimum of effort. Finally, demand enjoys the advantage of serving as a highly attractive alternative to need as equity. Need is fraught with the potential for political conflict. Demand is not.

Local governments are driven by a compelling need to suppress political conflict. The opportunities for such conflict are immense. Millions of people live in close proximity to each other. The differences among them are enormous. The conflictual relationships generated by vast disparities in income, status, and security are exacerbated by the fact that human interactions occur in narrow, geographic space. The threats posed by alien groups are perceived in an immediate and direct fashion. Minorities moving into an adjacent neighborhood are thought to influence property values. Substantial numbers of black students in the neighborhood school are perceived in negative terms. The personal and passionate concerns of home and family are paramount in local politics. Higher taxes, crime and the police, zoning and residential property values, and minorities and "quality" education are issues fraught with danger for political authorities.

Local public officials cannot afford to antagonize upper-class citizens. Disgruntled consumers enjoy a powerful option. If they become sufficiently disenchanted with the services provided by government, they can move to another jurisdiction. Power in urban areas is highly fragmented. Dozens of governments are in continuous competition with each other for select groups of citizens. Wealthy people can solve their problems (crime, high taxes, minorities, declining property values) simply by moving away from them. The suburbanization of urban areas during the past few decades vividly illustrates the powerful appeal of this option.

The political risks inherent in conscious choices about equity standards intimidate public officials. They abdicate responsibility for these major political decisions. Equity concepts are selected in the administrative rather than the political realm. The power of the discontented citizen in a fragmented and competitive system is sufficiently great to discourage public resolution of the equity issue. The bureaucrat solves the distributional puzzle by reducing it to a level that is susceptible to the application of technical-rational criteria. Administrators structure and routinize equity outcomes by concealing the distinctly political dimensions of their choices.

It should be emphasized, however, that it would be misleading to conclude that all public services are distributed on the basis of organizational routines. The above discussion with respect to the role of decision rules applies only to service resources such as police manpower, library books, park sites, recreational facilities, school equipment, and number of refuse collection pick-ups. Organizational routines are unlikely to ensure predictable behavior on the part of street-level bureaucrats. For example, senior administrators can control distributional policy by deciding upon a decision rule that assigns police officers on the basis of crime rates and calls for service. However, such organizational rules will be of little use in controlling the behavior of individual police officers in their interactions with citizens.

CONCLUSIONS

Public services do get implemented, of course. After cataloging the variety of factors that complicate the implementation process, it should be emphasized that dozens of vital services *are* delivered on a routine and daily basis. However, it is also significant that because of the difficulties associated with the implementation of public services, service delivery is reduced to an administrative task. Political conflicts are left unresolved. The fundamental issue of what constitutes equity is avoided. Consequently, services are delivered on the basis of demand rather than on the basis of need or equality. As a result, some citizens get considerably more in the way of public resources than others. Given the nature of the implementation process, it is unlikely that public services will ever be delivered any differently.

REFERENCES

Aberbach, J. D. and J. L. Walker (1970) "The attitudes of blacks and whites toward city services: implications for public policy." In J. P. Crecine (ed.), Financing the Metropolis. Beverly Hills, Cal.: Sage Publications.

Allison, G. T. (1971) Essence of Decision. Boston: Little, Brown.

Cyert, R. M. and J. G. March (1963) A Behavioral Theory of the Firm. Englewood Cliffs, N.J.: Prentice-Hall.

Eisinger, P. K. (1972) "The pattern of citizen contacts with urban officials." In H. Hahn (ed.), People and Politics in Urban Society. Beverly Hills, Cal.: Sage Publications.

Jones, B. D., S. R. Greenberg, C. Kaufman, and J. Drew (1977) "Bureaucratic response to citizen initiated contacts: environmental enforcement in Detroit." American Political Science Review 71(March):148–65.

———— (1978) "Service delivery rules and the distribution of local government services: Three Detroit bureaucracies." Journal of Politics 40(May):332–68.

Levy, F. S., A. J. Meltsner, and A. Wildavsky (1974) Urban Outcomes. Berkeley, Cal. University of California Press.

Lineberry, R. L. (1977) Equality and Urban Policy. Beverly Hills, Cal.: Sage Publications.

Lipsky, M. (1976) "Toward a theory of street level bureaucracy." In W. D. Hawley and M. Lipsky (eds.), Theoretical Perspectives on Urban Politics. Englewood Cliffs, N.J.: Prentice-Hall.

Mladenka, K. R. (1978) "Organizational rules, service equality, and distributional decisions in urban politics." Social Science Quarterly 59(June):192–201.

———— (1980) "The urban bureaucracy and the Chicago political machine: who gets what and the limits to political control." American Political Science Review 74(December):991–98.

—— and K. Q. Hill (1978) "The distribution of urban police services." Journal of Politics 40(July):112–33.

Nivola, P. S. (1978) "Distributing a municipal service: a case study of housing inspection." Journal of Politics 40(February):59–81.

Perrow, C. (1972) Complex Organizations. Glenview, Ill.: Scott, Foresman.

Simon, H. A. (1961) Administrative Behavior. New York: Macmillan.

Verba, S. and N. H. Nie (1972) Participation in America: Political Democracy and Social Equality. New York: Harper & Row.

Wilson, J. Q. (1968) Varieties of Police Behavior. Cambridge, Mass.: Harvard University Press.

PART V

IMPLEMENTATION ALTERNATIVES

IMPLEMENTATION AND MARKET REFORM

Mark E. Rushefsky

INTRODUCTION

One of the perennial issues in American politics revolves around the question of the role of government itself. Should government become involved in a particular issue? And, if the answer is positive, what is the appropriate form of that involvement? In some cases government efforts to resolve an issue create problems that require resolution. For example, a number of studies have suggested that programs established following the 1973/74 oil embargo to allocate oil supplies exacerbated the problem of inadequate supplies during the second oil shock of 1978–1980 (i.e., General Accounting Office, 1979). Perhaps allowing the market to allocate oil supplies would have created less disruption. Similarly, government efforts to supplement the health care system, such as Medicare, Medicaid, and the generous tax treatment of health insurance fringe benefits, may have aggravated the problem of the increasing cost of health care.

Deregulation and market reform advocates believe that the political system is in many cases the wrong locus for allocating resources or resolving problems. They see the political process as inefficient and ineffective. They also find that government programs often lack appropriate incentives, encounter political resistance, are complex, and so on. Reformers recommend employing economic incentives and private markets to replace or complement government programs. Such an approach, they argue, would permit the use of more appropriate incentives, require less information, reduce political disputes, lessen the use of coercion, and enhance free choice.

An underlying assumption of this view of government programs and the operation of markets is that markets work automatically and will not encounter the impediments attributed to the public sector. One thinks immediately of Adam Smith's famous passage (as paraphrased by Samuelson, 1964:36):

> Every individual endeavors to employ his capital so that its produce may be of greatest value. He generally neither intends to promote the public interest, nor knows how much he is promoting it. He intends only his own security, only his own gain. And he is in this led by an *invisible hand* to promote an end which was not part of his intention. By pursuing his own interest he frequently promotes that of society more effectually than when he really intends to promote it.

A more contemporary observer suggests that same phenomenon as "coordination without a coordinator" (Wildavsky, 1979).

Because of this key assumption, few market reformers have adequately considered the problems of implementation of their policy proposals. The growing literature on implementation of government programs has also not discussed policies designed to decrease or change the role of government. Because of these omissions, certain changes labeled as market reform have been ill considered from the standpoint of ease or difficulty of execution. This essay is an attempt to fill this gap by exploring the implementation problems of market reform. The area of health care policy will illustrate the general argument.

DEREGULATION VS. MARKET REFORM

Deregulation and market reform are related in the sense that they both rely on economic incentives and are suggested as replacements for government programs. But they differ in the types of programs they are directed toward and the role that would remain for government. They therefore also differ in their ease of implementation.

Deregulation is the elimination of a government regulatory program. As such, it is a form of organizational/policy termination (Mitnick, 1978) and is typically applied to economic regulation. This traditional form of regulation is applied to a specific industry such as trucking and governs economic behavior such as prices or allocation of markets. The rationales for government involvement in a particular industry are varied: to bring order to an industry, to protect or subsidize an industry, or to regulate a "natural" monopoly. In some cases, regulation might be undertaken to maintain low consumer prices. Numerous studies have demonstrated that such regulation is often counterproductive and a commonly proposed remedy is deregulation.

Market reform is the achievement of marketlike solutions through positive action. This type of reform is relevant to "new style" or social regulation such as in the areas of health, safety, and environment (Wilson, 1980). Social regulation encompasses a wide range of industries rather than a specific one, and though this regulation has important economic impacts, its goal is to change or limit the impacts of processes or product uses. The rationales for social regulation differ markedly from that of economic regulation and include various forms of market failure (for example, externalities, where the private cost of production does not include the cost to society of cleaning up the pollution from that process), the merit wants argument (where private markets produce a good or service but not to the extent that society desires), and equity considerations (of the distribution of impacts across, say, economic class lines). Again, there have been numerous studies documenting the inadequacies, inefficiencies, and high costs of social regulation.

It is often not feasible to eliminate social regulation entirely, because the problems remain that created the need for regulation in the first place. One solution is market reform, the use of government to create quasi-markets. The best example, and the one most frequently mentioned in the economics literature, is the effluent tax (i.e., Ramsay and Anderson, 1972). Instead of issuing pollution standards on a command-and-control basis as is presently the case, under such a system pollution emitted by a specific source is taxed to achieve a desired level. This internalizes the externality of pollution and creates incentives for the polluter to reduce pollution and lower the tax placed on it. Various forms of vouchers, such as in education or housing, are other examples of market reform proposals.

The important point of this comparison of deregulation and market reform is that the former is easier to implement. Deregulation is the simple termination of an activity. Opposition to such termination may well exist, but implementation itself is not a problem. With market reform, however, some form of government involvement remains and implementation problems might arise. For example, one problem, to be discussed below, is the extent to which various parties manipulate the rules within which marketlike activities will occur.

PUBLIC CHOICE AND MARKET REFORM

Public Choice

The implementation (and evaluation) literature demonstrated to many that government programs face considerable difficulties and frequently do not meet their goals. The alternative that appeared in the 1970s and 1980s was greater reliance on private markets or at least the creation of marketlike situations. The theoretical basis for a substitution of markets for government activities is as old as Adam Smith; more formally, it lies within the school of thought known as public choice or political economy.

Public choice is a relatively new paradigm in political science and it involves the use of economic analysis and reasoning to understand political behavior and the appropriate role of government. The essentials of the paradigm are readily summarized:

> Underlying [it] is a fundamental conception of politics as essentially an *exchange* phenomenon not totally different from economic exchange. In this view of politics, the economists are inclined to emphasize *rational choice* on the part of *individuals* and *organizations* as they engage in various types of exchange among themselves and with political parties and governments in pursuit of their subjective *self-interests*. The action and the choices are made under varying degrees of *uncertainty* concerning the specific *goals of others*, their *strategies*, and the *rules of the game*. While the individual is considered as the basic analytical unit and is self-interested, he does engage in *cooperative* as well as *competitive* behavior. Thus, he seeks allies to increase his bargaining strength but he also competes with his allies and opponents over the terms of the bargains. Governments want support, compliance, and resources while the individual citizen wants to improve his share of the benefits and/or reduce costs. All these individual choices and activity are products of *interdependent choices*, since one person's choice must take the uncertain choices of others into account (Mitchell, 1971:16; italics in original).

Public choice theory can be used for prescriptive as well as positive purposes. For positive purposes, public choice describes and analyzes political behavior. The prescriptive aspect goes one step further and suggests appropriate roles for government and policy mechanisms based on the positive analysis.

Public choice advocates believe that government programs in a wide variety of areas have failed to achieve their purposes. The problem is not excessive spending; rather, government intervention has grown, situations have become complex, and the intervention has taken the form of rules and regulations that are often inefficient and occasionally harmful (Schultze, 1977). The causes of failure are inherent in administered systems and the inability to devise plans and rules that can be followed (Levine, 1972; Wolf, 1979). While the goals are commendable, the means are often inappropriate. We rely on commands rather than incentives.

> Finally, and perhaps most important, we usually tend to see only one way of intervening—namely, removing a set of decisions from the decentralized and incentive-oriented private market and transferring them to the command-and-control techniques of government bureaucracy. With some exceptions, modifying the incentives of the private market is not considered a relevant alternative. For a society that has traditionally boasted about the economic and social advantages of Adam Smith's invisible hand, ours has been strangely loath to employ the same techniques for collective intervention. Instead of creating incentives so that public goals become private interests, private interests are left unchanged and obedience to the public goals is commanded (Schultze, 1977:6).

Economic incentives and markets have important advantages over public programs (Levine, 1972; Schutze, 1977). For example, markets involve unanimous-consent arrangements. That is, market transactions are voluntary whereas public sector arrangements are not (for example, one's child goes to the assigned public school). In addition, markets are relatively unplanned and decentralized as compared to governmental programs. Markets are not laid out in advance by external authorities, various actors make their own decisions (markets are self-administered), and these are decentralized. By contrast, public programs require some planning and at least some centralization; schools in a particular district are under central control and follow a mandated curriculum. Markets also require less information and detailed case-by-case application than do government programs. For example, a pollution control program requiring utilities to employ scrubbers in coal-fired power plants depends on knowing how well scrubbers work and under what conditions, what the contributions of a particular plant are to pollution, the sulfur content of coal, and so forth. An effluent tax would require only that a plant or group of plants meet a specific standard and leave the details of control to the owners. Finally, private markets can direct innovation toward desirable directions (because of the lure of additional profits) and sidestep questions of equity. Government programs often attempt to ensure that people are not disadvantaged by a particular action, often leading to detailed rules and inflexibility. All of these advantages of markets over government programs are powered by actors being motivated by economic self-interest in the case of markets and other motivations (power, larger budgets, etc.) in the case of government.

We can draw a number of generalizations about public choice theory on the basis of this brief discourse of the literature. First, public choice or political economy has as its foundation the idea of methodological individualism. That is, the analysis starts from the perspective of the individual. Second, public choice theorists see actors as behaving rationally on the basis of what they perceive to be their own self-interest. Third, and this follows from the first two generalizations, is a concern for choice. An important consideration is the lack of coercion and the ability of consumers to select from a number of different providers of a good or service. Such competition assures freedom. Fourth, there is a preference for private markets over political systems. Related to this is a minimization of the role of government, particularly central governments, and the view that the political system is the greatest threat to freedom (Friedman, 1962). Finally, public choice evinces a concern for efficiency, the provision of a good or service for the least cost.

How public choice theory can be applied to define a policy problem, critique inappropriate efforts, and recommend policies that conform to the theory can be seen in the area of health care. After looking at this application, we then explore implementation problems of the proposed public choice/market reform remedies.

The Problem Defined

From a policy standpoint, the most important health care problem is the question of cost and its impact on government budgets. The critical point seems to be 1965, with the passage of Medicare and Medicaid. In 1965 health care expenditures as a percentage of the gross national product were 6%; by 1981 they were 9.8%. And the pace seems to be increasing: in 1981, health care expenditures increased by 15.1%. Prices have shown similar increases: overall medical prices increased by 11.4% for the year ending March 1982, even though overall price inflation continued to moderate. The largest category of expenditures and the largest increases in prices occurred in hospital services. Hospital expenditures increased by 17.5% in 1981; hospital and medical services prices increased by 14.3% and hospital room prices by 15.5% for the year ending March 1982 (see Waldo and Gibson, 1982; Health Care Financing Administration, 1982).

In 1981, Medicare cost $44.8 billion, up from $30.3 billion in 1979. Medicaid cost the federal government $14.6 billion and state governments $13.8 billion in 1981. The comparable figures for 1979 are $13.0 and $9.8 billion, respectively. This represents increases in two years of 47.9% for Medicare, 12.3% for the federal portion of Medicaid, 40.8% for the state Medicaid share, and 36.7% for the total Medicaid program. These figures clearly exceed, by a large margin, overall increases in either health care expenditures or prices. Thus much of the health care problem as a policy issue revolves around the impact on budgets.[1]

Government and Health Care

Governments at various levels have attempted to come to grips with the problems raised by health care inflation. These programs include planning (such as the federal and state certificate-of-need laws designed to limit capital expansion), utilization review programs (such as the Professional Standards Review Organizations, which sought to limit unnecessary use of hospital services), and rate regulation by some states and, for a brief period, by the federal government during the Economic Stabilization Program of 1971–1974. Although some programs, such as certain state rate regulatory programs, have reduced the health cost problem somewhat (Coelen and Sullivan, 1981), on the whole, government efforts to alleviate the problem have not been effective (Pearson and Abernethy, 1980).

In addition to these attempts to reduce costs, governments have also been involved in increasing or enhancing the capacity of the health care system. One of the most important issues of public policy is the role of government. Part of this issue, aside from the public choice question of the appropriate nature of government's role, is the extent to which government policies themselves cause problems that require some solution. From a public choice perspective, a number of governmental policies have exacerbated the health cost explosion and changes are needed in those policies to help alleviate the problem.

In the case of health care, there were several policies adopted by the federal government that have been implicated in the health cost problem. A relatively minor policy involves subsidies for research and manpower training that emphasizes biomedical research, technological development, curative medicine, and specialty training, all of which direct medical care toward the delivery of expensive services (Altman and Blendon, 1979).

A more significant policy, and in a sense one established by Congress without health directly in mind, is the subsidy of the purchase of health insurance through laws and regulations that make employer contributions to health insurance a business deduction and treat them as nontaxable fringe benefits to employees (Ginsburg, 1981). These laws also enable employees to deduct part of their contributions to insurance premiums and medical expenses over a certain percentage of income. The result is a tax expenditure representing some $23 billion of lost revenue to the federal government for fiscal year 1982 (Minarik, 1981).

More importantly, the tax laws decrease the price of health insurance to the employee so that, according to economic logic, he would buy more insurance than if faced with the real price. The effect of insurance is to lower the cost of health care by spreading or socializing the risk. Purchasing more insurance and more comprehensive insurance effectively lowers the cost of health care, at least for covered services. Cost consciousness on the part of either consumer or provider is diminished because both know that a third-party will pay the bulk of the bills (Feldstein, 1977). This problem was compounded by the passage of Medicare and Medicaid in 1965 (a second major set of policies), which reproduced the reimbursement policies of the private sector.

Thus the critique of government policies takes two related paths. On the one hand, programs designed to enhance the capacity of the health care system exacerbate the cost problem. The solution, according to advocates of market reform, is to design programs that take into account the perverse incentives that exist in current programs.

Structural Incentives Analysis

The public choice theory underlying the critique of government programs and market reform health care proposals is structural incentives analysis (Falkson, 1980). Structures are "arrangements and relationships between individuals and organizations (and) the process by which these arrangements are created." Incentives are motivational forces (McClure, 1981:120). The basic proposition is that actors in the medical care system behave according to the way they are rewarded. The incentives in the system are presently skewed toward specialization and high technology care, and include third-party reimbursement for consumers, fee-for-service for doctors, cost reimbursement for hospitals, and government policies that support these incentives (Enthoven, 1978a). These motivational forces remove cost-consciousness on the part of consumers and providers and are weighted toward institutional and curative care rather than office-based, home-based, or preventive care. Providers cannot be blamed for this situation. Society makes and changes the rules and thus the problem is structural, rather than conspiratorial.

Public choice analysts also employ structural incentives analysis to explain why government regulation has failed to alleviate the cost problem. Because consumers have diffuse interests and producers have concentrated interests in the outcome of regulation, regulatory efforts are unbalanced in the direction of producers (or providers). Agencies exist in an environment to which they must respond or they will be constrained in their activities. The problems of the Federal Trade Commission

(FTC) are illustrative. In the 1970s, the FTC became an aggressive pursuer of consumer interests, initiating investigations and proposing rules for such varied industries as funeral homes, used cars, and television advertisements aimed at children. The response to these investigations and proposed rules was heavy lobbying on the part of the affected industries, resulting in congressional action limiting FTC ventures into these areas and the imposition of a congressional veto over proposed FTC rules (McClure, 1981; Wines, 1982).[2]

As a complement to the view that government is responsive to well-focused producer interests, government subsidy programs also have political problems. As one market reform advocate argues, when every dollar is a federal dollar, every dollar is a federal case (Enthoven, 1978a). The dispute over abortion and whether the federal government should use Medicaid funds to pay for abortions became a politically touchy issue and over a four-year period delayed appropriations bills for the Department of Health and Human Services. Thus, public choice theory and structural incentives analysis point to the impotence of government programs to resolve the major health policy problem, increasing costs.

Procompetition/Prochoice Proposals

Public choice theory, embodied in structural incentives analysis, has been employed, as we have just seen, to explain the problems of the health care system and government's failure to alleviate those problems; indeed, government is viewed as an important cause of those problems. Market reformers go beyond this critique and propose corrective actions for these maladies. The fundamental purpose of these proposals is to apply economic incentives to consumers, providers, and insurers in order to stimulate the development of diverse and competing health plans that will provide health services efficiently and enable consumers to select the types of services they genuinely want. One additional impact of some of the plans (the voucher and tax expenditure limitations) is that they may, at least theoretically, provide a control for government health expenditures; thus competition could alleviate the cost problem. The proposals contain various combinations of four elements: (1) cost-sharing, (2) choice among competing plans, (3) competitive regulation, and (4) private sector initiatives.

The first element is increased cost-sharing on the part of consumers. The rationale for this is that comprehensive third-party reimbursement eliminates economic considerations on the part of consumers and providers. Increased cost-sharing by consumers in conjunction with the second element of the competition proposals, choice among competing plans, restores economic considerations and encourages consumers to purchase the health care that they really want at a price they are willing to pay.

The granddaddy of the competition proposals (the second element) is Enthoven's (1978b) Consumer-Choice Health Plan (CCHP). What he proposed was a national health insurance scheme based on a voucher system. Each family unit would receive a piece of paper, or voucher, on a quarterly basis equal to some percentage of average health care costs or insurance costs based on a particular actuarial category (i.e., young family of four, elderly couple, etc.). The family would then purchase a health plan from one of a number of offerings, including a health maintenance organization, a conventional insurer, a health care alliance, etc. The key to this choice element is that various health plans would charge different premiums and none would cost as little as the voucher was worth. Thus the more expensive the plan chosen, the more the family would have to pay in addition to the voucher. This would force the family to purchase the amount of insurance or health coverage it truly desires. The various health plans would compete for subscribers on the basis of price and benefits and thus have an incentive to keep their costs and prices low.

More incremental choice proposals utilize the workplace as the major source of health insurance by mandating that employers offer at least three different plans by three different insurance carriers. Furthermore, there could be limits on the tax deduction for health insurance contributions by employers (say to $150 a month for a family plan) and requirements for equal contributions to the plans. That is, employer contributions would be the same whether an employee chose a more or less expensive plan. In addition, there could be provisions for employees to receive some of the employer contributions for selecting less expensive plans.

Provisions are also made for those covered by government insurance programs. For example, the Reagan administration has been considering a Medicare voucher program, and there has been a bill introduced in Congress to that effect. For Medicaid recipients, a voucher equal to 100% of the average actuarial costs could be provided. The choice situation would remain, even for them. Any plan selected over the value of the voucher would cost the recipient additional money.

These first two elements of the competition proposals are clearly based on public choice theory. First, consumers are motivated by financial considerations to select from an array of plans the one that best meets self-identified needs. Second, many of the proposals allow consumers to switch plans because an alternative becomes more financially attractive, has more desirable benefits, or delivers services in a more preferred manner. This "exit" option (Hirschman, 1970) encourages plans to be competitive (on price, services, or benefits) or fail. Consumer sovereignty (producers responsive to consumer demands) drives the health care market (as opposed to the responsiveness of regulatory agencies to producer interests). Finally, consumer sovereignty encourages providers and insurers to develop cost-efficient plans. Thus, competition has both external (competition from other plans) and internal (development of cost-efficient plans) incentives. All this is engineered by consumer choice and not coerced by government policies. Increased cost-sharing and competition among health plans are the heart of the prochoice proposals. The next two elements, competition-strengthening regulation and private sector initiatives, are intended to supplement the effects of competition.

The regulation–market dichotomy has informed debates over the years in many policy areas. This dichotomy, an ideological polarization of liberal and conservative views, masks the reality that regulation is sometimes needed to ensure that the market approach works. One major market reform proponent has labeled this mixed market–regulation approach as "constrained markets" (Enthoven, 1980). Unconstrained markets would eliminate, for example, state occupational licensure laws that restrict the practice of medicine to certified physicians. This totally free market approach has been advocated by Milton Friedman but not by the more modern market reformers (see Friedman, 1962; Reinhardt, 1982). The task of the market reformers is to identify and eliminate those regulatory programs that are either ineffective or impede the growth of competition and promote those programs that enhance competition.

The first set of programs, those targeted for elimination or diminution, include state rate regulatory programs, state restrictions on competitive practices (i.e., that restrict advertising or group practice), state and federal certificate-of-need laws, and the Professional Standards Review Organizations. An incremental strategy would be to effect changes in some of these programs that would foster competition or at least not inhibit it. The 1979 amendments to the National Health Planning and Resources Development Act (the federal certificate-of-need act) placed new emphasis on strengthening competitive forces, giving greater leeway to new providers and innovation by insurers. Utah has moved strongly in this direction with its certificate-of-need program. This "market-forcing" strategy has the advantage of utilizing already existing regulatory mechanisms to bridge the transition to a more competitive environment (Havighurst and Hackbarth, 1980; Havighurst, 1982).

The other part of the regulatory element is the strengthening of certain programs that enforce competition. For example, the Stockman–Gephardt bill (introduced in Congress in 1980 and again in 1981) is based on the CCHP and is clearly the most far reaching of the competition bills. It calls for a sweeping elimination of many regulatory programs and specifically preempts any state laws that might contravene the bill. However, the bill contains numerous references to the secretary of Health and Human Services ensuring that only qualified health plans could participate in the new program. For instance, plans must meet certain financial qualifications, they must permit open enrollment (a specified month each year when subscribers can enter or leave a plan), and so on. In a sense, this is regulation redirected at insurers and other organizers of health plans.

An equally important area of market-forcing regulation is the application of antitrust law, particularly by the FTC. "Antitrust law is a response to situations in which markets would perform adequately were it not for attempts by marketplace participants to monopolize or restrain trade through contracts, combinations or conspiracies" (Drake and Kozak, 1978:329). FTC efforts have recently focused on the problem of "the interface between health plans and physicians." Such measures are concentrated on "a series of control mechanisms by which the organized medical profession has effectively manipulated its own economic environment, preventing third-party financing mechanisms from becoming aggressive purchasers of inputs needed by their beneficiaries and from embarking on the reorganization of health care delivery and its closer integration with financing" (Havighurst, 1982:100). These mechanisms include direct control over Blue Shield plans, direct control over other financing entities (e.g., foundations for medical care and individual practice associations),[3] boycotts and related restraints, collective bargaining between medical societies and health insurers, professional prescription of third-party practices, restraints on physicians' sale of their services, and restraints on health maintenance organizations (Havighurst, 1982). Thus market reformers see the need for a considerable amount of regulation to ensure that competition is allowed to work.

> The role of government is to make the necessary temporary interventions to create this new, restructured, effective marketplace; to alter public financing programs to be compatible with it; and then to exercise modest continuing oversight (antitrust enforcement, etc.) to assure that health competition is maintained (McClure, 1981:111).

The final element of the market reform proposals are cost-controlling initiatives by the private sector. These are to serve as a substitute for public sector regulation (Havighurst, 1977). Employers' concerns are in alleviating their cost problems as health care fringe benefits become a growing part of their production costs. Corporations have sponsored health organization innovations such as health maintenance organizations, redesigned their health insurance benefits to control costs, replaced insurance company administration with self-insurance (thus reducing administrative costs and fostering tighter utilization reviews), had corporate members participate on health planning boards, and participated in the Voluntary Effort to control health costs (started in 1978 as a response to the Carter administration's hospital cost containment bill) (Caulfield and Haynes, 1981). While these private sector initiatives cannot be considered successful (based on the continued trend in health care costs), should the competition proposals be enacted the private sector would have a vital role in fostering competition.

The various choice proposals contain important assumptions. The emphasis of the proposals is on the consumer or demand side of health care. The theory of the program is that if an environment is created in which consumers are faced with a choice among competing health plans and that choice has financial consequences to consumers/subscribers, then the choices they make will force changes in the delivery and financing of health care, without anyone (particularly a government agency) having to specify in advance what forms of organization and financing are preferred (Rushefsky, 1981). The major problem facing competition advocates, should the proposals be enacted, is the assumption that markets work automatically. This failure to consider implementation problems leads to predicting "the valued consequences from policies *as if they were implemented*" (MacRae and Wilde, 1979:224).

IMPLEMENTATION

Implementation or administration or execution is the carrying out of a policy or program. The literature on implementation can be divided into three types. There are, first of all, those studies that examine implementation of specific programs; Feder's (1977) study of Medicare is an example of this type. A related subtype are those works that study the implementation of a whole array of programs; Thompson's (1981) work on a variety of health care programs exemplifies this category. The second general type of implementation study involves a general discussion of implementation without concentrating on a specific program or set of programs; Edwards's (1980) work is an example of this type. Finally, there are those works that utilize the analysis of a specific program to make general comments about implementation; Bardach's (1977) study of mental health policy in California is a case in point.

What conclusions can be drawn from the implementation literature that are helpful in understanding implementation problems, or possible problems, with market reform? First, successful implementation of a program, one that operates as originally intended, is problematical, certainly rare. Those affected by a program seek to utilize that program either to create advantages for themselves or limit possible adverse effects. Resources are frequently not adequate to ensure meaningful compliance with a program's intent, regulations, etc. Some actors have independent political resources that enable them to limit programs enacted elsewhere. Second, the literature focuses almost exclusively on governmental programs. Politics and policy are largely identified with the public sector, and it is therefore natural that scholars concentrate on positive public sector programs. The third conclusion follows from the second: there is very little discussion of deregulation and market reform [for an exception, see Ripley and Franklin (1982)]. Thus, at first glance, the implementation literature does not appear very helpful.

However, a useful perspective on implementation is that provided by Elmore (1982). He suggests that implementation can be examined fruitfully from the perspective of "backward mapping." Most implementation studies employ forward mapping, where one starts from a given piece of legislation (or court or executive order) and works downward to see how the policy was implemented. Divergence between the intent of the legislation or order and the execution of the program is seen as programmatic or policy failure.

Elmore states that one should start from the perspective of those who administer a program and work upward in the organization and finally arrive at the legislation. The weakness of forward mapping "is its implicit and unquestioned assumption that *policymakers control the organization, political and technological processes that affect implementation*" (Elmore, 1982:20). This is the 'noble lie' of public administration and attempts to make directives and statements clearer, such as Sabatier's and Mazmanian's (1980) emphasis on the ability of a statute to structure the problem or Lowi's (1979) recommendation that clear directions limit discretion, reinforce this myth. Backward mapping concentrates on dispersal of control and factors that can only be indirectly influenced by policymakers, incentive structures, bargaining relationships, and the use of funds to affect choices. While those who advocate market reform would generally agree with this analysis, Elmore warns in an important passage that reliance on markets is too simplistic:

> Those policy analysts who are economists, impatient with the complexities of bureaucracy and the lack of precision in organizational theory, have tried to reduce implementation analysis to a simple choice between market and non-market mecha-

nisms. Schultze states the basic argument when he says that the 'collective-coercion component of intervention should be treated as a scarce resource' in the formulation of policies, and that policymakers should learn to 'maximize the use of techniques that modify the structure of private incentives.' Wolf furthers the argument, stating that the whole enterprise of implementation analysis can be reduced to a diagnosis of the pathologies of nonmarket structures, or as he calls it, 'a theory of nonmarket failures.' The simplicity of the argument is comforting, but its utility is suspect. It seeks to solve one kind of organizational problem, the responsiveness of large-scale bureaucracies, by substituting another kind of organizational problem, the invention and execution of quasi markets. There is little evidence to suggest that the latter problem is any more tractable than the former. One would hardly expect, though, that a detailed framework for analysis of organizational alternatives would emerge from an intellectual tradition that regards organizational structure of any kind as a second-best solution to the problem of collective action (Elmore, 1982:22–23).

Pressman and Wildavsky's (1973) conceptualization of implementation is also useful. Policy, they write, can be considered as an hypothesis. The enactment stage constructs the initial conditions of program, the 'if' stage of a policy syllogism; implementation is the 'then' stage. Market reform, whether in environmental protection or health care, can be seen as a set of hypotheses that are, in theory, at least, amenable to testing (Rushefsky, 1981). An analysis of market reform and implementation can likewise profit from this hypothesis conceptualization; that is, rather than accept the assertions of market reformers, we should view them instead as hypothetical statements that remain to be verified. For example, market reformers suggest that structuring the situation facing consumers so that the health plan they select has financial consequences for them encourages them to select cost-efficient plans and that competition among health plans for subscribers forces the plans to become cost-efficient. Both these propositions, which are at the very core of the competition proposals, can be tested empirically. One can seek situations or create experiments to see what kinds of choices consumers make (Farley and Wilensky, 1982). Similarly, one can relate penetration of health maintenance organizations (HMOs) in specific markets to the response of other providers and insurers in those markets (Christianson, 1980).

Pressman and Wildavsky also see implementation as the "complexity of joint action." That is, their sympathetic discussion of the Economic Development Administration project in Oakland showed that most participants were supportive of the project, a construction grant to employ minority group members, though each participant had his own reasons for that participation. What Pressman and Wildavsky demonstrate was that even under relatively favorable conditions, implementation was difficult because of the number of decision points involved. The more decision makers, both public and private, the less likely implementation will be successful.

IMPLEMENTATION AND MARKET REFORM

To what extent have market reformers considered implementation problems? The answer, in short, is "not very much." One can find statements in the literature suggesting that the full impact of the choice proposals would probably not be felt for 10 to 15 years after enactment (Enthoven, 1980a). Elsewhere, one can find statements that suggest that the end result of the competition proposals, particularly in terms of health care expenditures, might not be very different from the present situation, and that this is an acceptable outcome if it actually expresses revealed consumer preferences (Havighurst, 1982).[4] Others who have carefully considered implementation problems understand that some difficulties might exist but can be prevented or overcome. The biggest barrier appears to be enactment of a competition proposal (McClure, 1977, 1982). Nevertheless, in general implementation problems have been considered very little.

The proposals and their supporting discussions suffer from the problem of focusing "too much on how things *should* work out, and not nearly enough on how they may go awry. . . . [T]he more complex the system, and the more the system includes intelligent beings pursuing their self-interest, the more difficult it is either to predict outcomes or to obtain the desired results" (Luft, 1982:52). Thus two questions need to be addressed. First, why is there so little consideration of implementation problems? Second, what kinds of implementation problems exist?

The first question is readily answered. Implementation problems are cursorily considered because of a belief that once the appropriate conditions are established, the medical marketplace will automatically produce desired results. Recall the Adam Smith quote about the "invisible hand" of the market and compare it to this more contemporary version quoted with great approval by a prominent market reformer:

> One of the most conspicuous features of organization through exchange and free enterprise, and one most often commented upon, is the absence of conscious design or control. It is a social order, and one of unfathomable complexity, yet constructed and operated without social planning or direction, through selfish individual thought and motivation alone. No one ever worked out a plan for such a system, or willed its existence; there is no plan of it anywhere, either on paper or in anybody's mind, and no one directs its operation. Yet in a fairly tolerable way, 'it works,' and grows and changes. We have an amazingly elaborate division of labor, yet each person finds his own place in the scheme; we use a highly involved technology with

minute specialization of industrial equipment, but this too is created, placed and directed by individuals, for individual ends, with little thought of larger social relations or any general social objective. Innumerable conflicts of interests are constantly resolved, and the bulk of the working population kept generally occupied, each person ministering to the wants of an unknown multitude and having his own wants satisfied by another multitude equally vast and unknown—not perfectly indeed, but tolerable on the whole, and vastly better than each could satisfy his wants by working directly for himself (Frank Knight, quoted in Havighurst, 1982:108).

What follows from this view, again, is that once the structural incentives facing the various actors (consumers, providers, employers, unions, and insurers) are formulated correctly, desired outcomes result.

Because of this assumption of the automatic working of the market, implementation problems have not received sufficient attention from market reformers. Yet, there are four types of implementation problems likely to be encountered and that require discussion. First, the theory of the proposals is extremely complicated. Second, actors may not behave as predicted. Third, proposals adversely affect almost everyone. Finally, affected actors may seek to fix or change the rules by which the newly created competitive markets would operate. Each of these points is elaborated below.

The Complex Theory of Market Reform

The first generation of health care market reform proposals was embodied in the Health Maintenance Act of 1973. The theory behind the program, based on structural incentives analysis, was that HMOs would be efficient and effective deliverers of health care services; that HMOs, because of competitive pressures, would be responsive to consumer demands; and that consumers would be able to make rational decisions about the choice of health plans. Subsidies might be necessary to implement an HMO strategy and some actions (i.e., antitrust) might be needed to remove barriers to HMO formation (Ellwood, 1974; Brown, 1981; Falkson, 1980). In short, HMO proponents hoped that simply making HMOs available would result in consumers selecting them, and the external competitive and internal efficiency effects of HMOs would change the system and alleviate the cost (and other) problems.

The second generation choice proposals (the subject of this essay) are based on a much more complex program theory. Rather than simply make a favored option available (indeed, market reformers envision an array of options), the choice proposals seek to "stack the deck" in favor of cost-efficient options through the manipulation of financial incentives and, in some cases, constraining choices. If the choices consumers make have financial consequences for them, they will, in the long run, select cost-efficient plans. More expensive plans will have to restrain their costs and utilization to remain competitive. The causal chain of market reform theory is indeed long (Rushefsky, 1981) and changes the nature of the program; rather than working automatically, government must deliberately establish a program and structure incentives appropriately.

> Efforts to achieve efficiency and cost control by means of incentives, markets, and competition would not be, if taken seriously, an inconspicuous exercise in constructing new consumer choices. They would instead demand extensive social engineering that would impose large changes on the structure of the American health care system. . . . The so-called market approaches recommended to policy makers today as a means of employing private interests in the service of public ends . . . invite the central government to design with care and specificity a set of top-down rewards and penalties which, when applied to the system from above, may be depended on to change millions of individual choices significantly in directions that government prefers. . . . If the new approach were described accurately—as, for example, 'centrally planned social engineering by the federal government involving the manipulation of material rewards and penalties to trigger major behavioral changes'—instead of in code words with ancient and honored libertarian connotations, the nature of the enterprise . . . would be clearer (Brown, 1981:178–79).

The more complex the program theory and the more chains in the causal sequence, the more difficulty there is in implementation. One reason for this, discussed below, is the "complexity of joint action" that Pressman and Wildavsky (1973) discuss. Note also, from the above quote, that the program theory contains the same flaw that Elmore (1982) states is typical of implementation research, reliance on *forward mapping*. The perspective adopted here, based on Elmore, is that of *backward mapping*—starting from the people directly affected by a program rather than from the policymakers.

Complexity of Joint Action

Consumer choice is the focal point of the competition proposals and illustrates the problem of the "complexity of joint action" that Pressman and Wildavsky (1973) emphasize. If competition is to work as predicted, then the choices that consumers make become critical. The two problems of complex theory and complexity of joint action are obviously related. The major difference is that the former operates at the "macro" level. This means that the competition theory assumes that on the basis of the choices that consumers make, certain desired changes will occur in the organization of health care delivery systems and in health care markets. The complexity of joint action has a "micro" perspective; certain behaviors on the part of individuals must occur for the macro effects to appear. According to public choice theory, such behavioral changes in consumer choices would be based solely on self-interest, with the primary motivator being financial. Yet the reality of consumer selection is much more complex than market reformers picture (Brown, 1981).

Enrollment choice is a function of many factors: the economic characteristics of the family (e.g., income), risk factors (i.e., family size, age, chronic and acute medical conditions, perceived health status, and precine, preferences about patient–physician relationships and choice of physicians, expected utilization patterns (types of services and frequency of use), delivery system characteristics (access, continuity, and comprehensiveness), and insurance characteristics (benefits, premiums, and out-of-pocket expenses). Additionally, selection of plans may be made on the basis of the subjective health risk facing a family, the appropriateness of available benefit packages, and the cost of service in relation to income. The evidence to date on how consumers select plans is mixed; that is, different studies produce contradictory results (Berki and Ashcraft, 1980). Some people select a plan because of perceived future health risk, others because of a satisfactory relationship with a provider, still others because of the characteristics of the delivery system, and so on. To base a complex proposal on one motivation, financial self-interest, is to ignore these other dimensions of self-interest. In addition, one major survey suggests that while employees had great incentives to select more expensive plans, some chose less expensive plans even though the difference in cost between plans was considerably less than the difference in benefits. "The number who chose less expensive plans, despite rather significant economic incentives to the contrary, stands as an important reminder of the many other considerations which influence a person's desire for health insurance" (Farley and Wilensky, 1982:21). This finding also suggests that the ability of consumers to intelligently select among a wide array of plans is questionable.

One final note on this point is that the idea of insurance is precisely to ensure against risk and to spread (or socialize) that risk among a large group of people. Certainly one possible response to increased cost-sharing is for consumers to purchase supplemental policies to reduce it (Brown, 1981). If choice is to have cost-restraining effects, the differences among plans must be considerable, yet consumers may act to reduce those differences, possibly driving up health costs by once again reducing the true cost of health care to the consumer.

Proposals Adversely Affect Everyone

The previous problem, complexity of joint action, suggests that the decisions consumers make in their choice of plans are much more complex than an emphasis on economic self-interest would lead one to believe. Compounding this type of problem is one that asks how the competition plans affect various parties. Will these actors (consumers, providers, insurers, employers, unions, and states) be better off after a competition proposal has been enacted and put into place? If the answer is no, affected actors will seek, during implementation, to change the rules by which competition operates and obtain a more favorable (for them) result. This section considers why adverse affects may appear; the next section examines how actors might seek to ameliorate those impacts.

Consider the elements of a typical proposal. A model plan might include a voucher for Medicaid and Medicare, requirements that employers offer employees a range of options of health plans, equal contributions by employers to the health plan, open enrollment (specified periods when subscribers can switch plans without penalty), readily available information to enable subscribers to intelligently select among offered plans, taxation of employer contributions to health plans over a desigated amount, preemption of state laws interfering with the development of competition, application of antitrust laws, and regulation of health plans to ensure compliance with competition purposes (i.e., financial qualifications, open enrollment, and preparation of adequate consumer information).

Based on such a plan, the number of individuals and groups affected is enormous. If health politics can be, perhaps oversimply, described as a war over money and control (or power), then political opposition is readily understandable. Whatever other impacts the competition proposals might have, the one definite impact is to limit the amount of money available to the medical care system. If the "law of medical money" that "medical costs rise to equal the sum of all private insurance and government subsidy" (Wildavsky, 1977:109) is a valid statement, then the competition proposals utilize that "law" by restraining insurance and government subsidies and allowing costs to be passed more directly to consumers. How would this work?

From government's standpoint, the voucher plan at the very least changes the open-ended subsidies to a budgeted plan and one that can be reliably forecasted (Rushefsky, 1981). The limitation on tax-free employer contributions to health plans and the requirement for equal employer contributions for health plan premiums have the effect of increasing the real cost of insurance to employees and making cost-efficient health plans more attractive. Perhaps we should look at health expenditures as health income, that is, each dollar spent on health care respresents a dollar of revenue to providers of health care. Thus, when one talks about limiting health care expenditures, one also means, by definition, limiting income to providers. Put in that perspective, one can readily see why providers have not wholeheartedly embraced the competition idea (Reinhardt, 1982).

Opposition from others will also appear. For example, a number of market reform advocates suggest that state laws may need to be preempted to allow the choice plans to work. Thus the states as a group may well oppose that aspect of the proposals on several grounds. First is the federalism issue of interference by the federal government with state prerogatives. Second, states may be concerned that removal of regulatory programs might aggravate the health-cost problem, especially if the competition idea is not successful. A way to handle this is to use regulatory programs as a transition to a competitive environment (Havighurst and Hackbarth, 1980). But that raises all the problems of regulatory programs that public choice advocates decry.

Insurers may balk because a fair amount of the leverage and control exerted by the choice proposals will be concentrated on them. This is one area where more rather than less regulation is expected. Recall the discussion of the Stockman–Gephardt bill. State regulation over health insurers might be replaced by more restrictive federal legislation. Insurers could be faced with a situation in which government would prescribe a minimum set of benefits and set administrative standards that are overseen by a watchdog agency (Demkovich, 1981). Additionally, some of the ideas, such as the Medicare voucher, are opposed by insurers because insurance plans cannot be written for anything nearly as inexpensively as the value of the voucher. The problem is exacerbated in future years because the value of the voucher (as set by the federal Health Care Financing Administration) would be increased by only a portion of health care price increases. To make up the difference, insurers would require rate increases. Because of the political repercussions and visibility of state rate increase proceedings and thus the very real possibility that rate increases might be denied, one response to a Medicare voucher on the part of the insurance industry might be a decision not to offer such plans (see Subcommittee on Health, 1981).

Employers may not be pleased with the choice ideas, especially those that mandate three separate plans offered by separate carriers. This would create large administrative costs for them. Employers might also face tax penalties and lose advantages of self-insurance. As the Washington Business Group on Health put it, "the competition bills tend to require more regulation of employers than either the status quo or the more centralized (national health insurance) proposals supported by labor" (quoted in Demkovich, 1981:1389).

Employee groups may view the choice plans as eroding an important fringe benefit and in some cases removing their control over that benefit where unions negotiate and provide benefits rather than employers. Consumers could well be displeased because they might perceive the need to spend more money out-of-pocket for health care. The plans literally affect everyone and attempt to affect the behavior of essentially the entire population (see Subcommittee on Health, 1981). We have already been warned by public choice advocates about the implications of attempts at massive social change.

> The single most important characteristic of the newer forms of social intervention is that their success depends on affecting the skills, attitudes, consumption habits, or production patterns of hundreds of millions of individuals, millions of business firms, and thousands of local units of government. The tasks are difficult, not so much because they deal with technologically complicated matters as because they aim ultimately at modifying the behavior of private producers and consumers. The boundaries of the 'public administration' problem have leapt beyond the question of how to effectively organize and run a public institution and now encompass the far more vexing question of how to change some aspect of the behavior of a whole society (Schultze, 1977:12).

Fixing the Rules—Politics Remains

A basic problem facing market reformers is that, in an attempt to depoliticize the medical industry (i.e., reduce government regulation and involvement at the state and federal levels), politics itself is ignored. Recall the earlier comment that public choice advocates believe that people behave the way they are rewarded, the way incentives are set up. But incentives to increase health care costs are due to societal demands, not provider actions.

> Providers of medical care cannot be blamed for this situation. It is society who changed the rules, it is we the people who are establishing health care as a right. Until the last decade or so, we were content with our medical care system and with health care as a market good. Our expectations have changed. But the structure and incentives of the medical care system have not changed, and cannot cope with health care as a merit good. Thus the problem is structural rather than conspiratorial. It is not that providers will try to do us ill; it is that they will try to do us too much good. And when someone else foots the bill, we will all want the very best. The system is therefore doing exactly what society rewards it to do (McClure, 1976:25).

In the words of Pogo, we have met the enemy and he is us.

The problem with this type of "societal" explanation is that precisely because it is historically apolitical it is fundamentally flawed. For example, the federal programs alluded to in the previous quote (Medicare and Medicaid) were financially modeled after the private health insurance system to maintain the support of the medical profession (Marmor, 1973). Furthermore, the growth of private health insurance was shaped by provider organizations either through direct controls (Blue Cross, Blue Shield) or pressure against insurers who might impose cost controls and therefore restrict the practice of medicine. Private health insurance (third-party reimbursement) was thus an accommodation on the part of the insurance industry to provider demands (Starr, 1982) and served the interests of providers. Even critics of government occasionally note that public policy may serve particularistic ends. In the words of George Stigler, 1982 nobel laureate in economics:

> We economists have traditionally made innumerable criticisms of the inefficiency of various policies, criticisms which have often been to their own (and my own) utter satisfaction. The meager success of these criticisms in changing these policies, I am convinced, stems from the fact that more than narrow efficiency has been involved in almost every case—that inexplicit or incomprehensible goals were served by these policies and served tolerably efficiently. Tariffs were redistributing income to groups with substantial political power, not simply expressing the deficient public understanding of the theory of comparative costs. We live in a world that is full of mistaken policies, but they are not mistaken for their supporters . . . (Stigler, 1982).

The fatal flaw in the market reform proposals is thus the failure to think through the political implications of the proposals. Recall the distinction between deregulation and market reform. The former is the simple elimination of a regulatory program; the latter is the use of government to create quasi-markets. The changes required to create a competitive market in health care are enormous and in many respects affect all parties adversely. The politics of the system remains because various actors, seeking their own self-interest (as theorized by the public choice literature), attempt to limit any costs placed on them, even if society as a whole would benefit (Dahl, 1982; Olson, 1982). In this "zero-sum society" (Thurow, 1980), the task is to convince the relevant groups to sacrifice short-term considerations for longer-term societal benefits. That task has yet to be accomplished, but it seems to be the type of problem facing market reformers.

That groups seeking their self-interest will work to limit the effects of market reform proposals (discussed in the previous section), which are based on taking advantage of this best-understood motivation (Levine, 1972), is the logical contradiction of the market reform proposals. Group incentives are not to maximize the size of the pie for society but rather to maximize their slice of the pie. They do this by manipulation in free markets, the same way they try to manipulate the rules of regulatory agencies.

The point is this: firms are political instruments—it is in their self-interest to be so—
and they are *very good* political instruments. In the absence of strategies to constrain
conduct or alter structure (e.g., antitrust laws), firms will be able to tilt the rules
substantially to their advantage and produce a world that is a far cry from the
apolitical ideal of economists. It is naive to expect otherwise. Why would an organization that is actively seeking profits *within* the rules of the game not seek further
profits by *altering* the rules of the game as well—especially when its structure makes
it likely that it will succeed? The restraining strategies . . . must be evaluated not
against the standard of the apolitical competitive market but against what the unconstrained firm would otherwise have attained (Goldberg, 1974:479).

Groups (firms) have a variety of resources available to influence institutional change: financial wealth, voting, ability to withhold services,
and so forth.

These resources are differentially distributed—some groups will have a substantial
bankroll but few voters while others will have a different endowment. Outcomes will
depend on institutional structure. So, self-interest would dictate that the participants direct their efforts at influencing this set of rules also. Groups will attempt to
have their affairs governed by rules that reward the resources with which they are
relatively well endowed (Goldberg, 1974:480).

Attempts at rule fixing can be seen in the implementation of the most
popular of market reform proposals, the effluent tax. This is a tax
placed on polluters depending upon the amount of pollution and desired reductions. The effluent tax would allow polluters to reduce pollution in ways that are the most economically sound for them. In addition,
the tax would have a competitive effect. If one firm developed a process
to reduce pollution and thus reduce the tax, the cost of that firm's goods
would be reduced. Other firms would have to match the effort or lose
their competitive position. The result is not the elimination of pollution
entirely, but reduction to an economically efficient or optimal level
(Ramsay and Anderson, 1972). The experience with such taxes, however, suggests that they are as subject to politics and bargaining as are
regulatory programs. For example, in France, the National Water Commission and the regional water basin commissions are partly composed
of major industrial interests (e.g., major polluters). The water basin
commissions, whose "approval is required to fix the basis of calculation
and the level of the effluent charges proposed by the basin agencies," are
characterized by considerable political bargaining (Majone, 1976:607).
At what level should charges be set? How often should resources be
monitored? And so on.

Because of the mixed nature of market reform, the political focus will shift to the rules under which competition will occur. And the various rules that need to be made are not only numerous but will continually need to be made—the policy process is reiterative (Lindblom, 1980). What kinds of rules are we talking about?

If the voucher proposal is fully (CCHP) or partially (Medicare/Medicaid) enacted, then one question is the level at which the voucher will be set. Under CCHP, the basis for calculation is the average actuarial health cost for a particular family unit.[5] The voucher would then be set at some percentage of that cost. What is the percentage? If set too high, say at 85–90% of the average actuarial cost, then the effect of choosing among different plans with different premiums is minimized. If the voucher is set too low, say 30%, then the amount of cost-sharing on the part of consumers becomes prohibitive. In either event, here is one area where affected interests are likely to try to fix the rules of competition. Consumers, if they see a low percentage as economically harmful, might pressure for higher percentages. Providers and insurers might also prefer the higher percentage if they see it as minimizing choice: the more generous the voucher, the less incentive there is for consumers to search for cost-efficient plans and the less urgency there is for insurers and providers to consider the cost of their services.

A related question is the indexing of the value of the voucher. If the voucher is indexed at less than the increase in health care costs, the voucher becomes less valuable over time and consumers must pay more of the premiums. From government's standpoint this might be desirable because it reduces its expenditures. Indeed, this is one of the few ways that government has of controlling health care expenditures. From the consumer's standpoint, this might not be a desirable result. The problems of Social Security indexing should be enlightening for market reform advocates.

The broader question that indexing raises is how health care cost increases should be distributed among government, insurers, providers, consumers, and employers. Each group will seek to push off all or some of the increases on others. If, as market reformers believe, it will be some years before the full effects of competition are felt, then health care inflation will be not be alleviated soon. A likely response on the part of the nongovernmental actors is to attempt to push most of the costs onto government.

Other problems revolve around the question of choice and benefits. How much choice among plans should be allowed? The workplace-based plans specify limits, say three different plans offered by three different carriers. CCHP sets no limits on the number of alternatives.

Should some types of choices be proscribed? For example, medical soci-ety-sponsored plans such as individual practice associations are not fa-vorably viewed by some market advocates (Havighurst, 1982). Should they be prohibited from offering plans? Would such a prohibition lead to reactions by providers that would stifle competition?

The benefits questions also raise interesting political questions. Should a minimum set of benefits be prescribed? If so, then the choice among plans is limited. If minimum benefits are not to be prescribed, then the range of choice could be overwhelming and intelligent selection among plans minimized. What benefits should be included or excluded? Os-teopaths and chiropractors would certainly like to be included. Nurse-midwives and free-standing birth centers might make a case for inclu-sion. If these alternative providers did attempt to be included in some of the plans, they would undoubtedly meet opposition from more conven-tional providers. Should abortion be included in the plans? Right-to-life groups might attempt to eliminate abortion payments from governmen-tally regulated plans, as they have done with the Medicaid program and are seeking to do with the Federal Employees Health Benefits Program. If this should occur, in what ways would the politics be any different from what currently exists?

The "market strengthening" regulation required for competition to work would face the same kinds of problems that current regulatory programs face. Enhanced application of the antitrust laws in the health field will meet opposition from those it is applied against. The attempt in 1982 to restrict FTC regulation over state-regulated professions is a precursor of what might happen should the competition proposals be enacted. One interesting political question that the FTC might face is whether to allow providers to continue to be on the boards of some Blue Shield agencies. The new oversight of insurers that competition would bring would create a situation analogous to Medicare, in which providers and insurers played important political roles in deciding how payments would be made and on what basis. What is most noticeable about the Medicare situation is the lack of participation by the ostensible benefici-aries of the program, the elderly (Feder, 1977). These attempts at fixing the rules of competition change the very nature of competition. Quasi-markets do not work automatically but must be deliberately established. Yet the very ones most likely to be affected by the new rules are precisely the ones in the best position to help set those rules. If competition is enacted, as time passes the impact of the rules will be felt. The various relevant political actors may very well seek to change those rules to limit those impacts.

CONCLUSION

Market reform policies have been suggested as an alternative to government regulatory programs. These programs are viewed as failures and inherently flawed, even if implemented by zealots [those convinced of the merits of the program and seeking to make it successful—see Downs (1967)]. Industries are too complex for detailed oversight, necessary information is often unavailable, and, most important of all, regulatory agencies are responsive to concentrated producer or industry interests. In addition, in the case of health care, government programs such as tax laws governing fringe benefits and Medicare and Medicaid have exacerbated the cost problem by reinforcing the perverse incentives already existing in the system.

The favored alternative of market reformers, in health care and elsewhere (housing, education, poverty, environment, etc.), is market-correcting policies, the creation of quasi-markets. The major virtue of quasi-markets, they argue, is that the incentives built into the system will automatically influence various parties to move in desired directions (e.g., select cost-efficient plans, reduce pollution to optimal levels). But because of this "automatic" assumption, the "invisible hand" of Adam Smith, market reformers have not seriously considered implementation problems. Similarly, the implementation literature has had little to say about market reform (or deregulation), primarily because of its focus on government programs.

But implementation problems exist because market reform is not deregulation. Deregulation is the elimination of government's involvement in a particular area. As of 1983, for example, the Civil Aeronautics Board (CAB) no longer has authority over fares charged by airlines. Indeed, by 1985, the CAB will cease to exist. Implementation is not a problem. But market reform is different; an important role for government remains. Indeed, government must take positive action to create the quasi-markets, and the role does not disappear but continues.

Health care illustrates the argument about market reform and implementation. In some respects market reform in health care is more difficult than in other areas. Government's current role has three components. First, some programs are undertaken for merit wants or equity reasons (the health system does not provide adequate services or insurance for certain sectors of the population, such as the poor and the elderly). Second, other programs such as the tax laws ratified previous agreements (the treatment of fringe benefits during World War II). And third, because these programs and private insurance contained cost-increasing incentives, regulatory programs were undertaken to limit the costs, particularly to government budgets. Again the rationales for these programs vary. Rate regulation and certificate-of-need programs are examples of economic regulation and attempts to limit costs. Antitrust enforcement was undertaken to correct defects in medical markets. Thus, policymakers are faced with a bewildering array of programs. By contrast, airline deregulation and regulatory reform for pollution control (i.e., effluent taxes) are relatively simple undertakings involving only one type of change. Health care is a mixed bag of some regulation and some subsidy; the result is a complex situation. No simple solution is sufficient to remedy the defects that market reformers correctly point out. And market reform is not a simple solution.

Market reform is faced with four sets of implementation problems. First, it is based on an extremely complex program theory. The more complex the program, the more difficulty there is in implementing it. Second, the complexity of the program requires that numerous actors behave appropriately, which may not happen. Third, opposition to market reform exists because various actors are adversely affected by it (indeed there appear to be few positive short-run effects for anyone of political consequence), and they will seek to limit the impacts during implementation, much as occurs with other government programs. Finally, the politics that market reformers decry remains because affected actors, especially those whose interests are most directly affected, will seek to fix the rules within which competition occurs.

The basic problem facing market reformers is to convince all actors that reform is in their best interests and that of society in the long run. But precisely because of the financial incentives, the only short-run interest served by competition is government, e.g., it provides a means to limit and control health budgets. The argument of this essay suggests two possible and related solutions to implementation problems.

First is the "evolutionist" perspective that suggests that we eliminate regulation that hinders competition and allow the market to work but do not constrain choices or try to force the health care system to respond in a desired way (Havighurst, 1982). Second is a "minimalist" strategy consisting of a limit to tax subsidies, a voucher for Medicare and Medicaid, and regulatory reform (Meyer, 1982). Even here, we will encounter many of the same problems that more comprehensive reform confronts (as discussed in this essay), but not to the same degree. These alternatives affect fewer actors and control government expenditures. Either of the two related paths moves a bit closer to deregulation and its relative ease of implementation and away from the difficulties of implementation that would undoubtedly characterize comprehensive market reform.

NOTES

1.   The current policy response to this budget problem is cuts in Medicaid and Medicare benefits. But this response has little rationale apart from reduced government expenditures and does not address the problem of perverse incentives that public choice advocates see as the cause of the cost problem. In addition to budget cuts, a prospective reimbursement system has been proposed for the two programs. While this may change some of the incentives in the system, it is, again, not competition (see Meyer, 1982).

2.   An alternative view suggests that agencies are responsive to congressional desires, particularly to the dominant congressional committee or subcommittee. In the case of the Federal Trade Commission, the dominant partner is the Senate Commerce Committee's Subcommittee on Consumer Affairs. As the composition of this subcommittee changed, so too did the actions taken by the FTC. Calvert and Weingast (1982) argue that the makeup shifted twice in the 1970s, first to consumer-oriented actions and then later in the 1970s away from consumer issues. Their point is that the FTC and other regulatory agencies may not be "runaway bureaucracies" but rather highly responsive to policy cues.

3.   Competition proposals may indeed not alleviate the health care cost problem, yet market reformers would still support these proposals because the results would express actual consumer preferences. This alone—ethics, freedom, and expressions of consumer preferences—is ground enough for market reformers to prefer markets to government programs (Havighurst, 1982).

4.   Foundations for medical care (FMCs) and individual practice associations (IPAs) are medical societies' responses to the growth of prepaid group plans (PGPs). The latter, more recently known as health maintenance organizations (HMOs), provide comprehensive services to subscribers for a fixed premium from a closed panel of providers. FMCs and IPAs combine elements of PGP and the predominant fee-for-service system. For example, subscribers pay a premium to the group, but providers receive a fee from the premiums for providing services. FMCs and IPAs also contain features more typical of PGPs such as fixed-fee schedules and utilization or peer review controls. Market reformers do not favor IPAs or FMCs because they tend to include as many providers in the area as possible and thus limit competition. In addition, while IPAs are growing faster than PGPs, they tend to have both higher costs and higher hospital utilization than PGPs (though lower than the fee-for-service system) (Enthoven, 1980a; Wilson and Neuhauser, 1976).

5.   The average actuarial health cost is the average amount of money spent on health care (from all sources) for a family unit depending upon the category of the family unit. For example, this cost would be higher for an elderly couple than for a young couple. The percentage that the voucher would be worth would be the same for the two units, but the actual dollars would be higher for the elderly couple, because their expected health costs would be higher. The number of different actuarial categories actually employed in a competition proposal is also one of the rules subject to political debate. For instance, for the elderly, one can distinguish between the young-old (65–74) and the old-old (75+). This would mean that the old-old would face higher out-of-pocket costs.

REFERENCES

Altman, S. H. and R. Blendon, eds. (1979) Medical Technology: The Culprit Behind Health Care Costs? Proceedings of the 1977 Sun Valley Forum on National Health. Washington, D.C.: U.S. Department of Health, Education and Welfare, Public Health Service.

Bardach, E. (1977) The Implementation Game: What Happens After a Bill Becomes a Law. Cambridge, Mass.: MIT Press.

Berki, S. E. and M. L. F. Ashcraft (1980) "HMO enrollment: who joins what and why: a review of the literature." Milbank Memorial Fund Quarterly/Health and Society 58:588–632.

Brown, L. D. (1981) "Competition and health cost containment: cautions and conjectures." Milbank Memorial Fund Quarterly/Health and Society 59:145–89.

Calvert, R. L. and B. R. Weingast (1982) "Runaway bureaucracy and congressional oversight: why reforms fail." Policy Studies Review 1:557–64.

Caulfield, S. C. and P. L. Haynes (1981) Health Care Costs: Private Initiatives for Containment. Washington, D.C.: Government Research Corporation.

Christianson, J. B. (1980) "The impact of HMOs: evidence and research issues." Journal of Health Politics, Policy and Law 5:354–367.

Coelen, C. and D. Sullivan (1981) "An analysis of the effects of prospective reimbursement programs on hospital expenditures." Health Care Financing Rev. 2:1–40.

Dahl, R. (1982) Dilemmas of Pluralist Democracy. New Haven, Conn.: Yale University Press.

Demkovich, L. E. (1981) "No deregulation here." National Journal 13:1389.

Downs, A. (1967) Inside Bureaucracy. Boston: Little, Brown.

Drake, D. F. and D. M. Kozak (1978) "A primer on antitrust and hospital regulation." Journal of Health Politics, Policy and Law 3:328–44.

Edwards, III, G. C. (1980) Implementing Public Policy. Washington, D.C.: Congressional Quarterly Press.

Ellwood, P. M., Jr. (1974) "Models for organizing health services and implications of legislative proposals." Pp. 67–95 in I. K. Zola and J. B. McKinlay (eds.), Organizational Issues in the Delivery of Health Services. New York: Prodist.

Elmore, R. F. (1982) "Backward mapping: implementation research and policy decisions." Pp. 18–35 in W. Williams (ed.), Studying Implementation: Methodological and Administrative Issues. Chatham, N.J.: Chatham House.

Enthoven, A. C. (1978a) "Consumer-choice health plan (first of two parts)." The new England Journal of Medicine 298:650–58.

_____(1978b) "Consumer-choice health plan (second of two parts)." The New England Journal of Medicine 298:709–21.

_____(1980a) Health Plan. Reading, Mass.: Addison-Wesley.

_____(1980b) "Supply-side economics of health care and consumer choice health plan." Paper present at A Conference on Health Care—Professional Ethics, Government Regulation, or Markets? Sponsored by the American Enterprise Institute, September 25–26, Washington, D.C.

Falkson, J. L. (1980) HMOs and the Politics of Health System Reform. Bowie, Md.: Brady.

Farley, P. J. and G. R. Wilensky (1982) "Options, incentives and employment-related health insurance coverage." Paper presented at annual meeting of the Eastern Economic Association, May 1, Washington, D.C.

Feder, J. M. (1977) Medicare: The Politics of Federal Hospital Insurance. Lexington, Mass.: Heath.

Feldstein, M. (1977) "The high cost of hospitals—and what to do about it." The Public Interest 43:40–54.

Friedman, M. (1962) Capitalism and Freedom. Chicago: University of Chicago Press.

General Accounting Office (1979) Iranian Oil Cutoff: Reduced Petroleum Supplies and Inadequate U.S. Government Response. Washington, D.C.: General Accounting Office.

Ginsburg, P. B. (1981) "Altering the tax treatment of employment-based health plans." Milbank Memorial Fund Quarterly/Health and Society 59:224–55.

Goldberg, V. P. (1974) "Institutional change and the quasi-invisible hand." The Journal of Law and Economics 17:461–92.

Havighurst, C. C. (1977) "Controlling health care costs: strengthening the private sector's hand." Journal of Health Politics, Policy and Law 1:471–98.

———(1982) Deregulating the Health Care Industry. Cambridge, Mass.: Ballinger.

——— and G. M. Hackbarth (1980) "Competition and Health Care: Planning for Deregulation." Regulation 4:39–48.

Health Care Financing Administration (1982) Health Care Financing Trends. Baltimore: U.S. Department of Health and Human Services.

Hirschman, A. O. (1970) Exit, Voice, and Loyalty: Responses to Decline in Firms, Organizations, and States. Cambridge, Mass.: Harvard University Press.

Levine, R. A. (1972) Public Planning: Failure and Redirection. New York: Basic Books.

Lindblom, C. E. (1980) The Policy Process, 2nd ed. Englewood Cliffs, N.J.: Prentice-Hall.

Lowi, T. J. (1979) The End of Liberalism: The Second Republic of the United States, 2nd ed. New York: Norton.

Luft, H. S. (1982) "On the potential failure of good ideas: an interview with the originator of Murphy's Law (response)." Journal of Health Politics, Policy and Law 7:45–53.

McClure, W. (1976) "The medical care system under national health insurance: four models." Journal of Health Politics, Policy and Law 1:22–68.

———(1977) "An analysis of health care system performance under a proposed NHI administrative mechanism." Pp. 11–36 in William R. Roy (ed.), Effects of the Payment Mechanism on the Health Care Delivery System. Proceedings of a conference held at Skyland Lodge, Shenandoah National Park, Virginia, November 7–8. Washington, D.C.: U.S. Department of Health, Education and Welfare, National Center for Health Services Research.

———(1981) "Structure and incentive problems in economic regulation of medical care." Milbank Memorial Fund Quarterly/Health and Society 59:107–44.

———(1982) "Implementing a competitive medical care system through public policy." Journal of Health Politics, Policy and Law 7:2–44.

Macrae, D., Jr., and J. A. Wilde (1979) Policy Analysis for Public Decisions. N. Scituate, Mass.: Duxbury Press.

Majone, G. (1976) "Choice among policy instruments for pollution control." Policy Analysis 2:589–613.

Marmor, T. R. (1973) The Politics of Medicare. Chicago: Aldine.

Mazmanian, D. and P. Sabatier (1980) "The implementation of public policy: a framework for analysis." Policy Studies Journal 8:538–60.

Meyer, J. A. (1982) "Health care reform and market discipline—federalism strikes back." Regulation 6:16–20.

Minarik, J. J. (1981) "Tax expenditures." Pp. 271–75 in J. A. Pechman (ed.), Setting National Priorities: The 1982 Budget. Washington, D.C.: Brookings Institution.

Mitchell, W. C. (1971) "The shape of political theory to come: from political sociology to political economy." Pp. 12–25 in R. S. Ross and W. C. Mitchell (eds.), Introductory Readings in American Government: A Public Choice Perspective. Chicago: Markham.

Mitnick, B. M. (1978). "Deregulation as a process of organizational reduction." Public Administration Review 38:350–57.

Olson, M. (1982) The Rise and Decline of Nations. New Haven, Conn.: Yale University Press.

Pearson, D. A. and D. S. Abernethy (1980) "A qualitative assessment of previous efforts to contain hospital costs." Journal of Health Politics, Policy and Law 5:120–41.

Pressman, J. L. and A. B. Wildavsky (1973) Implementation. Berkeley: University of California Press.

Ramsay, W. and C. Anderson (1972) Managing the Environment: An Economic Primer. New York: Basic Books.

Reinhardt, U. E. (1982) "Table manners at the health care feast." Pp. 13–34 in D. Yaggy and W. G. Anlyan (eds.), Financing Health Care: Competition versus Regulation. Cambridge, Mass.: Ballinger.

Ripley, R. B., and G. A. Franklin (1982) Bureaucracy and Policy Implementation. Homewood, Ill.: Dorsey Press.

Rushefsky, M. E. (1981) "A critique of market reform in health care: the 'consumer-choice health plan'." Journal of Health Politics, Policy and Law 4:720–41.

Samuelson, P. A. (1964) Economics, 6th ed. New York: McGraw-Hill.

Schultze, C. L. (1977) The Public Use of Private Interest. Washington, D.C.: Brookings Institution.

Starr, P. (1982) "The triumph of accomodation: the rise of private health plans in America, 1929–1959." Journal of Health Politics, Policy and Law 7:580–628.

Stigler, G. J. (1982) "The economist as preacher." The New York Times (October 24).

Subcommittee on Health (1981) Proposals to Stimulate Competition in the Financing and Delivery of Health Care. Washington, D.C.: U.S. House of Representatives, Committee on Ways and Means, 97th Congress, 1st Session, September 30, October 1–2.

Thompson, F. J. (1981) Health Policy and the Bureaucracy: Politics and Implementation. Cambridge, Mass.: MIT Press.

Thurow, L. C. (1980) The Zero-Sum Society. New York: Basic Books.

Waldo, D. R. and R. M. Gibson (1982) "National health expenditures, 1981." Health Care Financing Review 4:1–35.

Wildavsky, A. (1977) "Doing better and feeling worse: the political pathology of health policy." Pp. 105–23 in J. H. Knowles (ed.), Doing Better and Feeling Worse: Health in the United States. New York: Norton.

———(1979) Speaking Truth to Power: The Art and Craft of Policy Analysis. Boston: Little, Brown.

Wilson, F. A. and D. Neuhauser (1976) Health Services in the United States. Cambridge, Mass.: Ballinger.

Wilson, J. Q., ed. (1980) The Politics of Regulation. New York: Basic Books.

Wines, M. (1982) "Squelching the FTC." National Journal 14:1589–94.

Wolf, C,, Jr. (1979) "A theory of non-market failures." The Public Interest 55:114–33.

THEORETICAL PERSPECTIVES ON CONTRACTING OUT FOR SERVICES:
IMPLEMENTATION PROBLEMS AND POSSIBILITIES OF PRIVATIZING PUBLIC SERVICES

Ruth Hoogland DeHoog

INTRODUCTION

Governments in the United States have a preoccupation with free enterprise. As Ira Sharkansky notes in his comparative study, *Wither the State?*, "The inclination to use business firms or other private units as government contractors is distinctly an American style of conducting public activities outside the borders of the state" (1979:4). In particular, during the last three years a preference for using nongovernmental agents has become a significant part of government theory and practice. Although for some years federal and state agencies have followed Office of Management and Budget (OMB) and state directives to rely on the private sector to supply their needs, only during the Reagan administration have we seen a major commitment to achieving public goals and implementing programs via private agents.

In the field of human services, private, nonprofit agencies are expected to increase their services to the needy. Urban enterprise zones are to be created to give businesses the incentives necessary to revitalize economically depressed areas. In its Government Capacity Sharing Program, the U.S. Department of Housing and Urban Development (HUD) has encouraged local governments to increase their use of contractors for a wide range of municipal services. A variety of mechanisms for privatization of public services has been suggested in the literature of public administration as well, including using vouchers, franchises, contracting out, and coproduction of services (Poole, 1980; Straussman, 1981; Savas, 1982). Governments at all levels have considered or adopted most of these mechanisms to cut back expenditures in view of fiscal constraints and to "get government off our backs." Perhaps the theme for the 1980s will be "less is best."

While all of these innovations warrant further examination, we will focus in this chapter on the process of governmental "contracting out" for the production and delivery of public services. The general term "contracting out" refers to the practice of having public services (those that any given government unit has decided to provide for its citizens) supplied either by other governmental jurisdictions or by private (profit or nonprofit) organizations instead of delivering the service through a government unit's own personnel. Several different types of contracts and different ways of granting them have been used in many kinds of services.[1]

Contracting for services from either the private sector or outside public agencies is not, however, a new method of service delivery. For years, many local governments have purchased such routine services as garbage collection, road maintenance, and street lighting from outside suppliers (Fisk et. al., 1978). Under the contract cities plan (or Lakewood Plan) several California cities for some years have contracted out for their basic municipal services, in most cases from the county government (Miller, 1981; Sonenblum et al., 1977; Warren, 1965). And almost all government units that require roads, buildings, or military weapons have long had contracts with profit-making firms for architectural and engineering services. On the federal level in the post–World War II era, the number of contracts for scientific research, complex technical or evaluative services, and defense-related services increased rapidly (Danhof, 1968). According to Bruce L. R. Smith, a foremost scholar of federal contracting, such extensive usage of private institutions is a central feature of *any* modern government (1975:1).

However, in the last two decades two new trends have been apparent. First, the purchase of human services for clients has become a more common method of service delivery in state and local governments, often as a result of federal laws and regulations.For example, it has been estimated that over half of the funds for Title XX of the Social Security Act have been spent by states for purchased social services, and increasing percentages of contracts have been with private, nonprofit agencies. In fact, federal regulations have encouraged states to use outside sources in many cases rather than build the capacity to produce these services in house (O'Donnell, 1978; Wedel, 1979). Some states have come to rely heavily on purchase-of-service arrangements for day care, protective services, family counseling, homemaker services, rehabilitation, housing programs, foster care, and institutional care for needy clients. The now-defunct Comprehensive Employment and Training Act (CETA) also used both public and private contractors extensively to deliver services. services.

Second, urban service analysts have more frequently suggested and considered contracting out as an alternative to conventional bureaucratic means for a wide variety of programs and services, particularly in the face of fiscal strain. Services supplied by this means run the gamut from the more traditional janitorial and sanitation services to management consulting, tax collection, training services, and highly specialized research and development. While some are purchased primarily for government agencies' use (e.g., janitorial services and research and development), many contracted services are performed for the general public or a specified client group. Thus, the contractor, whether another public agency or a private (proprietary or nonprofit) agency, acts as an extension of the responsible government unit.

THE CASE FOR CONTRACTING OUT

What then are the arguments in favor of contracting for public services? Why could this method of delivering services be considered by some to be superior to traditional methods? In the academic literature, representatives of one school of thought have provided much of the theoretical basis for this approach: public choice theorists in the fields of public administration and economics who have focused on the size of government jurisdictions and the economics of bureaucracies. Although there are differences in subject, methods, and emphasis, the major underlying arguments of scholars identified with this group are similar (Bennett and Johnson, 1981; Borcherding, 1977; Ostrom and Ostrom, 1971, 1977; Niskanen, 1971; Savas, 1982; Sonenblum et al., 1977; Tullock, 1965). Perhaps the best theoretical formulations directly supportive of contracting out have been written by urban service analysts (Fitch, 1974; Savas, 1974, 1982), while most of the other public choice scholars in public administration approach this subject from a more general and often more theoretical perspective.

Unlike other public choice academicians, this group has concentrated on analyzing and altering specific services and the structures by which they are supplied, with less concern for the voting and demand mechanisms or the patterns of metropolitan organization. Using a neoclassical economic framework, these public choice scholars argue that the competitive marketplace produces goods and services efficiently, whereas monopolies, whether public or private, tend toward both inefficiency and unresponsiveness. They assume that few theoretical differences exist between public and private sector goods and services in how they can be supplied.[2] (However, governments determine the demand for public services by acting on behalf of citizens and use taxation and coercive authority to prevent free riders.) Since in most program and service areas government agencies are service monopolies, the personnel are likely to behave in ways that promote their own interests at the expense of the interests of efficiency and the consumer/citizen. Niskanen (1971) has argued that public bureaucracies are inefficient and expensive burdens because bureaucrats use their monopoly of information vis-à-vis the legislature to maximize their bureaus' budgets, a goal that, if achieved, is most likely to increase their personal rewards. Consequently, bureaus tend to produce too much output, exceeding the point at which benefits equal costs, thus leading to larger budgets, the inefficient use of public funds, and bigger government.

The basic perspective of Niskanen and other public choice theorists is to encourage the use of quasi-market mechanisms for the provision of services that are usually produced by federal, state, or local government "monopolies." For the production of mainly private goods (those that are highly divisible and packageable) that the public sector has traditionally provided, governments could try to return both the financing and production of such services to the private sector entirely (e.g., garbage collection). Or governments could provide vouchers to consumers, thus subsidizing the consumer rather than the supplier of a service and thereby giving the consumer/citizen the opportunity for choice among various agents (e.g., education). Offering franchises to private firms and getting citizens involved in "coproducing" services are two additional means to reducing government's role in service delivery.

But these modes of privatization (sometimes called "load shedding"), according to some, are not as feasible and acceptable as contracting for public services either to other government units or to private companies. Unlike other methods of privatization, contracting out can be used for many services with either private or public good characteristics, according to public choice writers, since both types of goods need not be delivered to the public *by* a public agency *through* its public employees, even if the service is paid for by the taxpayers through a government unit.[3] Instead of using its own bureaucracy, the relevant government body can purchase the services directly from public or private sources through the use of competitive bids or competitive proposals, thus developing quasi-market conditions and achieving a desirable degree of both flexibility and responsiveness in the process.

For their part, bidders/proposers must calculate not only the actual costs of service provision for the specified services, but also the price and services of other competing firms or agencies. According to public choice (and market) theory, prospective contractors will be encouraged to bid near the true costs of production for the exact set of services desired by the government in order to obtain the contract. To get a contract, in public procurement parlance, the bidder must be viewed as *responsive* to the contract requirements and specifications as well as *responsible,* being capable of carrying through on the terms of the agreement. Given responsive and responsible bidders, contracting advocates assume that awards will usually be made to the lowest bidder, whether for garbage pickup, tree trimming, or employment services. Only then will there exist an incentive to keep costs to a minimum.

The essential role of the government agency or elected body would be to perform a "watchdog" function. Not only would it deal with revenue gathering or budget allocations and the transfer of payments to the delivery agent, but the unit would also choose the agents, continue to monitor and evaluate their performance, and engage in long-range planning. The threat of the government agency contracting with another supplier (or even producing the service itself) would, advocates believe, ensure that the producer is both efficient and responsive to the needs of the citizens and their representatives. Therefore, advocates expect contracting out to enable governments to achieve the best service performance at the lowest cost because of a direct monetary incentive, namely profit and/or the desire to stay in business. (The former incentive is usually associated with proprietary firms; the latter, with non-profit agencies.)

In part, this confidence in outside supply is based on empirical study, as well as deductive, formal theory and ideological predispositions. Researchers have examined several different policy areas to determine if the quasi-market approaches to service provision are less costly or more efficient than public monopolies. In the main, what limited evidence there is usually supports the arguments that the privately (or outside) supplied services are at least *less costly* (and in a few cases, more efficient) than in-house services in the cases of fire protection (Ahlbrandt, 1973), an airline (Davies, 1971), a utility (DeAlessi, 1974), refuse collection (Bennett and Johnson, 1979; Kemper and Quigley, 1976; Savas, 1977b), a range of municipal services under the Lakewood Plan (Deacon, 1979), and property tax assessment (Lowery, 1982).

Often proponents believe that even government services that have outputs that are more difficult to measure could lead to similar results in areas such as mental health, social services, and education (Bennett and Johnson, 1981; Poole, 1980). Unfortunately, few scholars have studied these services in terms of their supply structure. Moreover, seldom have the existing empirical works in any service areas gone beyond measuring the costs of outside supply to analyze service levels, service performance, or the political and administrative contexts of contracting. Nor have researchers examined the procedures of contracting to shed light on the problems governments may encounter in the contractual relationship. These unexplored areas of research are critical to our improved understanding of the contracting process and its outcomes. If scholarly research in this field is to be of some utility to practitioners and elected officials in their decisions, we must begin to identify the conditions and procedures conducive to contracting arrangements achieving the aims of improved efficiency and good quality services.

In summary, what then are the major arguments in favor of using outside sources to supply government services? First, proponents believe that private supply will lead to *lower government costs* for at least five reasons:

1. Competition for contracts would help to reveal the true costs of production and eliminate waste, since contracts would be awarded to those offering the most or best quality services at the least cost level.
2. Substitution of the profit motive for budget maximization and empire-building would help to limit budget growth in particular, and government growth in general, in the long run.

3. Economies of scale could be realized in some jurisdictions through the reduction of overhead, start-up costs, or high personnel costs by spreading supply over a large number of units or other agencies (e.g., contracting for specialized medical services).
4. High personnel costs would be reduced, primarily due to avoiding public employee unions and public personnel controls (e.g., civil service rules).
5. Greater flexibility in the use of personnel and equipment would be achieved for short-term projects, part-time work, specialized needs, or new problems, without a commitment to sustaining a bloated bureaucracy.

This anticipation of reduced costs of public services is the most compelling reason for both scholars and government officials to favor contracting out (Fitch, 1974; Savas, 1982).

Privatization advocates also see a second advantage of contracting out. They expect that competition for contracts among private contractors will also produce *better quality services* for the price paid, since a direct monetary incentive for good performance by suppliers exists (Bennett and Johnson, 1981; Fitch, 1974; Savas, 1982; Spaan, 1977). If the overseeing agency judges the delivered services to be inadequate, another supplier (either another private agent or a government agency) could be granted the contract. Thus, to use Albert O. Hirschman's (1970) terms, the contract relationship has a major advantage over the usual methods in that it allows for *both* exit and voice mechanisms to be activated in the event that the service quality delcines or does not meet the contract's specifications.

A third—some observers believe a major—advantage to purchasing services is that the rapid *government growth* of the last decades *could be slowed,* if not halted, by this means (Borcherding, 1977). Government would have greater control over its services. The anticipated cost of savings would keep budget growth to a minimum, while the size of public employee rolls could be limited. The power of the centralized bureaucracy at all levels could be somewhat reduced as well by allowing greater participation for private actors in public policymaking. Public choice economist James M. Buchanan argues:

> *Governmental financing of goods and services must be divorced from direct governmental provision or production of these goods and services.* There may be fully legitimate arguments for governmental financing but little or no argument for governmental provision. Through the simple device of introducing private provision under government financing, the growth of public spending may, figuratively speaking, be stopped in its tracks (1977:5; italics are in original).

ANALYSIS OF THE PROCONTRACTING ARGUMENT

The obvious question is: are these anticipated benefits of contracting realized in practice? As noted above, some empirical research in a few services lends support to these assertions, but much remains to be studied. Before these research results are available, however, another approach to evaluating this argument can be utilized. Some writers have implied in their descriptions of how contracting works that certain key conditions must be present for their positive expectations to be realized. Without them, the benefits of contracting would not be fully realized. These conditions, though usually not clearly stated, are implied by the writers on contracting, but they must be made explicit in order to understand the likelihood of attaining the expected benefits of contracting. In particular, at least three major conditions appear to be critical to any contracting arrangements: competition in the environment and in the government's contracting procedures; government decision making to attain the goals of cost reduction and service quality; and an effective "watchdog" role by government.[4]

First, public choice scholars emphasize that market competition is the key ingredient in reducing costs and improving service performance. Some writers seem to imply that the contracting "market" acts as an automatic mechanism, but this is a naive view. In particular, two aspects of competition in the contracting system appear to be essential: competition in the environment and in contracting procedures. These elements are not automatically present in all contracting situations; yet they create the competition that is supposed to produce beneficial results. The service environment determines the alternatives that can be considered by the government unit as well as the calculations made by potential contractors. At least two responsible and responsive independent bidders or proposers (and preferably more) are required to produce a basis for competition. If no other firm exists to offer its services, what incentive does the single bidder have to pare costs and provide high quality services? And how can the purchasing unit evaluate the proposed price and services when there is no method of comparison? (This task is particularly problematic when the government agency has never delivered the service itself.)

In addition, the procedures utilized by the government unit must promote, rather than reduce, competition. Wide advertising, a clear and complete specification of the services required, and the impartial consideration of contractors throughout the process are the primary methods of ensuring that purchasing services will ultimately benefit the service consumers and taxpayers. Usually maximum utility will be realized when the government has an adequate knowledge of: (1) potential service providers and their past performance; (2) the services themselves, especially as they relate to the needs of consumers; (3) the methods of service; and (4) the costs of various components of the services. With this information those who write the specifications and evaluate the suppliers' bids/proposals will understand what elements are essential, practicable, and sufficient for good service provision.

The second major condition for efficient contracting that proponents assume is that contracting officials will be rational decision makers who are motivated to adhere to the goal of maximizing cost savings with adequate service performance.[5] (This condition is hardly discussed in the contracting literature, partly, I surmise, because it is assumed that if contracting is considered by officials, it is to achieve this goal of cost reduction.) Individual public officials first would be able to rank-order the various alternatives according to this goal with the information they have obtained about cost, quality, needs, and past performance. Then they would select the best choice, i.e., the alternative that will result in the desired services at the least cost level. This outcome, however, depends on two key elements: the common goal of cost minimization with adequate service provision, and sufficient information to consider the major alternatives and to judge accurately the anticipated performance and consequences of each alternative in terms of this goal.

This form of rational decision making logically should be utilized in at least two critical contracting decisions: the choice between in-house service supply and contracting out and the choice among alternative outside delivery agents. It is obvious that cost savings via contracting can only be realized if it appears probable that outside sources *would* lead to reduced government costs (i.e., outside contractors should not be used simply because they are available or because politicians may benefit by using them).

The third condition required by the contracting argument is an effective "watchdog" role by the government, a role that has been inadequately treated in the contracting literature. Unfortunately, the methods and techniques of program evaluation and contract management have seldom been applied to the subject of purchasing services in the pro-contracting works.[6] The basic principle of contract administration is that the contracting officials should continuously monitor contractor compliance and service performance to ensure that the activities conform to the specifications of the contract. Where contractors are reimbursed for their costs, particular attention must be paid to verifying expenditures to prevent illegal activities and mismanagement of funds. Opportunities should also be provided for consumers of the services to express their suggestions and dissatisfaction directly to the responsible government unit. These monitoring operations are critical for spotting potential problems, keeping contractors "honest," and providing technical assistance to contractors when problems arise. For human services (and any other types of services where cause and effect relationships are more uncertain), independent, objective evaluations are also necessary to determine if the services are effective in meeting program goals. These reviews of cost, performance, and effectiveness constitute essential feedback information when contracts are considered for renewals. Only by these means can the government be certain that it is receiving the kinds of services it desires.

This analysis of the three major conditions—competition, rational decisions to achieve cost reduction and efficient services, and an effective government watchdog role—logically leads to this crucial question: how likely is it that these three conditions will occur in the real world of public bureaucracy? Since the positive expectations about contracting appear to rest on these assumptions, what will occur if these conditions are not always present? Eventually these questions should be answered by thorough empirical study across a number of services in various government jurisdictions. Then better judgments could be made concerning when, how, and where to purchase which types of services. As yet, contracting scholars have not considered the importance of these conditions, nor have they examined them in their research.

PROBLEMS AND LIMITATIONS OF CONTRACTING OUT

Thus far, we have presented only the arguments favoring contracting for public services. But what might lead one to oppose changing the organizational arrangements for service delivery, changes that many believe will result in lower costs, good services, and a slowdown of government growth? Various individuals and groups, including some contracting advocates, recognize several different types of disadvantages and limitations of contracting out. We will examine two categories of difficulties posed by the contracting alternative: (1) utilization limitations and (2) program implementation problems. The following section will introduce and apply three alternative theoretical perspectives to contracting out that suggest some additional difficulties with this privatization prescription. Some of these limitations address issues relating to the effects of frequent purchases-of-services on private contractors and public policy implementation, while others arise out of the failure of some policy and program areas to produce the conditions suggested as conducive to successful contractual relationships. These actual and potential difficulties associated with this alternative to public bureaucracy caution us that the rosy picture painted by privatization advocates may have a darker side.

Utilization Problems

A number of barriers to the adoption of contracting out for public services have frustrated proponents of privatization. First, various federal, state, and local laws may prohibit its use in the place of public service production. State constitutions, for example, often include provisions requiring service delivery by government employees, e.g., municipal police and fire protection. Even if it is permissable, the mind-sets of elected officials and bureaucrats may limit contracting out to a few traditional areas (Straussman, 1981). Local governments have frequently and successfully purchased garbage collection services, but many officials balk at considering contracting out for budgeting, police, or educational services.

Part of governments' hesitation to utilize this approach more widely may stem from their anticipation of employees' reactions. Politically powerful unions act as a major obstruction to some municipalities (especially in the Northeast and Midwest) engaging in contracting. Advocates of public employee unionization charge that this method of service delivery is a way of by-passing the municipal and state unions to use underpaid, nonunion labor. When governments decide to switch from public employees to private firms, union leaders accuse the offending agency of union-busting and putting public employees on welfare. In 1981, for example, when the city manager of Benton Harbor, Michigan, proposed laying off almost all public employees in the debt-ridden city government and replacing them with contractors, the most vociferous reaction came from the municipal union. (Obviously, the manager and his plan did not last very long once employees mobilized opposition to contracting.) To support their interest in maintaining the traditional mode of service delivery, unionists are likely to employ some of the criticisms discussed below in their arguments, often with the same type of ideological fervor that characterizes most procontracting works (Hanrahan, 1977).

Some who recommend contracting out as a good alternative to bureaucratic supply have also pointed to a limitation of this method, i.e., that it may not work equally well in all service areas. Niskanen states that in order to improve efficiency, payments to outside sources "should be in the form of per-unit output subsidies, and not lump-sum grants based on need or input costs" (1971:215). This criterion would eliminate from contracting consideration public services whose outputs are difficult to measure precisely (e.g., research, fire protection).

Due to the dearth of research in most policy areas, it is difficult to compile a list of requisite conditions and services amenable to contracting for use in public policy decisions. Some scholars make an important distinction between contracting for "hard" and "soft" services (Nelson, 1980; Straussman and Farie, 1981). Hard services are those that primarily deal with objects (e.g., garbage collection, tax assessment, pest control), while soft services are involved with helping clients/citizens directly (e.g., education, job training, drug rehabilitation). Hard services are usually purchased primarily to reduce expenditures. Officials in the soft services, however, are less likely to be concerned with cost, but more likely to desire effective service performance. Service quality is the key issue, yet for each type of service, its elements are not simply defined or measured. Thus, the implementation and evaluation of contracting may be more straightforward in the hard services.

Contracting Out and Program Implementation

Where contracting out has been adopted and utilized in government agencies, opponents have raised additional objections about its effect upon program implementation. Some analysts have suggested that a growing reliance on outside organizations, particularly in the more complex human services, has made the creation and implementation of coherent public policy an even more formidable task for government (Beck, 1971; Brilliant, 1973; Wedel, 1979). At the same time that federal, state, and various local governments began sharing more responsibilities and tasks, many private agencies were brought into public service delivery via grants and contracts in what Kettl (1981) calls the "fourth face of federalism." These changes have produced increasing complexity and diversity where governments utilize a variety of different service suppliers. Coordinating and planning for the multitude of private service suppliers, according to this view, only adds to the already confusing, overlapping, and complex divisions within our federal system of government.

Probably nowhere has this complexity been more evident than in the CETA programs. Because of the block grant nature of CETA, key decisions about types, levels, and quality of the services were determined by federal, regional, state, and local prime sponsor units. Not only were the program specialists throughout the system responsible for setting policy, but legislators, particularly at the local level, were also very involved in almost every phase of decision making, from planning to evaluation. Various titles of the original and revised act brought these officials into the business of purchasing many of its manpower and research services from outside suppliers, mainly public agencies (e.g., school districts, universities, other prime sponsors) and private organizations (e.g., labor unions, community-based organizations, technical schools). Some outside agencies received CETA grants and contracts from several sources for a variety of services, often with differing demands and expectations. With little consensus about program goals and methods, most communities had different, even contradictory, conceptions of the use of the federal funds. Consequently, awards were made for many reasons, including for political payoffs and friendships. It should have come as no surprise that the CETA program was the target of many accusations concerning mismanagement, corruption, and ineffectiveness.

The ever-present political problem of accountability in public administration is only magnified with the addition of nongovernmental organizations carrying out the work of government. In a contracting system whose structure (if it can be said to have one) is not at all hierarchical and where clear, straight lines of authority are often absent, political and legal responsibility or accountability to a chief executive or legislative body is said to be difficult to establish and enforce. Critics have charged that in almost any type of service it is often difficult for the public or program recipients to hold contractors responsible and to encourage them to react responsively when the service proves to be unsatisfactory (Fitch, 1974; Sharkansky, 1980; Smith and Hague, 1971). This problem is often complicated by the fact that nonprofit agencies can be torn in several different directions because of their need to be responsive to the various demands of the government, their boards of directors, contributors, clients, and the community (Brilliant, 1973). Where other public agencies are awarded contracts, similar tensions may surface, since each agency may have its own clienteles, programmatic concerns, and political responsibilities.

In some respects, the issue of control over contractors parallels the problems of controlling street-level bureaucracies (Lipsky, 1980). Lower-line public employees and contractual workers can have a great deal of discretion over actual delivery of services, directly determining service quality and effectiveness. Control over the employees of contractor agencies can be restricted by their physical distance from agency headquarters, their limited background or training preparation, and the difficulty in continuously monitoring their performance in the field. In addition, the fact that nongovernmental agencies deliver many human

services to the poor inhibits some feedback mechanisms of quality control, since clients usually do not select the contractors or judge their
services. (The major exceptions to this statement are in Title XX's home
health care, chore services, and children's day care, where clients may
choose among several approved service providers.) The result is that
service delivery is further removed from top-level appointed and elected
officials who must rely primarily on contractors' own information to
evaluate service performance.

Government's increasing reliance on nongovernmental actors has also
created the "dilemma of independence vs. control," to use the words of
Smith and Hague (1971). Those concerned about private autonomy,
particularly nonprofit institutions, complain that government control
can become excessive through the contractual relationship (Brilliant,
1973; Gilbert, 1971; Lourie, 1979; Manser, 1974). Neil Gilbert summa-
rizes how private human service agencies view this problem:

> A major concern from the perspective of voluntary agencies is the degree of autono-
> my they might have to forfeit in gaining access to public funds. The questions they
> ask are, How much constraint on private agency activities will accompany the receipt
> of government funds, and will private agency activities emerge ultimately as merely
> the instrument of government policy (1977:633–34)?

The issue of separation of church and state also enters the contracting
picture. While church-related agencies struggle with their autonomy
when under contract, strict separatists question whether constitutional
principles have been jeopardized. This concern does not call for the
elimination of human services contracting, but it does emphasize that
the granting of government contracts may produce difficulties in the
short run and negative consequences in the long run for agencies that
deliver public, as well as private, services. One of the real difficulties for
government agencies arises in delineating clear but not excessively restrictive specifications, guidelines, and regulations for private agencies
to follow in implementing public programs.

Some critics of privatization also respond to the argument that contracting helps to limit government growth and interference while at the
same time strengthening the private sector and private organizations.
They claim that the government's role in the economy, in private organizations, and in people's lives continues to grow, it is just that public
employees may be hired less frequently to produce and deliver the public services. For example, federal, state, and local governments have
often used contracting to comply with imposed hiring freezes, while they
use the contracts to expand programs and services that are increasingly
expensive and intrusive. Along with a flourishing government role

:omes a growing tax burden for services and programs that govern-
nents believe they must provide. In her critique of using private institu-
ions for public purposes, Brilliant concludes:

> Effectively, the mixing of public and private activities masks or screens the growth
> of government intereference with the private sector and thereby makes it more
> palatable to average Americans. This illusion maintains the myth of less govern-
> ment, while government actually whittles away at the essential substance of private
> autonomy (1973:394).

ALTERNATIVE THEORETICAL PERSPECTIVES

These various criticisms of contracting out have not been well-grounded
n theoretical approaches to the general issues surrounding the subject,
hough they sometimes contain vague ideological overtones. Other intel-
ectual traditions in the social sciences can be brought to bear on this
liscussion, however. Three different perspectives offer useful frame-
vorks for thinking systematically about contracting. To facilitate refer-
:nces to them, I have labeled the three perspectives the market imper-
ection perspective (from economics), the cooptation perspective (from
)olitical science), and the organizational decision-making perspective
from multidisciplinary studies).[7]
   In what follows I do not intend to describe fully the analytic and
listorical bases of these perspectives. I will highlight their major argu-
nents and then identify some of their conclusions that can be extrapo-
ated to the subject of contracting out. While they have different foci,
irise out of quite different contexts, and do not specifically address the
iubject of contracting, these perspectives suggest several ways in which
he required conditions may be absent in some contracting arrange-
nents. In so doing, they point out various disadvantages associated with
:ontracting out and the underlying problems that would have to be
)vercome for its successful implementation.

The Economics of Market Imperfection

   The works that might be considered part of this perspective on indus-
rial organization are extremely diverse, but they are commonly rooted
n a long-standing effort to move away from the idealized components of
:lassical and neoclassical economics and move toward a more suitable
`ramework for describing and explaining the realities of economic be-
iavior (Burns, 1936; Chamberlin, 1933; Robinson, 1933; Von Neu-

mann and Morgenstern, 1947; Bain, 1956; Shepherd, 1970; Shubik, 1959). A major thrust of these scholars has been to emphasize imperfections in the traditional model of competition, pricing, information, and automatic adjustments of the market—market factors that are believed to produce an efficient allocation of society's resources. This neoclassical, competitive model underlies much of the public choice tradition's desire for market mechanisms in the supply of public services.

For this analysis, it is most relevant to examine two areas of supposed market imperfections, i.e., competition and information. According to this perspective, the market in many industries tends to be dominated by monopolies or oligopolies and cannot be described as competitive at all. Decision making within such markets is not characterized by firms' automatic adjustments to the demands, prices, and competition of the marketplace; rather, it is marked by market control or power, interdependence, and interaction in an attempt to reduce uncertainty and risk. Moreover, natural and erected barriers to entry into some markets significantly reduce the number of firms and the degree of competition. Consequently, prices are too high, output is too low, innovation and responsiveness to market changes are reduced, and resources are allocated inefficiently. Thus, traditional claims about the virtues of private sector activity and the unhindered marketplace may not always be valid.

The perspective of market imperfections also points out that buyers in the marketplace frequently have imperfect information with which to assess the products and services they wish to purchase. Not only is information limited and costly, but sellers have many incentives to distract, obfuscate, and mislead consumers with their prices, product varieties, packaging, and advertising. Since consumers depend to a large extent upon sellers' information, they may frequently make unwise decisions in the marketplace.

Some economists take this problem one step further. They point out that while perfect competition requires that demand and supply conditons be independent, in reality producers influence demand. In this view, the classical approach to consumer tastes and preferences is naive, i.e., the belief that tastes for particular products and services are endogenous. Consumers seldom enter the marketplace with a self-defined idea of which products and services they require. Instead, sellers often use selected information to mold consumer values and preferences, thus frequently creating and shaping "needs" where none existed before.

Logical extensions of this perspective to contracting out lead us to question some of the major assumptions of the public choice proponents of contracting, especially the competition and oversight conditions specified above. In many professional and technical fields and in services that require large initial investments for specialized equipment, there are often only one or two potential firms that could produce the desired service. The Department of Defense, for example, regularly uses sole source purchase procedures, often because only one contractor can produce the specified product or service. Competitive market pressures would certainly be minimal when the number of potential providers is so limited. There is no compelling reason to believe that outside suppliers will necesarily provide services more efficiently than bureaucratic agencies. Market power, monopolistic behavior, and the unavailability of alternatives may easily translate into higher costs for taxpayers and lower quality services for consumers.

While in principle the government can replace unsatisfactory suppliers and contract with more efficient and effective ones or produce the service itself, this option will often be absent, sometimes because no other responsive and responsible contractors are available. When a municipality sells its own firetrucks, buses, or sanitation equipment in favor of contracting out, it greatly reduces the possibility that it can act as a potential competitor to private firms should performance prove unsatisfactory. Sunk contracting costs and the need for service continuity may mean that the government unit may have little choice but to utilize a particular supplier on a long-term basis. Therefore, the problem of service monopolies cannot simply be avoided by relying on the private sector, since the private sector itself may not be marked by competition among suppliers.

Part of the lack of competition in contracting out is due to the fact that government services often have some public good characteristics, as in fire protection, recreation services, and education. The problem is not simply that this inhibits the expression of individual demand. Government can perform this function, though suppliers may try to shape the process. The more critical problem is that there is often no independent free market for supply purposes. The private sector is underdeveloped precisely because demand is underexpressed. When the government first articulates demand for a service, therefore, it has no full-fledged industry to turn to and, as a result, can hardly reap the benefits of competition through contracting. Over time, its demand and preference for private supply can encourage the emergence of an industry which is, in effect, governmentally created and dependent. Supplier strikes, slowdowns, or bankruptcy are potential hazards to such government contracting. Reliance upon this kind of a "public–private" industry may produce far less efficiency and flexibility than the proponents of privatization expect.

This prediction of limited competition actually has been observed in state implementation of Title XX social services. One of the recurring themes in purchase-of-service studies is the absence of responsive and responsible contractors for many of the services the government wishes to obtain for clients. Because of the limited number of agencies in many areas, often the states have had to contract out with whatever organizations have been available, almost regardless of the suitability of the particular service being offered (DeHoog, 1984; Straussman and Farie, 1981; Wedel, 1979). Where new agencies have been created or expanded to meet the needs and obtain the federal funds, dependency upon government contracts and grants has been almost inevitable. Therefore, government attempts to increase competition, reduce funding levels, or eliminate contracts have been met with strong resistance.

Contracting out also requires a review process in which relevant, accurate, and complete information is essential for the government to judge costs, performance, and effectiveness. But the information it require for wise decisions is often difficult to obtain, for various reasons, including: objective information is so costly that only a limited amount can reasonably be purchased; service quality and program effectiveness are often difficult to define and measure; information is often collected through contractors themselves and other organizations that have many opportunities for screening, bias, and ineptitude; and private contractors have incentives to shape information about needs and outputs to their own advantage. Together, these sources of informational inadequacy suggest that the government may often make unwise contracting decisions.

In Michigan's Department of Social Services (DSS), for example, officials have lacked necessary, independent information about the needs of clients. In proposal, expenditure, and performance reviews, DSS has usually had to depend upon information from provider agencies, since department resources have been very limited. On-site field visits and thorough follow-up evaluations of effectiveness have also been relatively rare (DeHoog, 1984).

The main point of this application of the market imperfection perspective is that the public choice model of contracting is built on an idealized economic foundation. For various reasons, the conditions that are assumed to exist to produce efficient contracting, especially market competition and adequate information, are not likely to materialize in the real world. As a result, the favorable expectations about contracting will often be in jeopardy.

The Politics of Cooptation

While the perspective of market imperfections has dealt with economic matters, the cooptation perspective focuses on political issues.

Some interesting parallels, however, between the two perspectives and their targets are apparent. Like the economists, political scientists who are part of this perspective also reacted to the major paradigm of their discipline: pluralism. They did not accept the pluralists' idealized picture of competitive politics as a means of understanding the interest group system and its relationship with government (Dahl, 1961; Polsby, 1963; Truman, 1951). A reasonable extension of this perspective to contracting conditions dovetails neatly with the economic perspective to produce salient caveats to the contracting model.

In particular, these political scientists challenged the pluralist assumptions that (1) interests form spontaneously and naturally; (2) there is a natural balance of interests represented before the government; and (3) government acts as a neutral, mechanical referee of active interests in society. This perspective, especially as articulated by Theodore Lowi and Grant McConnell, emphasizes that different segments of government tend to be "coopted" or controlled by those interests that are most successful in organizing and articulating their interests (Lowi, 1969; McConnell, 1966; Schattschneider, 1960; Kariel, 1961; Connolly, 1969; Selznick, 1949).

For the cooptationists some interests have inherent advantages over others in achieving organized political expression. Voluntary associations are more likely to form around the intense material interests of relatively few producers, these scholars claim, than around the more diffuse interests of many consumers. In contrast to the well-organized interests of business, labor, agriculture, and the professions, a range of broader social interests (e.g., concerning consumers, women, the environment) have struggled unsuccessfully to achieve membership levels and financial resources that reflect their support in society as a whole.

These biases are compounded, cooptationists argue, by the fact that the policymaking process is neither as competitive nor as truly open as the pluralists believe. Because of their preponderance of valuable resources, such as votes, money, information, political support, and administrative cooperation, the producer groups become the favored interests in their "triangular" relationships with certain key legislative committees and administrative agencies. Relationships in these subsystems often tend to be cooptive in that each of the insiders gains through regularized, supportive relationships with each of the other like-minded parts and through insulation from outside interference.

Lowi emphasizes that in the administrative process cooptive politics is even more pervasive and deeply entrenched than in the legislature. Specialized interest groups often have so much to offer that they are formally incorporated into agency decision making, relied upon to perform governmental functions, and, essentially, delegated public authority. Ties of professional backgrounds, friendships, and common interests mean that it is often difficult to distinguish between the government officials and the interest group or industry representatives. Some analysts have pointed to the frequent career movements between the two sectors as a further indication of cooptation. Noticeably absent in all of this are inputs from diffuse social interests that have difficulty organizing and gathering resources.

From this perspective, contracting for services is likely to create more problems than it solves. To begin with, cooptationists would predict that potential or current contractors are far more active and organized than the recipients of public services or those who pay for them, the taxpayers. Thus, the inputs from the private sector about service needs, methods of delivery, and the relative merits of private vs. in-house provision would be heavily weighted in their favor. In the "competition" to land and retain government contracts, moreover, individual agencies and firms have every incentive to employ their resources strategically with bureaucrats and legislators to exclude competitors and gain privileged, regularized roles in the contracting system. They may also try to minimize any risk of competition by cooperating among themselves. With contracting, in fact, the incentives for noncompetitive politics are even greater than they might otherwise be, because many of the suppliers become dependent upon government contracts for their very survival. Unless they find a special place in the contracting system, they are condemned to a year-by-year insecurity.

Michigan's Title XX contracting illustrates how social services in particular reflect this prediction. Private agencies and their professional associations have direct and indirect (through other of officials) access to contracting officials, while clients and taxpayers have had little influence in decision making. The generally poor clients may have a major interest in certain types and methods of services, but they usually do not have the resources or opportunities to express their demands. (One exception to this rule was the case of a county department that was pressured by vocal senior citizens to spend its entire program allotment for a large contract for services for the elderly instead of for various services for the poor.) As a result, client needs and service evaluations are interpreted by providers and DSS staff subject to their professional and personal biases (DeHoog, 1984).

For their part, self-interested bureaucrats and legislators cannot fail to see the opportunities for developing mutually beneficial relationships with contractors. Legislators have strong incentives to assist those contractors who have something special to offer, either directly (e.g., political support) or indirectly (e.g., economic advantage to a legislative district). Bureaucrats can give contractors special considerations in solicitations and awards, and thereby achieve predictability, cooperation, and political support for their program areas. In addition, they may have the future opportunity to be employed in the very firms or agencies that they once awarded contracts.

This incentive structure generally means that, like the contractors, public officials will prefer to eliminate true competition in the contracting process. If they can, they will not design procedures that promote competition, objectivity, and fairness. And contracting decisions will not be characterized by officials seeking to lower costs, improve service performance, and slow down government growth. They have few incentives to make these their goals; they have many incentives to promote their own personal goals through contracting.

Thus, it is not surprising, as Smith notes, that federal contracts are "no longer predominantly set by competitive bidding as in an earlier and simpler day but are to an increasing extent negotiated between the government and the contractor" (1971:14). Senator Howard Metzenbaum (D-Ohio) has estimated that in the U.S. Department of Defense (DOD) approximately 90% of all contracts are not competitively bid, even when more than one responsible and responsive supplier is available. He claims that sole source procurement has become the standard because of friendships between DOD officials and contractors as well as loopholes in the federal procurement laws.[8] According to many analysts, these contracts have been the major cause of waste, inefficiency, and budget growth in DOD. Other observers argue that DOD weapon choices and other contracts are also influenced by congressmen who desire the political rewards that come from representing the interests of major producers (Adams, 1981). At the local level, city officials may confer contracts on hometown firms rather than outsiders for political reasons.

In addition, conflict of interests and the use of bribes, kickbacks, and other illegal activities have been observed in many state and local governments and can be a part of any contracting system. As Fitch states,

Contracts are one of the most common and lucrative sources of corruption in government. The abuse has been only diminished, not eliminated, by public bidding and other formalities designed to improve the integrity of the process. Private contractors doing business with the government are still one of the principal sources of campaign funds, and of support for shady politicians (1974:279).

Because of many contracting scandals, the public has become wary of utilizing outside suppliers for some services. Thus, officials must guard against even the appearance of impropriety, lest citizens become completely disillusioned with politicians.

The cooptive environment in which contracts are awarded also conditions the review process. Officials have few incentives to scrutinize compliance and expenditures or to conduct meaningful evaluations of service performance and program effectiveness. These types of information are not utilized for most contracting decisions anyway, since government actors often do not choose suppliers primarily on the basis of these technical factors. For political reasons, inefficient suppliers can be preferred to more efficient and effective alternative suppliers. Any incentive officials have to collect and employ evaluative data has less to do with truly objective evaluation than with constructing justifications for decisions that are made on political grounds. Thus, government oversight does not check cooptive politics. It simply contributes to the broader cooptive pattern.

Even in the large Michigan state bureaucracy of the Department of Social Services and its county offices, political factors have influenced some contract awards and renewals. When DSS made new contracts or tried to drop unnecessary or unsatisfactory agencies, political pressure was sometimes successfully exerted on department officials to make choices in compliance with the politician's wishes. "Sweetheart," "protected," or "heaven above" contracts have been made on behalf of department directors, state legislators, and local elected officials (DeHoog, 1984). This phenomenon is not only a characteristic of Michigan, but has been observed in social service administration in other states as well (Wedel, 1979).

All of this suggests that contracting can be a counterproductive response to government inefficiency and growth. Contracting authorities may not be interested in promoting the goals of contracting advocates, at least not in their own bastions of power. Nor are they concerned with designing and implementing competitive procedures or thorough review methods. They *are* interested in maintaining existing relationships of mutual advantage and promoting new ones. These narrow interests are facilitated by more money, more programs, and resistance to any changes in funding levels, service priorities, and contracting methods.

Interestingly, this emphasis on the consequences of politicians' and bureaucrats' self-interest is not unlike that developed by various public choice scholars who favor contracting as a method of getting away from the inefficiencies of bureaucracy. Tullock and Niskanen, among others, posit that bureaucrats in particular are motivated to behave in their own interests, but these writers fail to recognize that these motivations may not automatically change when contracting is introduced (Tullock, 1965; Niskanen, 1971). And contracting advocates generally dismiss the fact that officials may see opportunities for using outside rather than in-house supply.[9] Unless contracting systems incorporate new incentives to promote competition and maximize efficiency, why should we assume that contracting officials will change their behavior when purchasing services?

The Process of Organizational Decision Making[10]

While the first perspective of market imperfections analyzes markets, industries, and consumers, and the second perspective of cooptation deals with the political relationships between producer groups and government officials, the third perspective focuses on organizations and organizational decision making. This last way of examining the subject of contracting employs various concepts and conclusions from studies of organizations in the disciplines of sociology, psychology, economics, political science, and public administration. In particular, the works of scholars in the organizational decision-making tradition are useful for evaluating the three conditions under study here, especially the competitive procedures, rational decision making, and watchdog activities (Simon, 1957, 1961; March and Simon, 1958; Cyert and March, 1963; Lindblom, 1959; Lindblom and Braybrooke, 1963; Downs, 1966).

Paralleling the revisionist attempts of the market imperfection approach and the cooptationist "school," decision-making theorists also reacted to unrealistic, conventional approaches to their subject, in this case, to the study of individual and organizational choice. Before Herbert Simon's work, most economists employed a conception of rational man in which individuals and organizations select the best alternative, following a thorough review and ranking of goals, alternatives, outcomes, and probabilities. Simon introduced a modification of this picture of "economic man" with his "administrative man," one who is "boundedly" rational. Because of limits on time, information, and cognitive abilities, individuals cannot be expected to consider all alternatives and their consequences each time a problem presents itself. Instead, decision makers primarily rely on routine solutions (standard operating procedures) designed to reduce uncertainty, risk, and capriciousness. If an appropriate routine does not exist, one engages in a limited sequential search process marked by "satisficing" behavior. According to Simon, individuals to not *maximize* goal achievement by examining many alternatives and rank-ordering them, but they conserve time and energy by choosing the first satisfactory solution.

In this perspective, organizational decision making is determined by one's premises or goals, information content and flow, the standard repertoires, and the threshold levels of what is judged satisfactory. Political or organizational leaders do not provide the only means to control choices and behavior. Rather, organization theorists emphasize that personal (as well as organizational) goals, informal group pressures, and professional backgrounds are critical factors in shaping the premises of decisions. Cyert and March add that organizations often have highly ambiguous, nonoperational goals that make success difficult to define. The more operational, or actual, goals arise out of internal bargaining and learning, and, as a result, are often in conflict and several in number.

Lindblom's work on "muddling through" in public policy decisions points out that goal agreement and a rational policymaking process are particularly improbable when many different individuals, groups, and organizations participate in decisions. Instead of seeking optimal, comprehensive solutions, policymakers treat problems narrowly and choose alternatives that are most acceptable to all involved. As a consequence, organizational or policy change usually is a slow, incremental, and piecemeal process. Past goals, decisions, and budgets are the best predictors of the future.

Applied to contracting out, this brief summary of the decision-making model of organization theory suggests that contract decision making often may not be oriented toward optimizing efficiency because it takes place in an organizational setting. First, government units may choose to contract out for a service in response to artificial, organizational incentives and not because of inherent cost or service advantages. Agency ceilings on personnel numbers, government hiring freezes, and the need to commit funds by the fiscal year's end provide reasons for using outside service supply. Under such conditions, the contracted services may not be significantly better or less costly than those provided by in-house staff. Probably quite the reverse would often be the case.

Second, particularly under conditions of fiscal constraints, officials will not have the resources to make strictly rational decisions about outside supply, awards, and oversight. Instead of considering all available alternatives with a thorough search for relevant information about costs and service, they will satisfice. Only a limited amount of information will be obtained. Decision makers will cease looking for alternative service suppliers when a minimally acceptable contractor presents a proposal or bid. Unless clearly written into the law, they will design the procedures of contracting to find a suitable agent, not to promote competition through costly, wide solicitations and time-consuming procedures. Often officials will not need to pursue a thorough search since they can more easily use previous contractors. Generally they will try to avoid new contractors, different directions, and increased competition wherever possible. Standardized procedures and rules-of-thumb will help to simplify decision making, reduce conflict, and achieve contracting predictability for everyone.

In the third place, organization theorists would predict that government officials may not be interested in single-mindedly pursuing the goal of efficiency, as contracting advocates expect. Other, often conflicting, operational goals may take precedence. These goals may be determined by individuals' personal needs, professional norms, and group or organizational pressures. Whatever the goals (probably different for different organizations), they will determine not only whether outside supply is adopted and which contractors are awarded contracts, but also the oversight methods utilized to ensure efficient and effective service delivery. An inadequate watchdog function may be produced by limited organizational resources, a reliance on past decisions, and other decisional premises (e.g., desire to avoid conflict with contractors). Officials will find it unnecessary to secure information to change future contract language and choices. They will judge contractor performance by simple, obvious measures that flow from the goals of the organizational unit (e.g., number of program enrolllees), instead of by measures that may be more difficult to obtain but more accurately reflect program success (e.g., long-term employment as a result of job training).

If more than one organizational unit or government level is involved in contractor selection, contract administration, and oversight, the difficulties and time involved in purchasing decisions will multiply. The units' goals will conflict, communication will break down, professional and organizational clashes will recur, particularly where the units have differing priorities and vocabularies. In Michigan's state CETA program, for example, several different parts of the Bureau of Employment and Training were involved in some aspect of the contracting process. One unit set overall contracting policy, another group selected contractors (subject to the approval of the department head), and a third wrote and monitored the contracts. (Other units also were involved in more limited ways at various junctures.) Even though they had closer contact with contractor operations, contract monitors were left out of the key decisions, partly because of their lower professional status and partly because of the bureau's separation between policy and operations. As a result, they were resentful and, at times, uncooperative. Since officials sometimes selected service suppliers with little understanding of the realities of contractor compliance, the process of writing contracts was often delayed to the extent that programs were late in getting started and sometimes were poorly managed.

Moreover, often contractor agencies will have their own bureaucracies through which proposals are written and services are delivered. Not only does this fact make for a more complex process, but it also means that lines of accountability and communication may be more problematic than in direct service delivery or where a single unit is in charge of contracting. Therefore, contracting for refuse collection by a small city's council produces problems of a far smaller magnitude than when large bureaucracies, elected officials, and more than one level of government are all involved in purchasing human services from large private agencies.

This organizational perspective proves very useful in increasing our understanding of social service contracting. Limited information, time, and staff resources in Michigan's DSS have meant that routinely renewing contracts has usually been preferred to seeking out new services and providers. Formal regulations (such as a matching requirement for contractors) and informal organizational and professional norms have also inclined officials to limit their alternatives, and thus, to limit uncertainty, conflict, and change in the organization. An unfortunate irony of Michigan's fiscal squeeze was that while the necessity for closer scrutiny, better information, and complete evaluations increased, the resources available for them decreased (DeHoog, 1984).

This discussion of decision making emphasizes that privatization proponents should be aware of the variety of organizational contexts in which contracting takes place. Several organizational factors combine to suggest that the contracting approach to services is not an automatic mechanism for supplying services, but one that is affected by various goals, organizational routines, information flow, and organizational structures. Instead of avoiding the major problems of bureaucracy, contracting takes place in and is an integral part of an organizational environment. Consequently, at least some of the problems and outcomes of contracting will be similar to those encountered in traditional service supply.

CONCLUSION

Is contracting out a viable solution to the related problems of government inefficiency, ineffectiveness, and growth? Contracting supporters in the public choice tradition have emphatically answered this question in the affirmative. The three perspectives introduced in this chapter, however, lead to a different response. Taken together, the economics of market imperfection, the politics of cooptation, and the process of organizational decision making suggest that the various conditions assumed by contracting adherents are unlikely to occur in the real world. Consequently, the positive expectations of contracting will not materialize either. In this view, contracting could even exacerbate the already-serious problems of government.

The major difficulty with the contracting prescription is that too often proponents offer it as a panacea for the current ills of government with little explicit recognition of the requisite conditions and realities of implementation. At least four general deficiencies are evident in the contracting prescriptions. First, despite its major contributions to our understanding of public bureaucracy and privatization, in its advocacy of contracting the public choice school overlooks the motivational and organizational contexts of the contracting participants. Second, contracting proponents fail to recognize the critical role that the service environment can play in contracting, both in terms of the pool of potential providers and the inputs and feedback of service consumers. Third, many contracting advocates assume that quasi-market mechanisms will operate almost automatically, without exploring how and why contracting is actually utilized, what procedures are critical in producing the expected benefits, and under which conditions contracting works the best. The alternative theoretical perspectives suggest that some of the same problems that plague in-house supply also characterize contractual arrangements. Finally, most public administrationists have not fully considered the effect of wide-scale contracting on public policy implementation and the private agencies that provide public services.

The most obvious question is not so much whether goods and services should be purchased from private agents; rather, we should ask, under what circumstances should they be purchased? Contracting out has obvious utility for procuring goods and short-term, occasional, or seasonal services. But to what extent should contractors replace in-house delivery, particularly where citizens are to be directly served?

A variety of situations do appear to offer some potential for implementing contracting out: where officials can try out demonstration, experimental programs, services, or methods with no long-term commitment to continuing the programs; where government does not have the requisite experience, equipment, or expertise to provide the services, and these commodities are available in the private sector; where governments can realize economies of scale; where government officials can set priorities, service levels, and outcome goals, with the opprtunity to reward and punish if these are not met by contractors; where there is adequate competition in the environment to ensure government choice; where contracting agencies can adopt and enforce competitive procedures; where politically motivated awards can be minimized; and where government agencies have the resources and desire to implement effective review methods.[11]

This list is only a preliminary attempt to specify some of the conditions for successful contracting. Even in these circumstances, practitioners and scholars must realize that contracting does not work smoothly and automatically. Some of the contracting difficulties discussed above may complicate the process. More research is needed to examine various service areas in an attempt to understand the procedures, problems, and outcomes of contracting out. Only by studying contracting can we learn where to implement this alternative and how inappropriate conditions can be changed into beneficial conditions for the purchase of public services.

NOTES

1. I will not, however, include consideration of financial agreements that are sometimes confused with contracts, such as grants-in-aid to lower levels of government, vouchers, subsidies, research grants, and intergovernmental agreements.

2. See Savas (1982) for his discussion of common-pool, toll, collective, and private goods.

3. In addition, contracting out is a more feasible privatization method because government bears the decision and transaction costs, and, therefore, they are less than they would be if each citizen negotiated individually for services.

4. Other scholars might select a slightly different number or set of conditions from the literature, but I believe these three are the most obvious and critical features necessary for contracting ou to work as envisioned by proponents.

5. Admittedly, the goal of cost reduction does not necessarily require a maximizing assumption. Conceivably, the expected outcomes could often be realized with satisficing behavior by officials, in the Simon tradition. But most of the theoretical contracting literature implies a maximizing principle (see Ostrom, 1974:50–53).

6. These connections have been made in some of the more applied works in public administration and human services. See Nelson (1980) and Wedel et al. (1979).

7. In doing this, I am undoubtedly simplifying complex arguments, placing together scholars who do ot see themselves as members of a common "school," and making generalizations that may not accurately represent any single scholar's contribution. This is an inevitable consequence of any attempt to synthesize a complex, diverse literature.

8. Metzenbaum in NBC television interview, *Today*, May 21, 1981.

9. On the other hand, contracting opponents seem to blame most corruption and opportunism on the contractors and downplay the issue of gains by officials.

10. This perspective is similar to Graham Allison's (1971) second model, his Organizational Process model.

11. Obviously, all these conditions are not required to be present at the same time for contracting to meet the public choice goals of contracting. In some cases seemingly necessary conditions of contracting can be absent if other conditions are used to compensate for the void.

REFERENCES

Adams, G. (1981) The Iron Triangle: The Politics of Defense Contracting. New York: Council on Economic Priorities.

Agranoff, R. and A. Pattahas (1979) Dimensions of Services Integration: Service Delivery, Program Linkages, Policy Management, Organizational Structure. Human Services Monograph Series 13, Project SHARE. Washington, D.C.: U.S. Government Printing Office.

Ahlbrandt, R. (1973) "Efficiency in the provision of fire services." Public Choice 18:1–15.

Allison, G. T. (1971) Essence of Decision: Explaining the Cuban Missile Crisis. Boston: Little, Brown.

Ayres, D. W. (1975) "Municipal interfaces in the third sector: a negative view." Public Administration Review 35:459–63.

Baker, K. G. (1976) "Public-choice theory: some important assumptions and public-policy implications." Pp. 41–60 in R. T. Golembiewski et al. (eds.), Public Administration: Readings in Institutions, Processes, Behavior, Policy, 3rd ed. Chicago: Rand McNally.

Bain, J. S. (1956) Barriers to New Competition. Cambridge, Mass.: Harvard University Press.

Bartlett, R. (1973) Economic Foundations of Political Power. New York: Free Press.

Beck, B. (1971) "Governmental contracts with non-profit social welfare corporations." Pp. 213–29 in B. L. R. Smith and D. C. Hague (eds.), The Dilemma of Accountability in Modern Government: Independence Versus Control. New York: St. Martin's Press.

Bennett, J. T. and M. H. Johnson (1979) "Public versus private provision of collective goods and services." Public Choice 34: 55–64.

———— (1980) "Tax reduction without sacrifice: private-sector production of public service." Public Finance Q. 8: 363–96.

———— (1981) Better Government at Half the Price: Private Production of Public Services. Ottawa, Ill.: Caroline House.

Benton, B., T. Field, and R. Millar (1978) Social Services: Legislation vs. State Implementation. Washington, D.C.: Urban Institute.

Bish, R. L. (1971) The Public Economy of Metropolitan Areas. Chicago: Markham.

Borcherding, T. E., ed. (1977) Budgets and Bureaucrats: The Sources of Government Growth. Durham, N.C.: Duke University Press.

Brilliant, E. (1973) "Private or public: a model of ambiguities." Social Service Review 47:384–96.

Buchanen, J. M. (1977) "Why does government grow?" Pp. 3–18 in T. E. Borcherding (ed.), Budgets and Bureaucrats: The Sources of Government Growth. Durham, N.C.: Duke University Press.

Burns, A. R. (1936) The Decline of Competition. New York: McGraw-Hill.

Caves, D. W. and L. R. Chiristensen (1980) "The relative efficiency of public and private firms in a competititve environment: the case of Canadian railroads." Journal of Political Economy 88:958–76.

Chamberlin, E. (1933) The Theory of Monopolistic Competition. Cambridge, Mass.: Harvard University Press.

Connolly, W. E. ed. (1969) The Bias of Pluralism. New York: Atherton Press.

Cooper, P. J. (1980) "Government contracts in public administration: the role and environment of the contracting officer." Public Administration Review 40:459–68.

Cyert, R. M. and J. G. March (1963) A Behavioral Theory of the Firm. Englewood Cliffs, N.J.: Prentice-Hall.

Dahl, R. A. (1961) Who Governs? Democracy and Power in an American City. New Haven, Conn.: Yale University Press.

Danhof, Clarence (1968) Government Contracting and Technological Change. Washington, D.C.: Brookings.

Davies, D. G. (1971) "The efficiency of public versus private firms: the case of Australia's two airlines." Journal of Law and Economics 14:149–65.

Deacon, R. T. (1979) "The expenditure effects of alternative public supply institutions." Public Choice 34:381–97.

DeAlessi, L. (1974) "An economic analysis of government ownership and regulation: theory and the evidence from the electric power industry." Public Choice 19:1–42.

DeHoog, R. H. (1984) Contracting Out for Human Services: Economic, Political, and Organizational Perspectives. Albany: State University of New York Press, 1984.

Derthick, M. (1975) Uncontrollable Spending for Social Service Grants. Washington, D.C.: Brookings Institution.

Dobelstein, A. W. (1980) Politics, Economics, and Public Welfare. Englewood Cliffs, N.J.: Prentice-Hall.

Downs, A. (1966) Inside Bureaucracy. Boston: Little, Brown.

Drucker, P. (1969) "The sickness of government." Public Interest 14:3–23.

Fisk, D., H. Kiesling, and T. Muller (1978) Private Provision of Public Services: An Overview. Washington, D.C.: Urban Institute.

Fitch, L. C. (1974) "Increasing the role of the private sector in providing public services." Pp. 264–306 in W. D. Hawley and D. Rogers (eds.), Improving the Quality of Urban Management. Beverly Hills, Cal.: Sage Publications.

Florestano, P. S. and S. B. Gordon (1980) "Public vs. private: small government contracting with the private sector." Public Administration Review 40:29–34.

Friedman, M. (1962) Capitalism and Freedom. Chicago: University of Chicago Press.

Gilbert, N. (1977) "The transformation of social services." Social Service Review 51:624–41.

Hanrahan, J. (1977) Government for $ale: Contracting Out, The New Patronage. Washington, D.C.: American Federation of State, County and Municipal Employees.

Hirschman, A. O. (1970) Exit, Voice and Loyalty. Cambridge, Mass.: Harvard University Press.

Kariel, H. S. (1961) The Decline of American Pluralism. Stanford, Cal.: Stanford University Press.

Keehn, N. H. (1976) "A world of becoming: from pluralism to corporatism." Policy 9:19–39.

Kelso, W. A. (1978) American Democratic Theory: Pluralism and Its Critics. Westport, Conn.: Greenwood Press.

Kemper, P. and J. M. Quigley (1976) The Economics of Refuse Collection. Cambridge, Mass.: Ballinger.

Kettl, D. L. (1981) "The fourth face of federalism." Public Administration Review 41:366–73.

Kramer, R. (1966) "Voluntary agencies and the use of public funds: some policy issues." Social Service Review 40:15–26.

Levitan, S. A. (1980) Programs in Aid of the Poor for the 1980's, 4th ed. Baltimore: Johns Hopkins University Press.

Lindblom, C. E. (1959) "The science of 'muddling through.'" Public Administration Review, 19:79–88.

———— (1977) Politics and Markets. New York: Basic Books.

———— and D. Braybrooke (1963) A Strategy of Decision. New York: Free Press.

Lipsky, M. (1980) Street-Level Bureaucracy: Dilemmas of the Individual in Public Services. New York: Russell Sage Foundation.

Lourie, N. V. (1979) "Purchase of service contracting: issues confronting the government sponsored agency." Pp. 18–29 in K. R. Wedel, A. J. Katz and A. Weick (eds.), Social Services by Government Contract: A Policy Analysis. New York: Praeger.

Lowery, D. (1982) "The political incentives of government contracting." Social Science Quarterly 63:517–29.

Lowi, T. J. (1969) The End of Liberalism. New York: Norton.

McConnell, G. (1966) Private Power and American Democracy. New York: Knopf.

Manser, G. (1974) "Implications of purchase of service for voluntary agencies." Social Casework 55:421–27.

March, J., ed. (1965) Handbook of Organizations. Chicago: Rand McNally.

———— and H. Simon (1958) Organizations. New York: Wiley.

Michigan Department of Labor, Bureau of Employment and Training (1980) Annual Plan for Special Grants to Governors Comprehensive Employment and Training Act, Fiscal Year 1981. Lansing: Michigan Department of Labor.

Michigan Department of Social Services, Title XX Administrative Division (1979) Michigan Annual Title XX Services Plan 1979–1980. Lansing: Michigan Department of Social Services.

Michigan House Fiscal Agency (1979) Purchasing Social Services Under Title XX in Michigan. Lansing: Michigan House of Representatives.

Miller, G. J. (1981) Cities by Contract: The Politics of Municipal Incorporation. Cambridge, Mass.: MIT Press.

National Governors' Association (1978) Utilization of Governors' Discretionary Grant Funds Under CETA. Washington, D.C.: National Governors' Association.

Nelson, B. J. (1980) "Purchase of services." Pp. 427–447 in G. Washis (ed.), Productivity Improvement Handbook for State and Local Government. New York: Wiley.

Nelson, R. R. (1977) The Moon and the Ghetto. New York: Norton.

Niskanen, W. A., Jr. (1971) Bureaucracy and Representative Government. Chicago: Aldine-Atherton.

O'Donnell, P. S. (1978) Social Services: Three Years After Title XX. Washington, D.C.: National Governors' Association.

Ostrom, V. (1971) "Public choice: a different approach to the study of public administration." Public Administration Review 31:203–16.

———— (1974) The Intellectual Crisis in American Public Administration, rev. ed. University, Ala: University of Alabama Press.

———— and E. Ostrom (1977) "Public goods and public choices." Pp. 7–49 in E. S. Savas (ed.), Alternatives for Delivering Public Services Toward Improved Performance. Boulder, Colo.: Westview Press.

Polsby, N. W. (1963) Community Power and Political Theory. New Haven, Conn.: Yale University Press.

Poole, R. W., Jr. (1980) Cutting Back City Hall. New York: Universe Books.

Pressman, J. L. and A. B. Wildavsky (1973) Implementation. Berkeley: University of California Press.

Robinson, J. (1933) The Economics of Imperfect Competition. London and New York. Macmillan.

Rose-Ackerman, S. (1978) Corruption: A Study in Political Economy. New York: Academic Press.

Samuelson, P. (1954) "The pure theory of public expenditure." Review of Economics and Statistics 36: 387–89.

Savas, E. S. (1974) "Municipal monopolies versus competition in delivering urban services." Pp. 473–500 in W. D. Hawley and D. Rogers (eds.), Improving the Quality of Urban Management. Beverly Hills, Cal.: Sage Publications.

_____ (1977a) "An empirical study of competition in municipal service delivery." Public Administration Review 37:717–24.

_____ (1977b) The Organization and Efficiency of Solid Waste Collection. Lexington, Mass.: Lexington Books.

_____ (1979) "Public vs. private refuse collection: a critical review of the evidence." Journal of Urban Analysis 6:1–13.

_____ (1981) "Intracity competition between public and private service delivery." Public Administration Review 41:46–52.

_____ (1982) Privatizing the Public Sector: How to Shrink Government. Chatham, N.J.: Chatham House.

Schattschneider, E. E. (1960) The Semi-sovereign People. New York: Holt, Rinehart, and Winston.

Seidman, H. (1970) Politics, Position, and Power. New York: Oxford University Press.

Selznick, P. (1949) TVA and the Grass Roots. Berkeley: University of California Press.

Sharkansky, I. (1979) Wither the State? Politics and Public Enterprise in Three Countries. Chatham, N.J.: Chatham House.

_____ (1980) "Policy making and service delivery on the margins of government: the case of contractors." Public Administration Review 40:116–23.

Shepherd, W. G. (1970) Market Power and Economic Welfare. New York: Random House.

Shubik, M. (1959) Strategy and Market Structure. New York: Wiley.

Simon, H. A. (1957) Models of Man. New York: Wiley.

_____ (1961) Administrative Behavior, 2nd ed. New York: Macmillan.

Slawsky, N. J. and J. J. DeMarco (1980) "Is the price right? state and local government architect and engineer selection." Public Administration Review 40:269–74.

Smith, B. L. R. (1975) The New Political Economy. New York: St. Martin's Press.

_____ and D. C. Hague, eds. (1971) The Dilemma of Accountability in Modern Government: Independence vs. Control. New York: St. Martin's Press.

Sonenblum, S., J. J. Kirlin, and J. C. Ries (1977) How Cities Provide Services: An Evaluation of Alternative Delivery Structures. Cambridge, Mass.: Ballinger.

Spann, R. M. (1974) "Collective consumption of private goods." Public Choice 20:63–81.

_____ (1977) "Public versus private provision of governmental services." Pp. 71–89 in T. E. Borcherding (ed.), Budgets and Bureaucrats: The Sources of Government Growth. Durham, N.C.: Duke University Press.

Straussman, J. D. (1981) "More bang for fewer bucks? Or how local governments can rediscover the potentials (and pitfalls) of the market." Public Administration Review 41:150–57.

_____ and J. Farie (1981) "Contracting for social services at the local level." Urban Interest 3:43–50.

Terrell, P. (1979) "Private alternatives to public human services administration." Social Service Review 53:56–74.

Truman, D. B. (1951) The Governmental Process. New York: Knopf.

Tullock, G. (1965) The Politics of Bureaucracy. Washington, D.C.: Public Affairs Press.

Von Neumann, J. and O. Morgenstern (1947) The Theory of Games and Economic Behavior. Princeton, N.J.: Princeton University Press.

Wamsley, G. L. and M. N. Zald (1973) The Political Economy of Public Organizations: A Critique and Approach to the Study of Public Administration. Bloomington: Indiana University Press.

Warren, R. O. (1965) Government in Metropolitan Regions: A Reappraisal of Fractionated Political Organization. Davis, Cal.: Institute of Governmental Affairs.

Wedel, K. A. (1976) "Government contracting for purchase of service." Social Work 21:101–05.

———, J. Katz, and A. Weick, eds. (1979) Social Services by Government Contract: A Policy Analysis. New York: Praeger.

Weisbrod, B. A. (1977) The Voluntary Nonprofit Sector: An Economic Analysis. Lexington, Mass.: Lexington Books.

Williams, W. (1980) The Implementation Perspective. Berkeley: University of California Press.

Wolf, C., Jr. (1979) "A theory of non-market failures." Public Interest 55:114–33.

Woodward, J. (1965) Industrial Organization: Theory and Practice. New York: Oxford University Press.

Young, D. R. (1971) "Institutional change and the delivery of urban public services." Policy Sciences 2:425–38.

BIOGRAPHICAL SKETCHES
OF CONTRIBUTORS

Samuel Aroni is acting dean and professor at UCLA's Graduate School of Architecture and Urban Planning. He is an engineer and planner concerned with the social, economic, and technical aspects of housing policy and building technology. He has published widely in the fields of structures, materials, building systems, and housing.

Robert W. Backoff is associate professor in the School of Public Administration at Ohio State University. His research interests include strategic management in public organizations, incentive systems in organizations, and management of organizational innovation. He has published a number of articles in policy and public administration journals and research annuals, including *Public Administration Review* and *Administration and Society.*

Lawrence Baum is associate professor of political science at Ohio State University. He is author of *The Supreme Court* and has done research on several aspects of judicial policymaking, including implementation of judicial decisions, diffusion of innovative doctrines, and case screening by appellate courts.

Ruth Hoogland DeHoog is assistant professor of political science at the University of Florida. Her current research interests are in organization theory and urban administration, and she is the author of *Contracting Out for Human Services.*

261

George C. Edwards III is professor of political science at Texas A&M University. He has written widely on public policymaking and the presidency, and his most recent books include *The Public Presidency*, *Studying the Presidency*, and *Implementing Public Policy*.

Frederick A. Lazin is director of the Humphrey Center for Social Ecology and senior lecturer in behavioral sciences at Ben Gurion University of the Negev in Israel. He has written widely on urban politics and federalism.

Barry M. Mitnick is associate professor in the Graduate School of Business at the University of Pittsburgh. His research interests include theories of, design of, and strategic behavior under regulation; incentive systems in organizations; and the theory of agency. He is the author of *The Political Economy of Regulation: Creating, Designing, and Removing Regulatory Forms*.

Kenneth R. Mladenka is associate professor of political science at Texas A&M University. His research on urban services has been published in the *American Political Science Review*, *American Journal of Political Science*, *Journal of Politics*, *Social Science Quarterly*, and *Urban Affairs Quarterly*.

Mark E. Rushefsky is assistant professor political science at the University of Florida. His research interests include health policy issues, especially the impact of competition on health care, and environmental and regulatory policy, especially the problems of regulatory science.

Robert M. Stein is associate professor of political science at Rice University, specializing in intergovernmental relations, urban politics, and the federal aid system. He has published works on these topics in the *American Political Science Review*, *Journal of Urban Economics*, *Western Political Quarterly*, *Social Science Quarterly*, and other journals.

Frank J. Thompson chairs the Department of Political Science at the University of Georgia. He has published a variety of articles and books dealing with issues of public policy and administration. His most recent book is *Health Policy and the Bureaucracy: Politics and Implementation*.

INDEX